NO HEIL HITLER!

Winner of the National Seniors Literary Prize, 2012,
the inaugural annual prize from National Seniors Australia for an
unpublished manuscript written by Australians aged 50 years or older.

"I wish to acknowledge the help in writing this book given to
me by my friend Jeff Steel without whose literary skills
this book would not have been written."
—Paul Cieslar

NO HEIL HITLER!

PAUL CIESLAR

SIGNS
PUBLISHING®
Established 1885

SIGNS
PUBLISHING®
Established 1885

Proudly published and printed in Australia by
Signs Publishing
Warburton, Victoria.

This book was
Edited by Nathan Brown and Sara Thompson
Proofread by Lindy Schneider
Designed by Kym Jackson
Cover and internal photographs provided by Paul Cieslar
Cover design by Shane Winfield
Typeset in Berkeley Book 11.5/14.5

ISBN 978 1 925044 10 2 (print edition)
ISBN 978 1 925044 11 9 (ebook edition)

DEDICATION

To my two grandchildren, Amy and Caleb and to the grandchildren of my brothers and sisters. As they read this book, may they reflect on the leadership of the Almighty in our family during the dark days of World War II.

And to the memory of my parents, Paweł and Maria, who exemplified in their daily lives the living hope and spirit of true Adventism. They taught our family from earliest childhood to appreciate and understand "the faith which was once delivered to the saints." They gave their children the courage and inspiration to fight the fight of good faith.

CONTENTS

PROLOGUE

My only excuse for writing this book is that everything in it happened. I am writing this for my family—but if anyone else would care to look over their shoulder and read about the strange events in my life, they are welcome to do so. This is the story of my family—the family I grew up in—during World War II particularly. I believe it is a story that deserves to be written down.

What I have written is my chronicle of life under the Nominal Church in the pre-war Republic of Poland, the time of the Third Reich and the Communist era. It was a world where defiance led to a quick and unpleasant death; but compliance led to misery. In the middle of all of this evil, for such it was, my own family was the happiest that ever lived. To have been a part of that family was simply a privilege.

Is anything left out? Yes, some things are specifically omitted. This is because some of the material concerns events that—even seven decades later—are so controversial that to raise these points could cause negative feelings. Some names are changed for diplomatic reasons. But, with regard to myself in this book, you have the whole story.

I do want to write it and want to do so very much. The misery and destruction around us was of historic proportions. My homeland of Upper Silesia is very beautiful and yet we who lived there saw some of the worst crimes in the history of humanity. We were ordinary people born in exactly the wrong country at precisely the wrong time. That we survived with our lives, our families and our bodies intact is evidence of God's providential victory—so my family believes.

Like many true stories, you will find that some episodes do not make sense

1

according to any logic. Where these seemingly incomprehensible events occur I have not attempted to explain them. Quite honestly, your guess or interpretation is as good as my own. Perhaps strangest of all, there are four people in this story who bear the name Paweł Cieslar. Two were members of my family, another was my boss when I was a shepherd. These Paweł Cieslars were delighted and in small part amazed to survive the war. A fourth was taken to the concentration camp in Auschwitz.

I do not seek or accept any pity for the things I lived through. Ultimately the horrors and treachery brought me face to face with a love of such redemptive power that few human beings have ever experienced it. I have had the privilege of seeing with my own eyes the triumph of good over evil.

In part, I was motivated to write this book by a statement of a great writer who had written: "It is for our own benefit to keep every gift of God fresh in our memory. By this means faith is strengthened to claim and to receive more and more. There is greater encouragement for us in the least blessing we ourselves receive from God than in all the accounts we can read of the faith and experience of others" (Ellen White, *The Ministry of Healing*, page 100). So this is my story—but I hope there is also benefit and encouragement for those who will read these memories.

My life—including its many difficult experiences—has been a journey. The destination of that journey is a proven and unshakable belief in God's ultimate goodness and power. That is why—in the final analysis—you should envy me.

Redemption is possible. I have seen it and experienced it!

Paweł (Paul) Cieslar

Germany and Poland at the outbreak of World War II.
Source: Mountian High Maps modified

Our family portait (circa 1943/44): (seated front, left to right) Marta, Mum, Dad, Maria; (standing back, left to right) Ruth, Jerzy, Pawel, Josef, Jan, Anna; (top right, later added into the photo) Ruben.

THE GOLDEN POLISH AUTUMN

September 1, 1939, was a day that began like any other—except that this day was particularly beautiful. The sun shone brilliantly through the fresh morning air from a clear blue sky. The cutting wind and the flocks of migrating birds above were the only reminders that we had entered into the golden Polish autumn.

I was 10 years old, out watching our cattle as my father had asked me. The mid-morning train had just left the station, so I knew the time was 9.30. It was one of those lovely mornings when God was in heaven and everything around me—the lovely valleys and the streams—looked so beautiful.

But the tranquillity of the morning was suddenly shattered when three German fighter planes appeared from behind the mountain of Kubalonka. They were in strict formation, one slightly in front of the others, as if taking part in a demonstration, barely above ground level. I could see the grey fuselage, the pilots in the cockpits and the ominous black crosses on the wings. The noise was deafening.

The three planes flew toward me at terrifying speed. The noise alone felt like it would shake all my teeth out. I saw the flicker of flames as the first plane fired its guns, and I heard the trees above my head splintering as the stream of bullets hit them. Branches toppled down. Cattle panicked. Leaves and twigs sprayed across the field. The ricocheting bullets whined around the valley.

Terrified, I ran. I forgot about the sharp stones on the rough farm track that might cut my bare feet. I forgot about the cattle. I forgot that my father had shown special trust in me to look after them. I ran and ran as fast as I could from the frightening scene.

Then, as suddenly as the planes had appeared, the mountainside was quiet again. After the noise of the fighters, the stillness was eerie. I wondered for a moment if I had dreamed it. But branches were still falling from the shot-up trees, reminding me of the reality that I had just experienced. I kept running. Arriving breathless at the farmhouse, I hoped my father would not be angry that I had left the cattle.

My father already stood with the rest of the family in front of our farmhouse. We had been hearing rumours for some time. With growing German aggression, it seemed only a matter of time until something cruel and catastrophic happened. But it was clear that everyone was shocked by the attack.

"Dad, I'm scared!" I shouted, not caring who heard me.

My father remained cool. It was a great comfort to me—to all of us I think—that he remained calm, seeming in control of the situation. He gathered us around a large linden tree. He hesitated for a moment, gathering his thoughts, then spoke.

"The war has begun. It is going to be a tough time for all of us."

A view across the valley and town of Wisła.

He opened his Bible, which he had with him, and read, "And call upon me in the day of trouble: I will deliver thee and thou shalt glorify me" (Psalm 50:15). He then led us in family prayers, in which we all joined with heartfelt energy and seriousness.

I will never forget his face in that moment. It was so drawn. He had fought on the front line with the Austro-Hungarian forces in The Great War (as we then called it). He told us that this war would have a terrible impact on our family.

The morning was still so beautiful. The sky seemed infinitely blue. But the world we knew had ended with a broadside of bullets from three fighter planes.

On that lovely morning, my father could not have imagined just how long the war would go on or how terrible it would be. He did not yet know that it was extremely unlikely all of his family would survive.

In the following hours of that golden Polish autumn day, Germany invaded Poland. Our hard but pleasant way of life was about to be swept away into uncertainty, unfamiliarity, and an all-pervading atmosphere of threat, brutality and death.

Normally on a sunny morning, our farmyard was a happy place, echoing

The beautiful River Wisla, which rises in the Mountain of Barania.

with the lovely sound of children playing. Now it was silent. We knew that an ending had come to life as we knew it. In the same way, that ending was to come to thousands of lives in Silesia, millions of lives in Poland, and many millions more lives across Europe and the world.

LIFE
BEFORE

My name is Paweł Cieslar (pronounced Tseshlar) and I am from Wisła (pronounced Viswa), a town located at the foot of Barania Mountain in the Beskid Mountains, the source of the mighty Vistula River. Wisła is an area of outstanding natural beauty. To me, mention of the area conjures up pictures of beautiful rolling hills, romantic castles, and a family that was materially poor, but emotional and spiritual millionaires.

Our farm was known locally as "Breniok." The farm had been in the family for generations, but one ancestor had come from Brenna, all of 15 miles (25 kilometres) away. It was so unusual to have such a foreigner living in our closed community that the farm had taken its name—meaning "home of the man from Brenna"—from this outsider and the name had stuck.

In rural Upper Silesia—as in most of rural Europe—you were born into a farming community and rarely went outside it. You might go to the local market town for shopping or to sell produce, but that was all. There was no opportunity to visit Kracków, our nearest major city. Warsaw, the capital of Poland, might as well have been in a different galaxy.

We were subsistence farmers who made enough to support our lives—and little more. Electricity and gas were only available to wealthier people living in the centre of Wisła. Our country roads were still the medieval cart tracks, dusty in summer and frozen like concrete in the winter. Those tracks had been there when Upper Silesia belonged to Bohemia (1339–1526), then to Austria,

Austria-Hungary and then to Poland followed by the Third Reich, then to Poland again. Had there been any road signs, the language on them would have changed every 50 years on average. But there were no road signs.

Our water came from the well in the farmyard and was wonderfully pure. The water was cold but so very refreshing. In winter, the water was so cold it was painful to wash. I remember the screams of the children when our mother would wash them with the freezing water that had been brought from the well. Admittedly, she added a cup or two of boiling water to make it more bearable, but it did little good. This was doubtlessly character-forming—but we would have preferred warm baths. I especially came to this conclusion when I had my first warm shower at 17 years of age.

We wore traditional dress, and almost all of our clothes were homemade. My parents and other neighbours grew flax in their fields. Mr Troszok, a great friend and neighbour, was a naturally talented weaver, and his cloth made beautiful linen and woollen clothes for wintertime. My brothers had two or three pairs of trousers and two or three shirts and jackets. To maximise our limited clothes, as each child grew older the clothes would be handed down to the next eldest of the same gender until they crumbled into tatters. As my parents had nine children, they certainly got value out of those clothes!

Our shoes were moccasins, homemade from wool or rawhide, purchased from a local farmer or taken from one of our own cows that had been

The initial Adventist church orchestra in Wisla, of which four members were from the Cieslar family.

slaughtered. During the summer months from April to October, we children went barefoot.

Whatever possessions a farmer had on his farm were homemade. My father made his own wheelbarrow, as well as all of his tools and ploughs. He made all the plates, knives and forks in our house from Jasien wood, and also fashioned cups from a particular species of fir tree whose trunk was tube-like in the middle.

My mother made washing powder from burning hardwood and adding fat to the cold ashes. The chemical equation eludes me but it did produce an effective cleaning agent. At certain stages of this process, the material is highly corrosive. My mother's hands were rough and a pale white colour from making this mixture. The existence of gloves to wear in the kitchen remained as unsuspected as the future existence of television.

We did approximately five things in life. We worked, we ate, we slept, we worshipped daily, we went to church and, as children, we also went to school and would sometimes play. In summer, we boys rose at 4 am to cut the grass on our farm and also to help out neighbouring farmers' wives, whose men had been called into the German army. At 8 am, we ran to school.

The farm was an excellent place to grow up in. We loved playing around the

Open-air meeting around 1935 My oldest brother Jan is seen with a sousaphone around his shoulders.

farm and we loved our farm animals, especially our great big horse. Living on the farm taught us responsibility from an early age. Our "deprived" situation left us fit, both physically and mentally. We were neither sophisticated nor highly educated, but we knew the clear difference between right and wrong.

Fridays were particularly treasured, as Mother would bake bread. We loved the rough barley bread she baked. Two of us boys would grind the grain by hand between two stones. We would do it again and again until the grain was fine enough for cooking. Then we would give it to her to make into dough. It tasted so wonderful, particularly when it was fresh out of the oven.

When we took the bread to school some of the children from wealthier families would have bread that was resplendently white. We would look at this white bread and envy those rich children. Our barley bread stamped us as "poor people." I found out later, of course, that our brown bread had vastly better nutritional value but in the back blocks of 1930s rural Upper Silesia there were no nutritionists to explain this.

The milk we had was fabulous, coming straight from the cow. It bore little resemblance to the bland varieties we now buy in the supermarket. There was no chemical content in it and it was very good to drink. The cream was taken away for my mother to make butter, which she then sold. We only ever had butter during spring and autumn when we sowed the seed and harvested the corn. Mum was strict about that but sometimes when she wasn't looking we would help ourselves to a forbidden treat. It was so tasty!

Our simple life was, in fact, abundantly blessed. My father, mother and siblings were devoted to each other. No family could have been happier. Our inner needs as human beings were met wonderfully. We had human contact of the best kind in our family. We had love, respect and regard, and were so much the better for it.

My parents were also very wise. They devised ways to keep their children detached from the nastier aspects of small-town life in the late 1930s. They used their considerable abilities to keep us away from drinking, although alcoholism was endemic in the area, smoking—they were decades ahead of their time—and any kind of political involvement, because it usually led to violence of some sort. Their solution was to involve us in music. There were strong traditions of music in the area, especially brass bands. We all took to this readily and I discovered that I could be quite a handy trumpeter!

The problem was how to pay for expensive instruments. My mother sold a cow to raise the down-payment for my trumpet. My father cut down some trees and sold the timber to purchase a second instrument. I believe that some other church members also helped with the purchase. The instruments were purchased from the music shop in Cieszyn and took two years to pay off.

For my parents, this was such an important priority that they were more than happy to put up with whatever cost. As they expressed it, they wanted us to be engaged in something "profitable," developing our talents through mastering the instruments. They also wanted us to use our talents to glorify God as members of the local church choir and orchestra.

Pawel Cieslar Senior with Pawel Cieslar Junior (me) around 1929.

As children we were always taught to be respectful to people older than ourselves. If we met an adult or a woman in the street, it was customary to raise one's hat and to bow. It was a lovely custom that created a good atmosphere between people and helped to build firm friendships between people of different generations. In return for the respectful behaviour, adults would often give presents to the children such as cherries or apples.

As a Christian family, we conducted regular morning and evening family worship. The morning worship was predominately about placing ourselves in dependence on the protective care of God. Our father often prayed: "O Lord, take us as wholly Thine. We lay all our plans at Thy feet. Use us today according to Thy will. Abide with us, and let all our work be done by Thy grace." This was our family's daily commitment.

At evening family worship, we prepared ourselves for a peaceful rest by acknowledging our faults. As the head of the family, my father began the process of reconciliation and we children would follow his example. If one of us had disobeyed our mother or father or spoken unkind words to one of our siblings, he or she had to bring a basin, pour water and wash the feet of the person we had offended. There were always warm hugs and kisses after this.

NO HEIL HITLER!

We then sang an evening song and the whole family went happily to the night's rest.

In my memory, we had an idyllic life in many ways and in a naturally beautiful place. The local Protestant people were so affectionately attached to our region, giving rise to this haunting and moving song:

Father's home like paradise
The gift of heavenly father's grace
The length and breadth of the earth thou mightst travel
Only to find that no place will equal this marvel.

But the natural riches of our region also had a darker side. My homeland of Upper Silesia had massive mineral wealth and sits at an important crossroad of Europe. It seemed our paradise was doomed to be lost. Every neighbouring country was prepared to kill to possess it. And, throughout history, they did so with great gusto.

THE WAR BEGINS

Later on that September 1, the Polish town of Gliwice became Gleiwitz. Adolf Hitler sent an army of some 1.5 million men over the border into Poland, backed up by 1500 tanks, 1200 planes and, oddly enough, 200,000 horses. There was little that the small Polish air force and army could do. There were stories of Polish cavalry on horses charging German tanks. No-one seemed to know if these stories were true but they eloquently summed up the mismatch in the armed forces of the two countries. Poland kept fighting for more than a month but it was a losing battle.

In our Upper Silesia, which was close to Germany, it was all over much sooner. By the morning of September 2, General List's 14th Army had arrived in Wisła-Centrum, the central business district of the town. Wisła soon became Weichsel and, a month later, Paweł (pronounced "Powl") became Paul—at least, it did if I knew what was good for me.

It was as simple as that. They walked in. They took over. Yesterday we were Polish; today we were German.

The German army—the Wehrmacht—were impressive. They arrived overnight in huge numbers. Many local townspeople, particularly those of German descent or inclination, gave flowers to the soldiers. They were such pleasant-looking, fit young men. There was clearly a well-worked out plan. Every detail appeared to be under calm, authoritative management. Every soldier appeared to know his role within the plan. They occupied the town with an unhurried but clear discipline and were respectful to the townspeople.

As a young boy, the marching captivated me. Companies of some 120 men would march along in perfect step, their hob-nailed boots crunching up Oswald Street. I followed them as they marched from the centre of Wisła 3 miles (5 kilometres) to the suburb Głębce. They were so impressively presented, organised and disciplined. Their drill was impeccable. Their uniforms were well designed and smartly turned out. They sang marching songs with excellent harmonies. As they heard this wonderful performance, people would open windows and doors to hear and watch the wonderful spectacle unfold.

When the Oberfeldwebel commanded "Achtung, Halt!" the company would take three steps forward and on the final step would scrape their foot forward to rasp the hobnailed boots along the concrete road in front of the school. The performance did not apparently serve any great purpose other than to demonstrate the discipline and power of the German war machine, German pride and German superiority.

The whole display impressed the local townspeople and, to a young boy, it was overwhelming. We were to learn that the Third Reich offered a strange mixture of good things and—more commonly—bad things. But, in those early days, it was the first big excitement that Wisła had seen in a long time.

The senior officers in their immaculate Mercedes staff cars, with "cheese cutter" caps and long leather coats, looked confident and proud, possessing absolute authority. The whole German army gave an appearance that they were professional, irresistible and indomitable. When they talked with the townspeople, they were charming and intelligent. The early impressions were very favourable. We did not yet know that this was to be a completely different form of war, the likes of which we had not previously seen.

To our amazement we found that some townspeople had forewarning of the occupation. One woman named Maria already had her Nazi flag ready as the troops moved in. She waved it outside her house and shouted "Heil Hitler" at everyone who came by. In the ensuing days, she was to say "Heil Hitler" so many times that she became known locally as "Maria Hitler." Oddly enough, she was not German but Polish! Another man in town produced his Nazi armband as soon as the troops arrived. Every time we saw him in Wisła, he would have his armband on. To a young boy, this certainly seemed strange behaviour.

But there was a temporary upside to this sudden invasion. Some weeks before the German invasion, my Uncle Szalbot came to visit. He told my mother not to go to our Adventist church on that Saturday morning.

We discovered much later that Szalbot had got wind of a plot for a violent attack on the Adventists on their way to church. Encouraged by some clerics of the Nominal Church, the plotters also planned to completely wreck the church itself. It was to be highly organised, bloody and vicious. My family were in grave danger of being severely beaten or even killed.

The plotters were well versed in their methods. They had already attacked several Jewish businesses with grim success. The police had doubtlessly been tipped off to go and sort out something a long way away. But as the plotters were about to put their plan into action, a roar of tanks, transport trucks and motorcycles came into town, followed by horse-drawn supply trucks and lines of marching soldiers in shiny boots and singing inspiring and patriotic German songs.

In what might be the only case of a Nazi invasion having a truly preventive and beneficial effect for some people they invaded, the plot collapsed. We could have been killed but for the presence of the German army. In one of the most ironic twists in human history, they inadvertently prevented something extremely unpleasant being visited upon the people of the Adventist faith.

However, all of Wisła soon realised that the German presence would not remain a benefit for long.

WORLD WAR II HITS HOME

Although World War II had come with the declaration of war on September 3, 1939, we continued to do what we had always done on our farm. But this was not the way it was to stay.

Within days of the invasion, the Reichsmark replaced the Polish zloty and our Polish banknotes were replaced with banknotes featuring Hitler's head. Our Polish railways became the Deutsche Reichsbahn. And the police on the streets were now German police—the Ordnungspolizei—with their leather coats and strangely shaped helmets.

We now also had the SS. There were the general SS in their grey-green uniforms and some in the sinister black uniforms. There were the Sicherheitsdienst, the intelligence arm of the SS and could be recognised by the diamond-shaped badge on their left sleeve bearing the letters "SD".

I never saw an SS man smile. If you encountered them on the street, you were expected to give them a smart "Heil Hitler!" Unlike the civil police, they were not subject to any rules or regulations. They were outside the law and could do anything they wanted—and they wanted you to know it. I never found an SS man who even seemed like a human being. You could see it in their eyes. If you saw the SS sign—a silver death's head on a military cap or the "SS" letters on a collar—you went in a different direction, if possible.

In addition to these were the Gestapo, who dressed in plain clothes. They were concerned with suspected political crimes or anything to do with Jews.

Like most people faced with new forces of law and order, we were tempted to think that if we had nothing to hide, we had nothing to fear. We would discover that it was they who decided if you had anything to fear.

It was of no great concern that you might be innocent. Their job was to decide if you might be guilty and beat you up, send you to a concentration camp or kill you. And if the SS bashed you up or did anything else unpleasant, what they were doing was not a crime, it was legal. If you were subsequently found innocent of any charge, that was quite in order. From their perspective, you might have been guilty of something.

The Polish civil police had disappeared before the Germans arrived. Those who did not leave were rounded up by the SS and taken away. It seemed that anyone who had leanings toward Polish nationalist or leftist politics or was in any position of power in the town was taken away, as was my Uncle Szalbot.

We wondered how the Germans had been able to identify all of these people so quickly. We were to learn that when the Germans arrived they already had a list of some people to arrest. There was also much discussion as to where the people were taken to, but no-one really knew.

Some people disappeared in other ways. Some went to western Russia and the Ukraine, and for most this proved to be a death sentence. Others fled elsewhere.

There was a small cafe in the mountains, which—it was whispered—was a safe house for those trying to reach Hungary, which was not far away from our farm and remained open for tourists. But we did not talk about these things openly. Such conversations might earn a death sentence for the cafe proprietors and their whole family. One of our neighbours' sons, Adolf Pilch, disappeared suddenly. According to the rumours, he had gone in this direction: whether it was true, no-one could say.

Others from our community went to the General Government area, a Nazi slave state in Central Poland. Many who went there did not return. But we knew from an early stage not to ask too many questions.

The town square in Weichsel—known as Zdrojowy—was festooned with black, white and red Nazi flags. The German authorities placed loudspeakers in high places around the square so people in town could hear the permanent propaganda about how powerful and successful Germany was. These shouted at us all day long. The shopkeepers must have been on the verge of lunacy. These broadcasts were interspersed with rousing German marches and military songs.

Meanwhile it was clear from the start that the Third Reich had no respect for Poles, Poland or Polish culture. Performances of Polish music, such as the works of Chopin or Paderewski, were forbidden. Poland has a long tradition of great prose and poetry writers but suddenly these writers' books became unobtainable.

Polish radio went dead. Where there had been news items, music and weather forecasts, there was silence. We did actually know a few wealthy people who possessed a radio, a "Volksempfänger", which cost about the same as a labourer's weekly wage. To listen to foreign radio stations such as the Polish Service of the BBC in London or Free Europe Radio brought a summary death sentence. But we knew people who possessed radios and listened to the forbidden stations under blankets in their bedrooms, in cupboards or in cellars. They passed on details as to how the war was progressing. There was no point in reading newspapers as they were under Nazi-control and quite worthless.

The new regime inflicted its propaganda everywhere. Posters told us of the new wondrous age that had now arrived and of the inevitability of the German victory. The "German greeting" of a "Heil Hitler" with right hand held high stiffly became mandatory. Many were proud to give this new greeting. Those who did not could find themselves taken away at 4 am. A few came back. Most did not.

We quickly came under the tender care of the "Blockleiter," the neighbourhood warden responsible for our political supervision. This lowest role in the Nazi hierarchy was to ensure everyone was compliant and loyal to the regime; that everyone said "Heil Hitler"—in spirit, as well as deed—and also that no-one was doing anything of which the National Socialist regime would disapprove.

We suspected two things of our Blockleiter, both of which proved correct. First, he kept a file on everyone in the neighbourhood. Second, he had connections to the Gestapo and Sicherheitsdienst. The Blockleiter rapidly became a key person. If you wanted to buy property or were applying for a job in the civil administration, you needed his signature confirming that you were not Jewish. If the police or Gestapo came sniffing around, it paid to be on good terms with him.

In our case, we were fortunate. Our Blockleiter was Mr Polok. Although he worked for Nazis, he was fundamentally a decent man, and had a reputation of being fair in his dealings. Had he so wished, he could have made us disappear just because we were Adventists and did not say "Heil Hitler" enthusiastically enough—or, in our case, at all.

One of Mr Polok's earliest duties was to ensure that every house had a German flag. Some people had huge flags. We tried not to be conspicuous and to blend into the background but our flag was the smallest we could get away with.

Another local Blockleiter, Mr L___, was a man of a different disposition. He was widely suspected of sending people to places referred to as "the camps" on the most trivial charges or even no charge at all. One of Mr L___'s methods was to creep outside people's houses in the evening and listen to conversations. My father found him outside our house on several occasions.

"What are you doing here, Mr L___?"

"Oh, I was just coming to see that your 'blackout' was effective," he would explain disingenuously.

If he overheard someone saying anything disloyal to the Reich, he would report him or her to the SS. In one well-known local case, he had hitched a lift with a local farmer and engaged him in a conversation criticising the Nazi hierarchy. As they entered Weichsel, he got down from the cart, saying that he had to visit a local shop and bade the farmer farewell. Ten minutes later, the farmer found his cart surrounded by SS uniforms—and the farmer was not seen again.

Rumours continued to circulate as to where all these arrested people had disappeared. Some rumours were quite grisly but there were so many rumours that most people took most rumours with a pinch of salt.

Mr L___'s case gives an excellent example of how some human beings can become intoxicated with power and use it to malevolent ends. There is no doubt that Mr L___ thought he could get away with it in the long run. In one sense, this was typical of many people who sold their soul to Hitler. Their stupidity let them believe they could behave as they did and that there would be no consequence.

* * *

After the pomp and ceremony of the invasion, we settled down to life under the Third Reich. The atmosphere was negative, poisoned. It was as if the air we breathed was polluted by the propaganda, the evil presence of the SS and the rumours that circulated increasingly about those mysterious places called "the camps."

Polish law simply disappeared with the advent of the Wehrmacht. We were now under German law, which was not all bad. The drunken wife-beaters in the town got short shrift from the Ordnungspolizei. If a woman complained that her husband beat her, the man was subject to a process of law and was in a considerable amount of trouble.

Similarly, Wisła had been menaced by a gang of young men. They were always in town drunk. They would pick fights with people and beat them up for fun. If someone had a party, they would gate crash it. If anyone complained, they would be beaten. If no-one complained, they would start a fight anyway. The Polish police seemed to have no idea how to deal with them. But a couple of weeks after the German invasion, they were rounded up and taken away for a few days. We did not know where they were taken or what happened—but none of them ever gave the slightest trouble again.

Some people in Weichsel deluded themselves that the transference from Poland to Germany would lead to a higher standard of living. In that first year of occupation, this was apparently proving true. The coming of the Reich had given a modest boost to the local economy and Upper Silesia enjoyed a modest rise in living standards.

In the 1930s, Germany had undergone an economic miracle and they were promising to extend it to us. Hitler himself had come up with the concept of a cheap all-purpose car that was designed to be affordable to every family—the KDF-Wagen, later renamed "Volkswagen." Oddly enough, we never got to see one until after the war. There was talk of wonderful roads with flyovers where you could travel from one end of the country to the other in a matter of hours. German airships were crossing the Atlantic. From what we heard, the German railways were luxurious and very impressive. The *Bremen* was an ocean liner of wondrous proportions.

"What good fortune!" said some of the German people in Wisła.

Polish workers had gone increasingly to Germany to look for work. As Germany had now come to us, perhaps some of that prosperity would simply land in our laps. We remarked that the beggars who used to call on us had disappeared. It did not occur to us at that time that their disappearance might be sinister. Being part of Greater Germany was making Upper Silesia a little richer but at the cost of our meat, wool and timber, which were being stolen.

UNDER NEW MANAGEMENT

After the Nazi invasion in Silesia, we noticed a growing influx of "Reichsdeutcher"—Germans who came from inside the Reich. They had come to germanise us. The Reichsdeutchers cherished their attitude toward the Polish people as backward people, they even had an expression of "Polnische Wirtschaft"—"Polish management"—as they looked down on Polish people. The Germans believed their civilisation far superior to other nations, an attitude they demonstrated in demeaning and forceful ways.

An edict declared that all Silesians were now "Volksdeutsch" and that the Silesian territory belonged to Germany. We were required to sign the "Volksliste" in order to be officially recognised as "Volksdeutsch." To us, this was utter nonsense but the German Government had made it clear that this was compulsory.

There was a certain German logic behind this, tortured though it was. It stemmed from the German desire to have Upper Silesia as an integral part of the Reich. The embarrassing reality to the Germans was the fact that only a small percentage of the Silesian population actually spoke German as a first language. But, in order to justify the annexation, the rest of the Silesian population had to be classified as German.

Our new masters issued us with an identity card—the "Ausweis"—which we had to carry at all times or face punishment. This clearly showed our Volksdeutsch "Class 3" status. You could be asked for your papers at any time, and to be found without an Ausweis would result in arrest.

However, this created at least one advantage for people whose names were not on the Volksdeitschliste—they were exempt from German military service. It just meant that they were officially listed as "Polish." They should have known that if the Nazis were offering some leniency, something more deadly might be lurking below the surface. A short time later, the non-signatories made the interesting and unusual discovery that they had to wear a "P" badge on their clothing at all times.

From these earliest days, boys from the more German households began to appear at school in their Hitlerjugend uniforms with Swastika armbands. Similarly, we now had girls appearing in the girls' equivalent Bund Deutscher Mädel uniforms. The BDM uniforms were very smart and gave no hint that they were associated with a concerted attempt at mind control over a whole generation of young girls.

In the next few weeks, even more new uniforms and badges began to appear in the streets. One of the most intriguing was a blue cross that Reichsteutsch women wore. It was a Mutterkreuz or Mothering Cross. It was given to German women who had more than six children and meant that they would be served first in shops, would be saluted by officials in uniform and a whole host of other benefits. To our relief it turned out that my mother, as a Silesian woman, did not qualify.

Our schoolteachers were replaced with German schoolteachers. Several of our Polish teachers were among those who were arrested. We were not to see them again and do not know what happened to them. All we knew was that one morning we arrived to find that every classroom had a picture of Hitler, looking menacingly down on us.

Our new teacher, Fraulein Bramke, was one of the recent Reichsdeutsche arrivals. She was about 45 years old with blonde hair and pale blue Nordic eyes. Her hair was plaited and rolled into a bun in a very Germanic way. She was a determined follower of Adolf Hitler and always wore her Nazi Party badge. When Fraulein Bramke walked into the classroom, she would look adoringly at the mandatory picture of Hitler fixed to the front wall of the classroom. It was as though she was looking into the face of God.

No longer did our teacher enter our classroom with a greeting of "Good morning, children." Now Fraulein Bramke entered to a scraping of chairs as we all stood to the greeting, "Good morning, German children!"

Fraulein Bramke's right arm would shoot out enthusiastically. We children had to respond equally enthusiastically or face the painful consequences. Most of us actually thought we were Polish children. However, corporal punishment was part of life in those days and was applied with gusto. Being "German children" was less painful than being "Polish children," so we stuck out our arms and did as we were commanded.

Fraulein Bramke and another German teacher, Herr Heining, frequently walked along the streets where the children's parents lived, engaging the locals in light conversation. In a small community such as ours, the people soon suspected that they were passing information to the authorities. Word went around, quietly but quickly, "Be extremely careful when talking to them."

My sisters even found them taking photographs of our house on one occasion. We wondered what they were up to. Most people dressed in the traditional Beskids mountain cloths. Were they sending photos home to show how the quaint, old-fashioned Polish peasants lived?

After the invasion, the Germans continually emphasised one reality: everything in the Nazi state was for the state and if you assume something was innocent, you were gambling with death. Even a walk around the town centre was polluted with Nazi signage:

"Rader musen rollen fur den Sieg!"—"Wheels must roll for victory."

"Der Sieg wird unser sein!"—"Victory will be ours."

"Fuhrer befiehl! Wir gechorchen!"—"Hitler commands! We will obey."

Nazism crept into every corner of everyday life.

When the German army had its great victory after nine months of the most vicious fighting at Sevastopol in Russia, Fraulein Bramke almost knelt down in the classroom before the picture of Hitler. Her face was as radiant as sunshine. Her arm jutted out in the prescribed manner and she said "Heil Hitler! Heil Hitler! Heil Hitler!" Her eyes had the far-away look of a saint in a medieval painting.

We found the behaviour of Fraulein Bramke and the other Nazi believers both odd and obsessive. As she bent in an attitude of prayer before her beloved Hitler, a small number of children from a Nazified background also gave a "Heil Hitler!" Most of the rest of us found the whole spectacle funny, offensive and looked on with embarrassment at the antics of this woman.

Quite often she looked at us with her pale Nordic blue eyes and shouted: "Sing, children, sing!"

"Deutschland, Deutschland über alles, über alles in der welt."

"Germany, Germany above all, above all in the world."

Not all of the German newcomers were so possessed by Hitler. For instance,

Fraulein Tauber was a different young person. We liked her and looked forward to her lessons. Often she would take us out to enjoy the forests, the mountains and the wonderful natural surroundings. This was great fun. Even better, we would sing folk songs mostly about nature, instead of the politico-military songs the other teachers favoured so much.

While our German schoolteachers did not make such a big event of Christmas as we had been used to, they did not stop it. They appeared to tolerate it, rather than celebrate it. We noticed later that the biggest day in the German school was now April 20—Hitler's birthday. This was celebrated with lots of Nazi colour, flags and a parade with singing and shouting.

Fraulein Bramke would fuss and bother as if the celebration of Hitler's birthday was the most important event since the creation of the world. School children would line up in rows and march through town streets waving Swastika flags and singing, "Deutschland, Deutschland über alles, über alles in der Welt!"

They could call us fellow Germans as much as they wanted but the Germans remained alien to most people in Upper Silesia. They were strangers and enemies.

On the other hand, Poles had to know their place, which was toward the bottom of the pile. There were similar regulations for Jews who had to wear yellow armbands, later replaced by the yellow Star of David. Apart from these minor indignities and humiliations, it was not too onerous for Silesian people. There were, we clearly understood, punishments if you did not wear your badge of ethnicity.

At the same time, a very visible sign appeared in shops and railway carriages. It said: "Nur für Deutscher"—"Only for Germans." If you had "P" or other ethnic badges, you were not allowed into those shops or railway carriages on pain of the usual punishments. This was insanity of a high order. The ban applied most stringently to the Jews.

THE REICH TIGHTENS ITS GRIP

As we were now classified Silesian Volksdeutscher, our new Nazi masters decreed that the only language to be used for official business was German. Both the younger and the older folk had to learn German quickly. Lessons in the German language were compulsory, unless you could demonstrate some level of fluency. My father spoke German from his time in the Austro-Hungarian army and so was exempt. My mother, however, was not.

On the appointed day, she attended the first class. In the course of the lesson, the teacher started to shout at the class in German. Most of the ladies in the class had no clue what she was screaming about. After some minutes of being harangued in an officially approved manner, one woman got up and walked out. Others followed. Soon the entire class had walked out.

"Stop, stop!" screamed the teacher. This was met with suppressed chuckles, before someone burst out laughing. "Stop! Stop!" screamed the teacher, but by this time the class was down the corridor and into the street, laughing uncontrollably.

As an occupied people, we had one avenue of opposition and that was laughter. But we had to be very careful who we heard the joke from and even more careful who we passed it on to. The Nazi hierarchy looked down on the telling of jokes, political jokes in particular, and these could lead to swift disappearance. There were many jokes around at the time, for the Poles were good at them.

About this time, we began to hear rumours of a Russian massacre of Poles. The rumour was very vague and there were many rumours in those days. We took note of them but there was always a doubt as to whether they might be true. We were not to learn the word *Katyn* until much later—this was the name of the forest in which invading Soviet troops massacred thousands of Polish people in April and May, 1940.

Mr Baron was a local policeman who left when the Germans advanced. Mr Baron escaped into the part of Poland that the Germans had not yet occupied. Two weeks later, the eastern part of Poland was invaded by the Russians. Apparently, he was picked up by the Russian, then murdered in the forests of Katyn near Smoleńsk. He was my sister Maria's future father-in-law. He was a fine man and we young people liked him very much. He had done nothing remotely criminal to justify having his hands bound behind his back and having a bullet shot into his head.

* * *

The exiled Polish government in London had started to organise partisan activity against the German occupying forces. After a year or so, the Nazi regime had started a call-up system for forced workers. When the call up was not successful, people were just taken from the street. Because of these forced labour kidnappings, many people were happy to join the partisan activity. This involved sabotaging German vehicles and defacing German propaganda. They might disable railway wagons, vandalise German army trucks or write anti-German slogans on walls.

Usually the Germans were very revengeful in response to such activity. They would seal the exits to the town square and surround the people trapped there. They would pick out people who wore the Jewish yellow star or "P" badges. If these were not enough, they would simply arrest people at random. The selected people would be taken immediately into the surrounding forest and shot. The report of rifles would ring out in the distance. Many families lost their loved ones in this way and mourned their loss for years. There are many monuments in the forests that mark where so many people were taken out to be murdered.

One such incident will always be seared in my memory. It started on the Wisła-Głębce railway station one hot summer day. A young lady was waiting for a train in the sweltering heat. Suddenly, smoke came from inside her clothing and she appeared to burst into flames. She screamed for help and ripped off her burning clothing.

The other passengers naturally helped to put the flames out but there was something very odd about such an occurrence. The stationmaster came to supervise and began asking questions. It became apparent she had been carrying explosives for the underground movement. They were willing amateurs and not competent to play such a dangerous game.

Within minutes, a Gestapo car appeared at that station with a scream of brakes. Two men took her away. "We have ways to make a woman talk," said the Gestapo man.

I do not want to imagine what they did to her but they did make her talk. She gave them more than 20 names of men from the district of Cieszyn, who were involved in sabotage activity. They were arrested and tortured pitifully until the Gestapo were certain they could get no more information from them.

On this occasion, they were not taken to the forest for summary execution. A mass gallows was erected in the district town Cieszyn—or, as we now had to call it, Teschen. The townspeople were forced to assemble to watch the proceedings. The Gestapo wanted to set an example. They set out seats before each of the gallows. Each seat was for the mother of the person being hanged. Each mother was forced to watch while the tortured remains of a son or daughter were hanged just a few feet away.

One of our neighbours, Jan Halama, was hanged. His mother screamed and screamed and screamed in an inconsolable bereavement.

* * *

Some months after this event, I was at the bottom of the ski slopes in the Wisła Mountains, not far from home. The snow lay thickly on the ground and in the branches of the fir trees. The whole place was a classic winter wonderland. Many people had come out to go skiing. Hundreds of people enjoyed themselves so much as they climbed the hill and skied down to the bottom. The winter sunshine and the scenery below looked very beautiful. It was a truly wonderful scene in the midst of increasing gloom as Hitler's regime took over our lives.

A sudden thought flashed through my head. I could not stop thinking of it no matter what I did. The thought was a question: "How many of these people will survive the evil events in this country?"

I looked at the people once again with sympathy and sadness. I do not know, of course, how many of them did survive but, on average, a third of them would have been dead four years later.

Another depressing event that we learned about in the second part of 1940 was to have significance for us locally but also later on for the whole human race. The Germans were arresting an increasing number of people and needed places to imprison them. So the former cavalry barracks, some 40 miles (60 kilometres) away from our farm, provided a convenient foundation for such a facility of mass arrest and torture. They turned it into a concentration camp—or as called later "death factory"—where those who fell foul of the regime would be murdered and by the same token shown who was boss.

The concentration camp was established in the town of Oświęcim, better known by its new German name, Auschwitz. It was to become one of the saddest places on earth.

OUR CHURCH GOES UNDERGROUND

It was now some months since the Germans had moved into Upper Silesia. Many people had had their lives messed up in one way or another but, so far, we Adventists had been left substantially alone. This was to change dramatically.

One Sabbath, an SS officer in civilian dress came to our church. He asked politely for the elder and we introduced him. He handed the elder a piece of paper.

"You are to read this to your congregation," he instructed.

The elder read the paper and blanched. In an emotional voice, he read out these words: "You are permitted to have only one more sermon, one more hymn, and one more prayer. There will be nothing more. Then you will all leave this place and never return for any purpose of worship."

The SS officer nodded his head, indicating that the elder had read the paper out accurately, and looked across the congregation. Then he clicked his heels and went to stand by the front door, looking bored by the whole proceeding.

By now we knew how the Reich worked. If we disobeyed, the punishment would be fearful.

The congregation was silent. No-one knew what to say next. The elder thought more quickly than anyone and began to preach a sermon that lasted from 11 am to 1 pm. Then he found the longest hymn in the church hymnal. After singing, we all knelt to pray. Every boy and girl, every man and woman, every old person—we all prayed as if it were our last prayer ever. We prayed for an hour and, at 2 pm, we filed out past the German officer who had waited for three hours with commendable patience.

As we left, he nailed a notice on the church door "Entry Forbidden on Pain of Punishment." Some people were sighing, a few cried and everyone looked so terribly sad. We had been banished from this, the happiest place on earth for us. The words echoed through our minds: ". . . never return for any purpose of worship."

Small groups of Adventists walked away slowly in different directions, glancing mournfully at the church. They were saying a grief-stricken goodbye: not only to one another but also to the house of God, which they loved so much. They had congregated here every Saturday as long as anyone could remember. I recall particularly that several people lingered by the chapel for a long time, looking at the building as if they were chiselling an image of the building in their hearts and minds.

* * *

Some weeks later, two SS men knocked on the door of our house and demanded that all religious material be handed over to them. After we had complied, they searched the house for any Bibles, church hymnals or any other religious books. They knew exactly what they were looking for and took away all of our written material to be destroyed.

My parents had foreseen that something like this might happen. For the previous couple of years, they had taught us as children to memorise as many Bible verses as possible. Now they got us to write them all down. All of the adults in the Adventist community did the same thing and my parents hid the papers in secret places where the SS would never find them, if—or rather when—they came back to check on us. It was clear that they knew where all the Adventist families lived and performed spot checks on us but never found anything that would send us to a concentration camp.

However, we were able to replace our hymnals, Bibles and other religious books. Of all places, they came from Germany. The Adventist Church was allowed to carry on in Germany as normal but in Silesia it was banned. There was presumably some logic behind this but it eluded everyone. At any rate, the books came down a secret line of communication. We never knew where they came from or quite where they went to but they did turn up in our worship services. They were imaginatively hidden and never found. Everyone knew the ferocious risk that they could be betrayed at any time and without warning.

Some of our Bibles and hymnals were in the Polish language and others were in German. There is a certain irony that German language and culture was, on the one hand, the culture of terror and death and, on the other, the culture of civilisation and decency. By the same token, my father would pray both in the Polish language and in German.

The Adventist community decided it would carry on with our religious practices in a clandestine manner and in places of which our Nazi rulers were, we hoped, unaware. This was the point at which the 300-year-old folk memory of organised Lutheran civil disobedience was to serve well as an example to the Adventists.

First, it was safer for us to conduct services within our single family home. My family carried this out for the whole of the war. Even then, we proceeded with extreme caution and no little trepidation.

Second, it was customary for shepherds to sing songs, while watching their animals on the pastures. The Nazi regime tolerated this. Totally by "chance," a group of Adventist farmers would meet with their cattle on the pastures and

A forest church meeting remembering and celebrating the heritage of the faithful people of Wisła. Photo used by permission of Michal Pilch.

this "random" meeting would develop into an impromptu session of song plus some sessions of religious study and prayer. It was amazing how many such meetings occurred. If anything was written or if longer term plans were made, collaborators or Blockleiters would hear of it and the SS would be waiting to arrest us. And we knew what that meant.

Because we kept Saturday as Sabbath, we were very aware that we were suspected of being somehow related to the Jews. We know that the SS specifically suspected that we were hiding Jews as some Adventists in Germany had done.

Every day there was the possibility of the SS drawing up to the door and either shooting everyone immediately or arresting them for torture and disappearance into a concentration camp. As for "tomorrow" that was a concept you could not think about. "Tomorrow" was a luxury. You were still alive today and that, at least, was good.

It was about this time that people who had escaped from one of the camps in the Auschwitz slave labour empire began to appear. From time to time, a terrified escapee would head up into the mountain region near where we lived. He would come late at night begging for food and shelter. There was nothing in his stomach and utter terror in his eyes. We all knew that if we helped them we would be taken to a concentration camp and worked to death, if not immediately shot or hanged. Some prisoners were recaptured by the Germans and tortured to make them tell who had helped them.

It seemed almost every week that our neighbours would open the door to such people and send them up to us saying "The Adventists are good people and they have a farm. They may have some food for you." This was code. It really meant "The Adventists are the people who will be shot if they are caught helping you." It also got back to us that some of our neighbours were saying, "The Adventists believe in God, perhaps their God will help you." We were exposed to this danger on an almost daily basis for five long years.

It would be against our conscience not to help these unfortunate ones but the motives of some of the neighbours really come into question. They had got rid of the threat by sending it to us and possibly ensured the escapees got fed. And, of course, if anyone were to be caught and sent to Auschwitz, it would be us and not them who would go. By talking to some of the escapees, we knew what to expect if the SS caught us.

The world of horror with the Nazis seemed to know no boundaries. A friend of mine was walking through town one quiet afternoon. On the other side of the street was a young woman with a baby. A uniformed official, perhaps a policeman or an SS man, walked calmly up to her. He grabbed the baby from her, swung it around and beat its head against a wall, killing it instantly. He threw the pathetic broken little body into a ditch and walked on as if nothing had happened. The whole episode was over as quickly as you have read it. It filled me with a horror that persists to this day, seven decades later.

I wonder what that man did that evening. Did he share a few beers with his workmates and tell them the story, which they would all laugh about? Did his workmates come back with similar amusing stories of their own? I wonder what that man felt later in his life. Did he look back with joy to the golden age when criminality was legal? The sad conclusion is that he was most probably the willing victim of the collective psychosis called National Socialism of Hitler's reich.

THE HISTORY
OF OUR STORY

From that first morning when those three planes had shot away the treetops, our world changed completely. Apart from anything else, our church services were banned. But there were some significant historical background that added resilience to our faith and family amid these trials.

* * *

The first important story explains why Wisła was predominantly Protestant, while the neighbouring town Istebna was almost totally Catholic—and how our people have long experience with political and religious oppression, and of resistance to these outside forces.

In the 17th century, Duchy Cieszynskie was a Protestant area. The inhabitants had supported Martin Luther during the Reformation a century earlier but the Dukes of Cieszyn eventually fell under the influence of the Habsburg Empire, which meant the region would be forcibly returned to the Catholic faith. On April 1, 1655, the Duchy issued an edict to the inhabitants of Cieszyn banning secret church services on pain of severe punishment.

In 1663, a Religious Purging Committee was established to enforce the doctrine and authority of the church. As this committee became more powerful and expanded its operations, it was increasingly detested by the Protestant population. The committee's actions became counter-productive.

In order to retain the Protestant form of worship, Protestants began holding secret church services in caves and forest churches—and this dissenting faith continued to grow.

The local Catholic nobles signed a petition asking Emperor Leopold to send Jesuits to Cieszyn. In May, 1676, the Emperor's office informed the court in Wroclaw that the Jesuits Province agreed to send missionaries to Cieszyn, and that the church hierarchy in Duchy Cieszyn was to give them all material and moral support. On September 14, 1676, Jan Pisek and Pawel Beranek came to Cieszyn. The Catholic hierarchy and nobility were extremely welcoming and supported their mission wholeheartedly. Jan Pisek became the leader of the new mission and reported to the Jesuits hierarchy in Opawa.

After settling in Cieszyn, the Jesuits targeted those areas most likely to give immediate results. They attacked the nobles who had supported the Protestant religion. They prevailed on the local courts to issue a writ, ordering all the Protestant nobles to either give their children up to the Jesuits for education or send them away to their school in Lower Silesia.

Then they turned their attention to the religious studies of the adolescent children in Cieszyn. They developed a detailed list of all eligible children who had failed to attend their first communion, identifying the families who supported the Protestant cause. The children on the list were ordered to take part in Sunday school lessons. The local magistrate had parents imprisoned if their children failed to appear at Sunday school as required.

To further their goal, militiamen were placed on city gates in Cieszyn in an attempt to stop attendance at the secret meetings that still carried on, despite these methods used to control and convert Protestants.

There are many faith-filled stories recounted from the Protestants during this time. One tells of a young woman on her way to a secret religious meeting who was stopped by a guard.

"Where are you going?" the guard asked.

"Sir," the woman replied creatively, "I am going to my Father's home."

"And what will you do there?" the guard demanded.

Thinking quickly, she replied, "I will read my Brother's testament."

"In that case," losing interest, the guard said, "Go."

The young woman continued to the secret meeting with a quickened heartbeat. Her heart was lifted that she had not been caused to lie. "I am hurrying to a place that is a replacement for the House of God, who is our Father. And there we will read the testament of His Son, who is our Brother!"

* * *

It was clear that the efforts to stamp out Protestantism were failing. In 1672, the emperor issued an ultimatum. All those who would not convert to Catholicism within six months would be forced to leave town. The order received much opposition but was upheld. Father Pisek forced the implementation of the order. The Starost received the order on July 21, 1672. Several Lutheran families left Cieszyn immediately. House-to-house searches intensified and known Lutherans were fired by their employers.

However, in some smaller mountain villages, where Protestantism was strong, the edict was not enforced. So the Jesuits set their sights on these villages. They formally requested that the Catholic Bishop Franciszek Ludwik appoint a suitable missionary to bring the mountain areas into line. In response Leopold Tempest was assigned as missionary to the Cieszyn district.

To begin, Tempest targeted the poorest parish, Jablonkowo, which became the base for his activities. Tempest was appointed as priest in all parishes of the Cieszyn diocese. His mission was to convert the Protestant believers. This, of course, would save their souls but it would also increase the political power of the Catholic Church and their political allies.

This stone in the forest of Rownica was rediscovered at the beginning of the 20th century, marking the meeting place of a secret church. Photo used by permission of Michal Pilch.

Tempest proved to be a formidable opponent to the Protestants. The typical Jesuit strategies of coercion and manipulation drove Protestant practices underground. Tempest realised this and used entirely different methods.

Tempest's primary method of conversion and confirmation of the faithful in Catholicism was religious instruction and constructing church buildings. From early morning until late at night, Tempest visited people in their homes and taught them. Due to his gentle nature, some Protestants welcomed him into their homes. He worked ceaselessly to gain people's trust. He visited. He laughed and joked with people. He gave presents to people such as religious paintings or a bowl to hold holy water. He listened to what people had to say and, when he saw an opportunity, engaged in religious instruction.

Istebna was the most successful place for Tempest. Even today, the strong Catholic presence in Istebna owes much to the work of Tempest. Many other villages and towns were brought back, or at least closer, to Catholicism due to the salesmanship of Tempest. His intelligence and indefatigable nature won the day in every town. Until he showed up in Wisła.

Tempest's success ended in Wisła. He was unable to work his magic in this town. He wrote to his superiors complaining about the stiff-necked heretics in Wisła.

Re-enacting the worship and remembering the faithfulness of their ancestors, Polish believers meeting in the forest churches of the past. Photo used by permission of Michal Pilch.

The difference was the Bible study in their many underground forest churches and schools. The majority of the people were self-educated. They used the Bible and religious books to learn and to teach each other about God's Word and truth. In a time when nearly all religious education came from the clergy, these people were engaged in personal Bible study. In the church chronicles of Bukowa and Szymkow, it is recorded that they also occasionally received visiting preachers from Hungary, who conducted secret services for them.

With the Protestants in Wisła so strongly rooted in their knowledge of the Bible, Tempest had little impact. He failed to take Wisła back to the Catholic fold. His presence and new strategies served to strengthen, yet again, the resolve of those meeting in secret.

During the Nazi occupation, the Wisła Adventist church members faced religious bans much like their ancestors. But they knew how to weather the storm. They remembered their history and, again, faced the tempest with strong commitment to the Bible and its principles.

This chapter based on material in *The Society of Jesus in Silesia of Cieszyn* by Jozef Kiedos, pages 40–45, used by permission

THE STORY
OF OUR FAMILY

T he second part of our history was the story of our family. The "paradise" my family enjoyed in Wisła had been hard won.

My grandfather had been a *pijak*—a notorious drunk. Heavy drinking was a major social problem at the time. My grandfather kept the company of the other local drunks, who pulled him into the alcoholic maelstrom. The stuff they used to drink was Polish vodka that could be as high as 95 per cent alcohol. The effect on my grandfather and his boozing mates was that they were perpetually drunk. The alcohol ruined them. My father told me that many times he heard my grandfather, absolutely rotten drunk, shouting and swearing as he staggered home. If my grandmother used ill-chosen words, which might displease him, she would receive a quick punch or two. My father was disgusted.

At harvest times, the wives of the old *pijaks* would have to ask neighbours for help "because he is down the pub drunk, he can't even stand and he doesn't seem to care whether the harvest is taken in or not." If she had complained to him, she would have risked another flurry of punches. Even though the Nominal Churches had a strong influence on village life, for some reason they had a tolerant attitude toward *pijaks*, of which there were many.

My grandfather degenerated into the kind of hard drinker who beat his wife on a regular basis. He would throw her on the floor and kick her until he had no energy left. To finance his alcohol addiction, he sold much of the forest from the family farm. Fortunately for our farm, legal restrictions prevented him from selling the land as well. From time to time, teams of workers arrived and another chunk of timber disappeared to pay for my grandfather's drinking habit.

As children, we heard the story of how it all came to a turning point. My grandfather was giving my grandmother one of his regular beatings one night and my father—who was then 18—could not bear it any more. His loathing of my grandfather's behaviour and the anger at his pathetic lifestyle brought a volcano of passion out of him.

He grabbed my grandfather by the shoulders and pressed him against a wall so that my grandfather could not escape. "Stop it, Father, this is a disgrace!" he ordered.

My grandfather was screaming and cursing and shouting at my father to let him go. My father's emotions must have been so confused. On one hand, there was his love for his father. On the other was the dislike, contempt and pity for this degraded human being.

"Get your hands off me, you little creep." He swore for added emphasis.

"Father, I will not let you go until you promise me faithfully that what you did to my mother will never be repeated," my father replied calmly.

Then my grandfather began to plead in an ingratiating, whining voice. But my father knew my grandfather would attack him if he relaxed his grip. He held my grandfather firmly against the wall and asked my grandmother to open the outside door.

In one movement, my father released my grandfather and ran out of the house as fast as he was able.

In his drunken rage, my grandfather staggered to the fireplace and picked up a large block of wood. He threw it at my father as he ducked across the yard. Then my grandfather picked up an axe and chased him.

If he had caught my father, there is no doubt that murder would have been committed in our yard. But, in his drunken state, my grandfather could not run in a straight line and his chance of landing a blow was small. Nevertheless, my father dared not go back home.

My father escaped to Czechoslovakia and worked for two years in a factory in the town of Trzyniec until things quietened down. One day at this time, my father recalled, he knelt on the ground and prayed, "God! Please let me live a different life than my father."

It probably never occurred to my grandfather but, by his negative example, he instilled good values into my father. My father felt that as long as he was leading a life opposite to that of my grandfather then his life was heading in the right direction.

Like most of the rest of the people of the region, my father was a dedicated and staunch Lutheran. But, in 1912, a Seventh-day Adventist Church was planted in Wisła. The minister of the nominal church had a burning hatred of these new Adventists, whom he described as a pestilence on Wisła's territory. In reality, the Adventists were peaceful and hard-working people. But both the nominal church and later the Nazi occupiers confused the Adventist church with Judaism because of the Adventists' observance of the Sabbath on Saturday rather than Sunday, the first day of the week.

About a year after the Adventist Church was established, members of the nominal church solicited my father to lead a group of street thugs to harass and intimidate the Adventists. My father's plan was simple: his gang of thugs would go to the Adventist church to interrupt the worship service and beat up anyone they could get their hands on.

It was partly student prank and partly attempted murder. My father organised his thuggish friends to go to cut down a hefty tree trunk. They also made four stout cudgels. As the worship service began, four of the gang

My father and his gang attacking the Adventist church in 1913, painting by Katarzyna Mojak.

members lurked by the exit door with cudgels ready. The other four smashed the tree-trunk through the church window, aiming directly at the heads of those worshippers unfortunate enough to be in the way. The idea was that the people inside would panic and, as they came out the door, would have to run the gauntlet of the four bully boys who would be aiming their cudgels at heads, arms and any other body part they thought they could injure.

The tree trunk smashed through the window, glass shattered in all directions. "Filthy Jewish swine!" my father and the other boys yelled. "Take that, you scum! Kill the Jews! Kill the Jews!"

Some were hurt with gashes to the head as the tree trunk smashed into them.

"Kill the Jews! Kill the Jews!" the shout went on.

The worship service stopped but people did not shout and there was no panic. The members of the congregation looked around to try to understand what was happening. The thugs' scheme was not going according to plan.

The worshippers moved away from the windows. Looking in through the broken window, my father saw them fall to their knees and beginning praying for their attackers.

Despite himself, my father was touched deeply by this simple and honest demonstration of faith. He let go his hold of the tree trunk and ran away from the scene as fast as his legs could carry him. As the other thugs saw their leader running away, they ran after him.

"Hey! Where do you think you're going?" they asked him roughly. They swore at my father using colourful language and accused him of the worst kind of cowardice. They began beating my father with their fists, boots and the cudgels they had intended for the Adventists. In just a few seconds, his status had gone from being chief bully boy to chief whipping boy. The local thugs now thought of him as worthless.

It is probable that my father only escaped further beatings by being called up for military service, which meant he was already a member of the military when World War I broke out in 1914. He was sent to the front line in Italy and the Balkan countries. And it was during this period that his life truly changed.

It happened at the end of a day's fighting. The dead were being buried by the thousands. The wounded were screaming with pain, with no anaesthetics to ease their suffering. My father was living in a louse-infested uniform, tired, cold and wet, with nothing to look forward to tomorrow but more of the same—or worse.

He and some other survivors of the day's carnage were sitting around a campfire, deep in the forest. Another soldier—Paweł Nieboda—sat a short distance away from my father.

"Hey, Nieboda, what's that book that you keep reading so avidly?" asked my father. "That must be some great book if you've brought it into the front line."

It was just soldiers' banter, but the soldier replied, "Oh, it's a book that gives me peace, encouragement and hope in this hopeless situation. But the other reason I'm carrying it on the front line is that if I don't make it, then whoever buries me might read it and find the same hope and love that I receive from it every day."

This was not what my father was expecting. The book sounded interesting.

"Could I read it?" asked my father.

"Of course," replied Paweł Nieboda.

By the light of the campfire on that gloomy evening, my father read the book through. It was a German translation of *Steps to Christ* by Ellen White and the content made an indelible impression on him. It started a yearning in my father to know the love of God and to want to change his life for the better.

Paweł Nieboda turned out to be a preacher of the Seventh-day Adventist Church from Moravia. Between the fighting, the bullets, the advances, the shells, the retreats and near misses of the next few days, my father asked Mr Nieboda many questions about faith and the Adventist church. They became good friends and decided that if they survived the war, they would meet in Wisła and share this knowledge with my father's relatives and anyone else who was receptive to the Advent hope.

Against all the odds, both of them did survive and eventually the day came when they had to part company. Mr Nieboda shared some important parting advice with my father: "Paweł, our lives now lie in front of us like a path of untrodden snow. Let us be careful how we treat it for every mark will show." For the rest of his life, my father never forgot this powerful saying and it became part of the bedrock of his own Christian life. He was careful to pass it on to his future family.

Their intended reunion in Wisła occurred sometime later. My father was baptised into the Adventist Church and he and Mr Nieboda shared the Adventist faith in almost every home in our town. Their efforts met with extraordinary success and soon two congregations were organised.

Inevitably there came a backlash. Partly this was from the established churches. Opposition also came from the local *pijaks*. From time to time, a gang of thugs would pull my father by force into a bar and force alcohol down his throat. If he refused to swallow it, they would take him outside and beat him. There was also opposition closer to home. When my father and mother married in 1919, my grandparents expelled them from their homes, cut off all contact with the family and treated them as outcasts.

My mother's family were also opposed to the marriage. My mother's father had been killed in World War I. Left by herself to bring up the family, my mother's mother had fallen prey to the local curse of alcohol. She battled on alone but it was an unequal fight. The solace of alcohol gradually overtook the pain of the struggle and the poor woman succumbed to alcoholism. Nevertheless, she retained her strong Protestant belief and was horrified that her daughter would marry an Adventist.

"If you marry him, you are not part of this family," my mother was warned. But her love for my father was so strong that she accepted the terms.

My father was so poor that he was married in a paper suit, designed for one-off use and then thrown away. They both were excluded from their parents' wills. My parents had to live in a derelict hunting lodge for two years. In these poor conditions, two children were born: Jan and Ruben. They were so destitute that my mother had to tear up her dresses to make nappies for the young children. But they were fortunate enough to receive some help from friends and also from Adventists in Hamburg and they were able to survive.

From time to time, the local priest would visit. "If you will come back home, we can arrange a divorce," he offered.

"How kind," replied my mother, "—but can you find me a man like this one?"

After a few such visits, she firmly asked the priest not to return.

* * *

However, my father's reinvention was to serve him well. Back at the family home, my grandfather had been involved in yet another drunken brawl. This one was with my Uncle Jan. Although it was unlikely that either of them could remember the next day what it was all about, the climax was when Jan smashed my grandfather in the face in a serious assault. My grandfather might not have remembered the cause of the quarrel but he was very aware of the cuts and bruises his son had laid upon his face.

So, some years after being rejected by my grandfather, my father heard a knock at the door. To his astonishment, he found my grandfather standing at the door of the hunting lodge. My grandfather said he had disinherited Jan. If my father would come home, the farm was his. My father made a counter proposal that it was better if the farm could be divided between himself and his two sisters and so it was divided into three.

He continued to do exactly what his father had not. My father had taken my grandfather's example in life, gone the opposite way and found his own moral compass. The result was that, when he became a family man himself, our family was extremely happy.

By a quirk of fate, my grandfather died on the day I was born, so I never knew him. But immediately after his death, my grandmother asked to join the Adventist church and was baptised. Shortly after this, my father was elected senior elder in the Wisła church, a position he would hold for a quarter of a century. He had always been missionary minded and brought many people to the Adventist church including his two sisters.

And this was the heritage of faith and family in which I grew up and which gave us a foundation amid the challenges, trials and fears that came with the Nazi occupation.

FROM BAD TO WORSE AT SCHOOL

O ne of the constants before and during the German occupation was the same religious antagonism that carried on unabated, particularly in our schools. The major sticking point was that we would not attend school on Saturday mornings. The teacher, Mr Lipowczan, would single me out.

"Cieslar!" he would bellow in his well-practiced, vicious and intimidating manner. "Why did you not come to school on Saturday?"

"I went to church on the Sabbath, sir."

"Come to my desk, boy!" My heart sank as my schoolmates giggled behind me.

As soon as I got to his desk, he would grab me by the shoulder, lay me over the desk and beat me on the back and buttocks with a large stick, which he kept for such occasions. If the stick was not handy, sometimes he would simply hit me with his hand.

I suspected he enjoyed these encounters. If I cried out, it would lead to further punishment. This would take the form of forcing me to kneel facing the wall with my back to the class. The teacher would then encourage the rest of the class, in clever and insinuating ways, to ridicule me.

I would go home and show my bruises and welts to my parents.

"Children," they would say, "it is a great honour and privilege to suffer for Jesus' name."

Given that this beating became usual every Monday morning, I can only assume that I was enormously honoured and endlessly blessed. But, being only 10 years old (in 1939), I did not fully appreciate the privilege of suffering for Christ.

The other children called us all a number of names. They frequently called us "fanatics," which they had doubtlessly learned from their parents, and "filthy Jews" because we kept Saturday holy and also avoided pork and alcohol. The more interesting names were "sabbaticus" and "cats," after which they would make meowing sounds. This happened quite frequently but I have no idea where it originated. One girl in particular demonstrated extreme hatred toward the Adventist children at school, in a most disrespectful manner. She would often use the most dirty words against us and sometimes even spat on my sisters and me.

The school bullies were also in the habit of victimising Lona, the one Jewish girl in the class. For her it was even worse. "You crucified Jesus!" they would say among their other insults. I heard none of the teachers ever say anything overtly against the Jews. Many of the teachers, who by this time were all of German origin, did not allow children to bait poor Lona. But some teachers, to their eternal shame, did.

I liked Lona and used to befriend her to try to neutralise some of the bad treatment. On some occasions, I would take her part and urge my classmates to leave her alone. While not a close friend, I would ask her, perhaps, if she had had a nice weekend or what she had been doing with her family. As a schoolgirl, she did not have to wear the yellow Star of David on her clothes, which was a small mercy. In the Third Reich, you appreciated whatever small mercies you could lay your hands on. There were not many of them.

* * *

One particular Monday morning, the schoolyard jesting was to have near-fatal consequences. That winter was one of the coldest Eastern Europe had ever seen. I heard the grown-ups say that in Wisła it was 42° Celsius below freezing (about -44°F). Because it was so cold, the school had organised a group of women to serve us hot drinks as we entered the school buildings. While waiting in line, things began to go wrong.

Two boys behind me started with the time-honoured abuse with insults such as "Sabbatical cats" and "Jewboy!" and swore with some really choice language. Normally, this would have been something I simply tried to ignore.

Our parents had counselled us how to deal with this. The rule was that we did not retaliate; we were to suffer for the truth of Christ. Many Christians had suffered down the ages and it was our privilege to suffer for Christ as well. I felt I was on top of the situation. On this day, it passed off as on so many other days. I received my hot drink and ignored the louts behind me.

However, there was a flaw in our parents' teaching and my tormentors found it with the well-honed instincts of a Gestapo interrogator. As I lined up, they would stick a pin or a needle into the back of my neck. As I turned around, each boy would say, "Wasn't me, Cieslar" or "I didn't do it Cieslar." As I turned to the front, the stabbing pain of a needle would come again and I would wince in pain.

This took me out of the area in which I had been counselled. My parents had told me how to bear being called names, but they had not counselled me in how to deal with the stress of being stuck with pins, needles and spikes.

"For heaven's sake, will you stop that?" I demanded.

This resulted in a burst of merriment from the boys behind me and a spike stuck into my neck with such force that I cried out in pain. This time the boy could not retract it quickly enough and I saw who it was.

"That was you!" I hissed.

Anger welled up inside me. I forgot all my parents' teaching and punched him in the face. There was a certain satisfaction as I made contact and felt his nose collapse against my hand.

He staggered back and held his hands up to his face, clearly in pain. It felt good to get my own back on him. He would not try that again! But I was soon to learn that it was a mistake.

The boy began to scream that I had attacked him, as blood spurted from his nose. The others shouted, "Sabbatical did it! It was Sabbatical!" The boy continued to scream at the top of his voice that he—a poor innocent boy—had been attacked by this monstrous Adventist brute! By now there was blood all down his face and everyone gathered around to see what the commotion was.

Out of the corner of my eye, I saw my twin sisters, Maria and Marta, before they disappeared into the maelstrom developing where two lines of obedient children had stood only a moment previously.

Much worse, though, the teacher, Mr Lipowczan, appeared and it was evident that he was not amused. I could see the hatred in his eyes. Now he had all the evidence he wanted that the Adventist fanatics were dangerous animals.

Now he could give all his prejudices free rein. Now he could beat me as much as he wanted and really enjoy doing so.

I ran—and there was such a commotion that no-one tried to stop me. Running out of the school door into those freezing temperatures was almost like running into a brick wall. It was deadly cold. The snow crunched beneath my felt boots as I ran out of the school grounds. The snow continued to fall gently, obliterating all of the other footprints, even those only a few minutes old.

There was no traffic on the roads and only a few pedestrians on the street, presumably because they had urgent business. Anyone who had a choice would not have been outdoors in those conditions. There was an utter silence on a street that would normally have been filled with people, horses and even the occasional motor car.

I ran a hundred yards or so. I could not hear any footsteps behind me and turned, panting, to look around. There was no hue and cry. There was no sadistic Mr Lipowczan. There were no children coming to persecute me further. I was relieved but it also meant there was no-one stupid enough to venture out into those temperatures to chase me. It was too dangerous!

I tried to decide what to do next. The notion of returning to school was tantamount to suicide. If I went home, my parents would ask why I had returned so early. That would be embarrassing. I decided on a third course. I would walk briskly up and down the road to keep warm, then arrive home at the normal time. After that, I would decide on the next move.

Running out of the school had warmed me up a little but that wore off quickly. The slightly cold feeling I had experienced was replaced by cold of a kind I had not experienced before. It was penetrating, invasive, implacable. My feet were losing sensation and I realised that my hands dug deep into my pockets were also becoming numb, as were my ears. My breath made steam like the wheezy old steam locomotives on the railway line from Wisła. In time my mind also began to numb. I did not know it at the time but my entire cardiovascular system was losing the battle against the arctic conditions and was beginning to shut down.

I had to shake the snow from my head and also from my shoulders and off the sides of my clothes. I must have looked like a snowman. By now the swirling snow had started to affect my sight. I seemed to see swirling snow even in sheltered places where there was no snow. I closed my eyes but I could still see the swirling snow. It struck me as strange but probably nothing to worry about.

It seemed I was walking for an age but eventually the end of the school day approached and I could set off home. The snow still came down as I began trudging toward our farm. Away in the distance, I saw the dark shadow of another person battling his way head-down through the snowstorm. As he came closer, I could see that he was another Jack Frost, completely covered in snow. It went through my mind that this is how I must appear and it struck me as almost comical.

Then I recognised the walk. It was my father going somewhere in the opposite direction. I smiled at him and was about to greet him, but I noticed he was looking very stern. He came closer. Could he have heard about what had happened?

I was totally taken aback by what happened next. Without saying a word, he slapped me across the face, causing a flurry of snow to shower from my head. It hit me in a flash that my sisters must have gone home ahead of me and told him of the incident.

"I never taught you to do things that way! Why did you do it?" He may even have grabbed me by the arm but I did not feel it. The feeling in my limbs was gradually diminishing.

I lost my footing and fell into the snow. As I tried to stand up, he hit me across the face again.

"You have committed a horrible crime in your school!" he growled. "That is not what I expect of you!"

He left me and walked on, disappearing into the gathering gloom of that awful afternoon.

I was in despair. The other children were against me. The teacher absolutely hated me. My father, whom I genuinely loved, was against me. I was alone and desolate in the snowstorm in the gathering gloom of a dreadfully cold afternoon. I had been emotionally hurt by the encounter with my father but the slaps across the face had not hurt that much. Perhaps my face was numb from the cold. But the situation was worse than I realised.

I headed for home feeling very sorry for myself but the battle of the cold snow came first. It was getting deeper. I realised I needed to get home quickly if I was not to be stuck in the snow. I tried to move as quickly as I could but, as I did so, I realised that my body did not seem to react as quickly as it had before. I seemed sluggish. I put my head down against the wind and snow. I didn't care what happened when I got home. I didn't mind if I got into trouble. This was good. I did not care anymore.

I was liberated from all feeling. I remembered that I had been frightened and desolate. Now I was not. Why had I been frightened? I could not remember.

I did not care about anything. Then arms were picking me up. Was it an angel, who had come to look after me? I smiled, I think. It was all very far away.

I was wrapped in a fur coat. That did not make sense because I didn't have a fur coat. Whatever was happening was far away.

I was not cold anymore but an angel or something or someone was carrying me. It was exhilarating I seemed to be flying in the arms of the angel.

Then we were at my house. I realised it was no angel. Fortunately, my Uncle Andrzej had seen the footprints leading away from the track and thought it would be prudent to see if anyone was in trouble. He found me and had wrapped me in his huge fur coat.

But for him, I would have frozen to death.

* * *

But the immediate problem was that he had got me home. My mind was starting to ramble but I did hear him say, "Maria, this is important: work on him because otherwise he will be dead soon." Then my uncle left.

My mother and sisters rubbed snow on my feet and hands and ears to revitalise the circulation in an attempt to prevent frostbite. As the blood began to flow again and the circulation revived, I was to receive a salutary lesson in how the human body works.

First the blood flowed into the extremities of my hands and feet and ears. Then the feeling began to return to these areas that had been starved of blood for some hours. As the feeling came back, a dull ache came with it. Then the dull ache turned into a sharp pain. The sharp pain turned into a screaming scarlet agony and the screaming was mine.

The black patches on the soles of my feet meant frostbite. Fortunately, the black patches were only on the balls of my feet and did not extend to my toes. If the toes were frostbitten, gangrene would set in and I would either lose the toes that night or die in agony a few days later.

The pain was dreadful. I imagine that my mother and sisters must have been very worried but I cannot remember anything about them. I can only remember the pain and the difficulty in getting my mind to focus on anything.

Some hours later, I was in dry clothes and enjoying the warmth of the family home. My circulation was back in working order. I was dry and warm and almost back to my normal self, except that standing up allowed the blood to flow back to my feet, causing me to utter sharp screams of pain. My feet were swollen and an unhealthy dark colour made up of blues, blacks and browns.

My mother came and sat beside me. It was clear that she was troubled.

"Why did you do it?" she asked. My sisters had told my parents everything about the events of the morning and the "needle gang".

"It is a very shameful thing, which you did as an Adventist child," she continued.

The disappointment I read in my mother's face was more agonising to me than the pain of frostbite. Yet I did not believe I was entirely in the wrong. I explained to her the story, exactly as it was. It had not been my intention to hurt anyone. They kept on doing it and it hurt. I had lashed out in exasperation.

My mothers and sisters seemed to understand. They helped me into bed, which was no small task as I could only walk with difficulty. Within seconds, I fell into a deep sleep.

It must have been some hours later that I woke to find my father sitting on the bed. My mother had spoken to him.

"I forgive you for what you did, son," he said with such love and tenderness. "I want you to forgive me for hitting you. I should have found out the situation properly."

"Of course, I forgive you, Dad," I replied.

It was wonderful to be reunited with my father. I would have forgiven him anything and he knew that. It was also of immense importance to me that he had forgiven me as well.

Next morning, however, meant a reunion with the dreaded Mr Lipowczan and that was not destined to be so pleasant.

"Is Cieslar here?" he asked with malice in his voice as he entered the room.

"Yes, sir," I said.

The more revolting of the boys giggled.

"Come out here!" he yelled.

He overpowered me and pulled me face down over his desk. He took a cane and hit me with it until I cried out in pain. Then he stood me up and made me put out my frostbitten hands. He hit them again and again with the cane.

"If you hit one of the boys again, you will get worse. Do you understand?"

I sobbed that I understood. There was little point in telling my parents.

There was little point in them coming to school and remonstrating with this ignorant and sadistic man. The Adventists were fair game and Mr Lipowczan was just having his share of the fun.

* * *

Looking back, I cannot feel too sorry for myself. A short time later, there was a commotion outside our classroom. Outside stood a policeman and a man in civilian clothes. They summoned our teacher.

The teacher came back in and spoke to Lona. "Lona, you must go with these gentlemen," he said quietly.

Most of the Polish members of our class were shocked that she could be removed in this perfunctory manner, but the German classmates were uncaring. We Adventists knew what it meant. We had heard through the informal networks that deportations were starting. At that time, no-one knew where the deportees were going but we did know that no-one was returning.

At break time, some of our class ran the short distance up the hill to the railway station. We knew that was where deportees were taken.

We saw Lona waiting on the platform with a number of other Jews, including her parents. The train puffed in, an official showed the Jews which carriage to get into and the train left. We never heard any more of her.

The teachers tried to explain that the Jews had been "disturbing" the Germans, therefore they had been taken away to a special place. The teachers tried to lead us to believe that it was in order for her to be taken away. We were warned not to say anything about it. In all probability, the teachers had no more idea where she had been taken than we did.

As with adolescents the world over, we often found the ways of grown-ups strange. We had difficulty seeing how Lona could have disturbed any Germans. Rather, it had been the German children who had been disturbing her.

Lona was a quiet and nice girl who, as far as we could see, only wanted to get on with her schoolwork. It also intrigued us that if it was in order for her to be taken away, why had we been told not to talk about it to anyone. The world of the grown-ups was strange indeed.

But, in 1941, Lona was most likely taken to the concentration camp in Auschwitz—to be gassed. This was the fate of most people who were taken to that camp. Alternatively, she might have been sent to a slave labour camp—and worked until she died.

For the rest of the school year, her empty desk gave a silent reminder of what the Nazi regime was all about.

In quiet moments, I shed tears for her for many days afterward. I really did miss her. Her disappearance was painful and remains so seven decades later. She was not allowed to grow up or to enjoy a full life. She would never know the joys of motherhood or grandmotherhood.

She was of Jewish descent—and in Adolf Hitler's wonderful new Europe that was a capital offence.

THE NAZIS COME TO CALL

Woof!" Our blood froze.

It had nothing to do with the October Friday night, which was already extremely chilly and portended the oncoming winter. One of the benefits of living in Hitler's "Thousand-Year Reich" was that we were now equipped with a sixth sense, like an animal's sense of danger. Anything out of the ordinary could spell threat, arbitrary punishment and sudden death.

On that terrible night, our sixth sense kicked in. Dogs do not commonly bark with a single "woof." We could do little but look at each other. Our whole family— my father, mother, two brothers, three sisters and me—were in the house and just finishing our regular Friday evening worship.

Outside our farmhouse, we heard something like the sound of heavy stones rolling down the hill. We did not say anything but one question was in all of our minds. What could it be? The sound was exactly like an avalanche, but could not be. In any event, we knew that it was not good.

"Das Haus umstellen!" a brutal voice shouted somewhere in the darkness outside. "Surround the house!"

We felt an immediate and deep shock. We caught our breath. Our pulses raced. My father hid the Bible and religious books in an instant. My heart beat as if it would burst out of my rib cage.

Our front door was nearly knocked off its hinges as the butt of a machine pistol smashed into it. Whoever they were they were not to be trifled with.

My father opened the door. It was pushed rudely all the way open and a uniformed officer pushed his way in, followed by men pointing their weapons at us. They were wearing those grey-green SS uniforms that we had come to loathe and dread.

The sudden blast of cold air made the kerosene lamps flicker. In the flickering nightmarish light, we clearly saw the death's head badge on the peaked cap. He was an Obersturmführer, a First Lieutenant—judge, jury and executioner. At this moment, we knew our lives were worth less than our homemade moccasins. This hatchet-faced individual had the power of life or death over us. But why had he come to our farmhouse?

Our living room filled with SS men. One of them pointed a machine gun at us. We stood huddled together in the middle of the room, the younger children crying and clinging to my parents.

"Everyone into the kitchen!" the commander ordered.

"Mummy, what are they going to do with us?' asked one of the younger children in Polish.

"Just be quiet, darling," whispered my mother. She knew that to speak Polish in front of diehard SS men was to confess racial inferiority at best and suspicion of defiance at worst, with obvious consequences.

The SS man kept us covered with his gun and seemed content to chop us all into a mass of twisted mincemeat on a single word.

An SS soldier.

"Where have you just been?" demanded the officer, addressing my father and my elder brother, Józef.

"I have not been anywhere," said my father truthfully, his voice wavering with fear.

Józef also confirmed that he had not been outside.

The officer's face was a mask of hatred. This was no human face. The SS officer smashed my father in the face with his fist, sending him reeling across the room. The SS trooper continued to point his machine gun at us, his finger on the trigger, the safety catch certainly off. All it would take was the slightest command from the Obersturmführer and we were all dead.

"Lügen! Lies!" shouted the officer at my father. "This is your last moment. You will be shot!"

Our family gasped, literally trembling in fear. My mother's maternal instinct took over and she took the hands of the youngest two, Jerzy and Anna. Our parents and the older children had to keep quiet.

"No talking and your kids can stop that whimpering or you know what will happen," demanded the officer.

We had no idea what was going on or why they wanted to kill us but if an SS detachment said they were going to kill you, you were effectively already dead. There might be a genuine reason for killing you or there might not. It was largely of academic interest.

"Das ist das Ende!" screamed the Obersturmführer. "This is your end! Today is your last day," said the officer over and over.

We waited for the finger to tighten and the muzzle flashes to spit out bullets and kill us.

"Search the whole house and I want that barn outside searched as well. I want to know if there is anything in here that is suspicious in any way possible."

The soldiers made their way through our house, opening every drawer and throwing the contents on the floor. They ripped up the floorboards and looked inside every jug. They did not tell us what they were looking for. To address them in any way was merely a further avenue to death. They missed the Bible and religious books, which my father had hidden so quickly and effectively.

An SS man re-entered our farmhouse from outside. "Someone has been sleeping in the barn, Herr Obersturmführer," he reported. That must have meant partisans or, as the Germans called them, "bandits" who were trying to disrupt the work of the Reich. I hoped my father would not give them away.

They took my father to the barn to get more information out of him.

"Only my son has been sleeping here," my father explained. "We have had a lot of sheep stolen in this area and Józef has been sleeping here to scare off the thieves."

The officer seemed unconvinced—but at least he did not scream "Lügen" or hit my father in the face again. He returned to the house and the children started crying again.

"If you don't shut those brats up, we can end their lives very easily," shouted the officer, "or perhaps I will just lose my temper and you're all dead."

We waited for the crash of machine guns. We had never experienced such a nightmare and were extremely frightened of death within the next five seconds.

Oddly, the soldiers were men in their 40s. Perhaps they had children of their own and would not want other people's children to suffer as they killed them.

Our breath drew short. Our senses came to a heightened level: the grey-green of the SS uniforms in that flickering light; the shiny black, sinister magazines of the machine guns; the door of the house still open letting in a freezing wind. Ten seconds from now we could all be dead. The SS men would get a neighbour to bury us. The neighbours would take whatever tools, animals and food we might have. The Cieslar family would simply cease to exist. We waited for the final order to fire.

Then a German shepherd dog ran into the house, obviously in great pain. It was bleeding profusely from a deep gash under its forepaw and whimpering pitifully.

"There's someone out there!" shouted the officer. "After them!"

The SS squad ran out in a clatter of hobnailed boots. We realised it was the boots on the frozen ground that had sounded like stones rolling down the hill.

As we watched them fan out across our farm in the moonlight, we could see that they were about 20 strong. We now understood that this was an SS Bandenkampfverband unit in hot pursuit of a group of partisans. They had been trailing them and the partisans had led them to our farm. The whole terrifying episode was not involved with our faith in any way. We just happened to be in the wrong place at the wrong time.

The SS unit left as suddenly as they had arrived, without a word of apology for frightening us so terribly. But if you were still breathing at the end of an encounter with the SS, you were fortunate.

The tension in the house cooled. No-one in the family said anything. We were all too shocked to speak. My father bolted the door.

After a few minutes, my father and mother gave prayers of thanksgiving to God that we had survived the ordeal. When we went to bed, we children could not sleep. It seemed that we spent all night thinking and talking about it.

While the partisans had been lucky, our family had also been protected. If the SS had captured them, they would have revealed under torture that our family had helped them. Even if we merely knew they were there, the SS might have summarily shot us as an example to others.

We never quite knew who the partisans were. Some might come from the Związek Walki Zbrojnej—the Union for Armed Struggle—organised under

General Sikorski in London. They were involved in the war effort against the Nazis in intelligence gathering and sabotage. Other partisans were bands of marauding thieves or people dodging military service. Many were just robbers on the run who stole food and were a nuisance to the farming families of the neighbourhood.

Some partisans were also engaged in propaganda activities such as the distribution of clandestine newspapers and posters. This might have been what the SS men were searching for in our house. A single leaflet would have meant our immediate death.

A few days after our terrifying experience, the partisans appeared. They had been lucky. Two of them had hidden in a gully on the hillside and the SS troop had missed them in the darkness. Another two had run down into the valley on the other side, pursued by the SS unit's dog. One of them had stuck it violently with a bayonet in an effort to kill it. However, it had survived the attack and come back to its master: for which we were mightily grateful! The partisans told us that the dog was trained to give a single bark when it had found its quarry.

As the SS did not apologise for our near-death experience, neither did the partisans. In their view, we were just collateral damage. Other people's lives were "cheap," of no value, worth or interest whatsoever.

The partisans soon went on their way and we did not see that particular group or their SS pursuers again.

SUCKED INTO THE WAR

In the early 1940s, the Third Reich was experiencing a labour shortage. Trying to hide their agenda, the local government made and enforced an official announcement that all men aged 17 and older should register in the employment office for the purpose of preparation for implementing a policy of an employment benefit. In this way, they would find out how many men they could send to labour camps in Germany.

The local people suspected the German government of playing a trick on them. The question was whether people should comply with the local government demands. There was much confusion, uncertainty and various views among the local people regarding this matter. Some decided to escape to Hungary, which was not occupied at this time. Others went into hiding, living rough in the forest, believing that Great Britain would somehow liberate Poland from Hitler's occupation.

It soon became clear that the call-up method was not always working. The next phase was when the SS would turn up unexpectedly in a town, and a group of men would be surrounded and taken to a labour camp. My brother Jan had been already taken to a labour camp in Kovel, near Breslaw. The Seventh-day Adventist men knew they were not immune and, in several groups, they were praying together regularly about this situation.

Finally, by God's providence, they were offered a more favourable deal. There was a railway building and maintenance firm in Berlin, whose representative—a former inhabitant of Wisła—arrived in Wisła to recruit men for labour for his firm. He was well acquainted with the Adventist people in Wisła and was friendly with them, particularly with my father. He met with some of the various church leaders in the district and placed before them the following plan:

"Instead of being taken by force to any labour camp in Germany, the firm in Berlin will offer you a better deal. The Railway Building and Maintenance Firm in Berlin needs good, honest and faithful workers, and I have highly recommended you Adventists as a loyal work force. So, the firm in Berlin asked me to offer you an employment proposal and if accepted, I am to bring you to Berlin to be workers of the firm."

As volunteers, their status would guarantee them superior living conditions and better food than those who had been forcibly conscripted. They would also receive better wages and be allowed two trips home a year. They could send and receive letters as often as they wanted. But, above all, they were offered Saturday free of any work and could attend their church to worship.

The representative gave the Adventist people a few days to think it through and then expected to receive their decision. My father was the first who responded favourably to this offer. The other leaders soon realised there would be no better alternative in this situation and also accepted the offer.

Within one week, 30 Adventist men commenced work at the railway firm in Berlin. They worked to build new railway lines and also maintain the old ones. Later in the war, my brother Jan escaped from the labour camp in Kovel and, together with Ruben, went to Berlin to commence work in the same firm in which my father was already working. As such, my father and brothers were among as many as 1 million people in Poland who were taken to various labour camps in Germany during the war.

The Adventist workers in Berlin soon found out the reality of what happened to those who wore the "P" badge. They received one single Deutschmark per day—enough to buy a newspaper—and they were not allowed in crowded air-raid shelters. As there were no raids on Berlin at this time, this was somewhat academic. But it was not to remain so.

Having my father away from home made life difficult for my mother. She had to run the farm without her husband or her two capable sons. Apart from that, we missed all three of them terribly and waited eagerly for the letters, which we received from time to time. At least we knew they were alive, possibly safe and well.

One good thing about his being in Berlin was that my father sent me a wonderful broad-brimmed trilby hat. It was very stylish and good quality. It was not the kind of hat you would ever find in Upper Silesia—or Oberschlesien, as we were now called. I loved the hat and wore it all the time.

In Berlin, the situation for the Adventist workers at this stage was not too bad. My father had seen large cities when he had been in the Austro-Hungarian army and had visited Vienna. Now he and the other Adventists were in the other great metropolis of the Reich: Berlin. Even though their living conditions were basic, they were nearly as good as most of them had experienced for all their lives. The firm provided the workers with working shoes and clothing suitable for their work, making their situation quite bearable.

* * *

As well as being Germany's Minister of Propaganda, Goebbels was also the Gauleiter Nazi Party Leader of Berlin and, in that capacity, was my father's ultimate boss. Goebbels was an evil man in many ways. He was, however, exceptionally clever. He had anticipated that Berlin would be bombed severely when the British and Americans decided on this as a priority in fighting the war. And it was Goebbels' responsibility to provide air-raid shelters for the civilian population.

As a result, you could see the sign "Luftschutzraum"—"Air-Raid Shelter"—everywhere across the capital of the Reich. Throughout the city, there were massive flak towers, bristling with weaponry and waiting for the coming attacks. It seemed that there was an 88-millimetre anti-aircraft gun on every street corner together with the teenage crew who manned it with their Hitlerjugend Flakhelfer, who did the fetching and carrying. My father might have reflected that Berlin in 1943 was as dangerous as that terrible southern front in Italy in what was now called "The First World War."

When the Allied bombers returned to Berlin—on January 16, 1943—it seemed unexpected. There were no sirens. There was no scurrying around or searchlights. But a huge number of planes inflicted significant damage on the city. It was the beginning of a devastating campaign.

The Silesian Adventists were now working much harder on railway maintenance, clearing bomb damage on the tracks. The rubble was loaded onto trucks and taken to one of the four mountains of debris—die Trümmerberge. These were the slag heaps for the waste fabric of a great but disintegrating city.

My father was to discover that three things made this work onerous. First, the piles of debris could fall at any time. If you were underneath, you could be buried alive, killed or maimed. Second, the rubble was dotted with corpses and body parts. Worst of all was the third hazard: unexploded bombs. Some were "duds" but others might blow up when disturbed. Others had time fuses that could be set for any time in the following 30 days. They could go off at any time.

SS guards would bring in the black-and-grey striped prisoners from concentration camps to move the bombs. It was also their task to pick up the corpses. The guards and everyone else would take cover as the prisoners would pick up the bomb and move it to a place where Wehrmacht sappers could explode it under controlled conditions. If the bomb went off while it was being moved, that was unfortunate but routine. With that threat removed, the clearance work could continue.

Bit by bit, the city was being demolished, as key buildings, factories, landmarks and homes were destroyed. My father endured no less than 22 of these main force attacks. When the bombs dropped near him he did, of course, fear for his life but there was a certain grim humour at street level. Fortunately, of the Silesian group, only one person was to lose his life.

Despite the horrors perpetrated on the Polish people by the Germans, it was in my father's character to deplore the fact that death from the sky was now a nightly occurrence. Some of the streets that my father had known and walked along were simply gone. Other streets were cordoned off for "Unexploded bombs." Train and tram lines gradually stopped operating. Suddenly there were shortages of food. Electricity and gas supplies failed. If any German said, "This was not what Hitler promised us," they said it quietly. They knew the costs of being overheard.

In addition to the heavy menace of the main force raids, there were dozens of nuisance raids. There was no alarm or call to go to the shelters. Bombs would simply emerge from the clouds of the wintery skies and detonate at random across the city. As soon as people heard a crash of a bomb, the air-raid siren would go off and people would run for the shelters.

A nuisance raid might only last five minutes but the dash to the shelter and the several hours waiting for the all-clear meant that another night's sleep had been lost. Berlin was descending into a disoriented state of sleep deprivation.

THE
WORST RAID

The worst air raid came on the night of December 16, 1943. Berlin had been under tension of bombing raids for almost a year. The early raids had been sporadic and most of the following raids were as well. Heavy cloud, typical of Berlin in winter, often protected the city in a solemn partnership with the various state organs of air-raid protection. However, on this night, there was unusually little cloud.

The Lancaster bombers targeted the railway yards and there was little the air-raid defences could do to stop them. The sirens went in the familiar fashion. Everyone ran for the shelters. The flak, as was typical, put up a barrage of coloured tracer shells so thick that it looked as if the pilots could have got out and walked on it.

Occasionally a plume of flame was visible as a bomber was hit and a bright yellow-red streak of flame showed where it headed rapidly to earth. That night, at least one Lancaster was hit and its entire bomb load ignited with a massive explosion. The flash as 4000 pounds of high explosive detonated would have lit up the whole of Berlin.

But the bombers kept coming. The colourful Christmas trees floated down and the bomb-aimers got down to business. The Berlin railway yards were left a twisted mass of metal and burning railway cars and buildings. Buildings nearby were reduced to piles of burning rubble. Such devastation had not been seen in Berlin.

The Berlin rail yards held 1000 trucks of war material and supplies destined for the front. They were vital for trying to stop the westward march of the Russian army and now would not be delivered. West of Berlin, thousands more railway wagons were backed up in the system. The Royal Air Force had dealt a serious blow to Berlin and to Hitler's Reich.

The Silesian group, with hundreds of other workers, were ordered out to the railway yards as soon as they emerged from the shelters. They were becoming used to the aftermath of a bombing raid, the acrid smell of fires and the sounds of ambulances as they made their way as quickly as possible through the piles of rubble that had once been streets.

The bombing of the rail yards had been very concentrated and accurate. What had been an orderly marshalling yard was now a mess of craters, wagons on their side and at odd angles, railway coaches burning out of control, and hulking locomotives smashed like children's toys. From underneath the rubble came the cries of people who had been buried. The fire brigade and other helpers tried to get them out.

From time to time, the blast of an unexploded bomb would interrupt the proceedings and everyone would duck for cover as rubble, unidentifiable chunks of metal and body parts rained down on the scene of destruction. The craters alone would require hundreds of tons of earth to fill. The smashed locomotives and wagons would have to be lifted out of their piles, cut up and taken to the Trümmerberge.

On that freezing December morning, the Railway Maintenance and Repair supervisors instructed my father's team to unpick the mangled trucks, take away the broken lines and clear the site so the rail yards could be rebuilt as quickly as possible. The task would involve men from work service units, fire service, police, ambulance, Hitlerjugend volunteers and medical staff to work with any survivors. The SS would have brought in concentration camp prisoners to clear unexploded bombs. In all there must have been several thousand people set to work on the site.

The work was filthy and relentless. At daybreak they were not allowed back to their hut but were ordered to keep on working. Fortunately, they were tough men. The Adventists also often prayed together for respite in their dangerous and helpless situation. It was legal for the Adventists to do this publicly in Berlin, as the Adventist church was allowed.

My father did not know it at first but he came to realise that the weather was a powerful ally. The rain and sleet were unrelenting. The cloud was barely above the level of the ruins of the Kaiser Wilhelm church. But while it was like this, the bombers would not be back.

As the rail yards were cleared, my father would have seen troop train after troop train depart for the East. All the people on the work detail noticed that it was almost solely one-way traffic. Train after train after train of fit young men went off to the east. Few came back and then it was only the occasional hospital train full of war wounded.

For the Adventists—including my father and brothers Jan and Ruben—it was a week of toil and total exhaustion. The clean-up in the rail yards went on for six days and six nights, with crews working around the clock. They worked until the yards were back in commission but, to the company's credit, they did not push their employees to work until they dropped.

Then, on December 23, the last night of the clean-up, the air-raid sirens sounded again. There had been a marked improvement in the performance of the air-raid warning system. It was possible for an orderly entry into the shelters before the planes could be heard. Simultaneously, the soldiers on the flak batteries and their Hitler Youth auxiliaries would be running to man their batteries.

"Now, you lot, your orders are to keep on working," the supervisor shouted above the wail of the sirens. "You can't stop now, you have to keep going. We're nearly finished."

For a moment, all the lights on the site were extinguished to prevent them acting as a beacon for the bomb-aimers. "OK, men, take cover where you can," was the only order.

The droning of the bomber squadrons was audible, away to the west. The weather was still very bad on that night and few night fighters took off. That meant that the flak batteries were free to fire at anything in the sky, knowing that if they hit something it must be British.

Powerful searchlights tried to pick the bombers among the clouds. As soon as a plane was highlighted, dozens more lights would suddenly light up and target the hapless plane at the apex of a cone of light. Immediately the tracer shells, red, green, white would shoot up in a vast pyrotechnic display. Often a plume of flame could be seen shooting out behind the plane. Then the plane would falter in its flight, dip and plummet down in tighter and tighter circles until it fell out of sight beyond the horizon. This would be followed by a vivid flash of light as the plane crashed to the ground.

Through the occasional breaks in the cloud, my father could see that there were hundreds of four-engine bombers. They did not break formation, flown by crews of young men like his sons!

He must have thought of his family at this time. He must have hoped these young men would not kill him that night and that he would see his own family again. On that night, the bombing was scattered and nothing came too close to him. He would survive for another day.

And he would have begun to hear more reports of how the war was beginning to turn. Kiev was about to fall. The Third Reich had lost 600 miles (1000 kilometres) of territory in less than a year. The German army was losing ground by the day and there was nothing the Third Reich could do to stop it. The Russians were almost halfway to Berlin.

Even worse the Russian soldiery, whose barbarism was well known, would be at his farm some months before they made it to Berlin.

RUBEN RISKS
HIS LIFE

While working in one of the large railway stations in Berlin, my brother Ruben encountered hundreds of Russian prisoners of war being held in a compound. Russia was not a signatory to the Geneva Convention, which set out rules for dealing with prisoners and the Nazi hierarchy took this as permission to treat them in whatever manner they chose. Nazis were invariably brutal to those who opposed them, and these Russian prisoners of war had no shelter, food or sanitation. This was a humanitarian disgrace.

Ruben knew where there was a blanket store in the station and surreptitiously "borrowed" two large bags of blankets when no-one was looking. He took them hastily to the compound and passed them through the barbed wire to the grateful Russian soldiers. The desperate Russian prisoners pleaded for more. He knew the terrible risk he was running but "borrowed" as many blankets as possible and passed them through the fence. Eventually he knew he was pushing his luck and left the scene of his "crime".

A couple of days later a man in plain clothes approached Ruben.

"Herr Cieslar?"

"Ja."

He showed Ruben a round identification disc. It bore the word "Gestapo". Someone had given him away.

The Gestapo man gave him a stark choice. He could go immediately to a concentration camp and work as a slave labourer, in which case he would have lasted the average four months or—as a Volksdeutscher—they could extend to him the more attractive offer of joining the German army. The latter was the obvious choice.

* * *

About six months before the nasty incident, Ruben had been attached to a German firm in Berlin that was engaged in important work for the war effort. They sent him as a team worker to the Ukraine for a war project. Completing this assignment, he returned to Berlin, where he was taken into military service and posted to France for military training. Ruben was then given 10 days leave at home, before he was ordered to report to his allocated division in Berlin. Chances were that this division—like most others—would go straight to the Russian Front.

On that last morning, the atmosphere in our house was as heavy as lead. Ruben cleaned and pressed his Steingrau battledress. He polished his jackboots until they had a mirror-like shine. He checked his equipment: gas mask, rifle and bayonet.

I offered to help him clean his bayonet. This simple but deadly device was designed to press into another human being's entrails and to disembowel them. I took it out of the leather sheath, began to polish it and burst into tears like a child. I pressed myself into the cold ground and begged God to prevent Ruben from using it for its intended purpose. I could not think in terms of Russians being enemies, only that this weapon would be used to skewer another young man. It was vile.

The neighbours came around to say goodbye to Ruben. Everyone tried to be optimistic—but not successfully. We talked a little, then lapsed into silence. All our thoughts were sombre. We knew the realities of what happened to soldiers who went to the Ostfront—the Eastern Front. They did not come back.

Visiting home some months before he was eventually released from the labour camp in Berlin, Father offered a final prayer and commended his son into the arms of Almighty God. Barely able to fight back the tears Ruben embraced my parents and the rest of us one by one. He said simply, "Goodbye! I love you all!"

He walked slowly down the road that led to Głębce station, then back to his unit in Berlin and on to the Eastern Front. Other parents' sons were not returning and he had no reason to expect better. He knew the realities, as did we. Orders were orders. War was war. "Goodbye" was "goodbye." Ruben left home with a heavy heart and left us with a heavy hearts, too.

From the few news sources we had, we knew that by the time his train had gone east, the Russians had swarmed across the Dniester River and were already in eastern Poland. He would have been disembarked somewhere, sent up to the line and told to keep firing until he had no more bullets, then use his bayonet. At this time, complete divisions were being sent to the front and simply disappeared. There were no survivors to tell their story.

The rest was silence. We received no letter from him. There was no notification of death or any other official communication, which was not unusual. There were no survivors in administration positions to report what had happened. Our brother had disappeared and there was no-one alive to tell us what had happened. But we continued to remember him every day, without fail, in our family prayers.

My second oldest brother Ruben, a few days before going to the Eastern Front.

NO HEIL HITLER!

While my father and brothers were working in Berlin, the rest of our family had our own trials closer to home. Despite the apparent tide of the war, Mr L__—the Blockleiter for the neighbouring area and a Nazi party member—remained dedicated to the cause of Adolf Hitler right to the end of the Third Reich.

"Heil Hitler!" he would shout at my mother. "Mrs Cieslar! Heil Hitler!"

She considered this form of greeting to be stupid, not to mention blasphemous, and would not reply in the prescribed manner. "Guten Tag, Mr L__," she would say cheerily, as she studiously avoided the hated Hitler salute.

"Mrs Cieslar, I said 'Heil Hitler! Heil Hitler!'" When Mr L__ spoke like that, people would freeze. They knew that their next sentence could take them to Auschwitz.

But my mother remained steadfast. "Oh, Mr L__, I don't really understand the 'Heil Hitler' greeting. I will stay with 'Guten Morgen' or 'Guten Tag'—I understand those. Thank you, Mr L__."

He watched her as she moved down the road and away from him as fast as she could.

One Saturday morning in April, 1942, an SS man in a long grey-green great coat walked up to our house. As he walked, he kept a careful eye on the woods, the farm buildings and any lane ways. We knew the uniform and the cautious behaviour: for the SS man, every tree hid a potential assassin.

We were chilled to our souls. Our family were preparing for home worship. The SS man clearly knew that and timed his visit just as they knew we would be beginning. We did not understand the agenda, merely that it bode badly for us.

"Stay inside, children!" said my mother urgently. "Go into the kitchen!"

My two sisters, Marta and Ruth, did not need telling twice. She kept looking out of the window and was clearly extremely frightened at the sudden appearance of someone whose very uniform meant incarceration, torture and death.

The officer was curiously handsome with the blonde hair of the "Master Race" and glittering blue eyes. A cruel cast to the mouth made him all the more sinister. He looked like someone you did not want to meet.

I ran into the kitchen in fear, huddling with Ruth. Our hearts were beating loudly and we did not dare speak.

The SS man banged on the door roughly. As my mother opened it, the man pushed her aside and walked into the house as if it was his personal property. In his right hand, he carried a rifle and from the look in those evil glittering eyes, he was perfectly happy to use it if there was any noncompliance. He had the power of life and death over us, and wanted us to know it.

"Alle Kinder 'raus!" he screamed in a voice that suggested he might benefit from immediate psychiatric care. "All children outside! The children are coming with me, is that understood? Come on, all of you, I want to see you in front of me."

My mother's immediate thought was that we were being rounded up for random execution, which was common at that time. As we came out from the kitchen with great trepidation, we could see that our mother was in a state of abject panic. To our astonished eyes, she leant forward in a gesture of supplication.

"Please, sir, do not take my children," she said. "They are innocent. They are not guilty of any crime."

Without a word, he responded with a vicious kick from his extremely well polished, black, hobnailed boot. The thud of the boot and the violence of the act made me suddenly want to be sick. He had kicked her as someone might kick away a disgusting cockroach.

For a moment, there was silence in our front yard. We children looked at my mother, her face showing the physical pain she felt. Much worse was the prospect of her children being taken away.

The man in his grey-green uniform did not waste time on niceties. "Kommen Sie mit! Come with me!" He gestured to Ruth and me, older by two years.

My mother feared the worst. As the man pushed us rudely in front of him I heard her voice. "Children, my prayers are with you. My prayers are with you!"

It was voice of a mother who had every possible reason to fear that her children might be put to death.

Without a further word, the officer walked us for 40 minutes to an old school in the Głębce Valley. I was in a state of complete fear. My stomach was tied in knots of terror. I did not know what would happen, barely understanding that I was entering a world of brutality, pain and possible death.

The SS man's violence against my mother reverberated through my mind over and over. How could he do that? Did he not have a mother of his own? The motto of the SS to which he belonged was "Meine Ehre heisst Treue"—"My honour is loyalty." In his world, it seemed honour included violence against a harmless and decent woman.

As we walked, I did not speak to Ruth and she did not speak to me. We were much too frightened to utter a single word.

"Hinein!" said the man as we approached the school building. "Get in there!"

We were outside a newly built administrative block and ushered into large room, possibly a gymnasium.

As it was Saturday morning, other children were in classrooms. As we waited, we heard some of the different classes singing, "Deutschland über alles."

But then there was us—the "special cases" who had been brought in. Our

Taken for interrogation, painting by Katarzyna Mojak.

75

group were sullen, frightened and cowed. They seemed to have selected mainly children from Adventist and Jehovah's Witness families. I knew many of them.

A German-language teacher from our school brought in a large painting of Adolf Hitler. In the picture, Hitler looked handsome, statesmanlike and was looking into the middle distance. He had the vision of a man destined to bring order and, no doubt, honour to the lucky countries he was overrunning.

A man in plain clothes barked instructions. "When you are called," he ordered, "you will take three steps forward in front of this picture of the Führer. You will raise your right arm so . . ." he demonstrated, "and you will say 'Heil Hitler!' three times, loudly and clearly."

Some children complied immediately and were sent into one of the regular classes. They had relief on their faces that they had been able to do something that did not result in physical violence or being screamed at by a Nazi thug.

Others of us would not say "Heil Hitler" and were sent into the corner of the gymnasium. Ruth and I did not comply with the order and were sent with a few other recalcitrants into another corner.

The problem was that my father had explained something to us, conscientiously and clearly. "Paul," he had said, "this 'Heil Hitler' thing is blasphemy. A person may only use 'Heil' to Jesus Christ and absolutely no-one else."

It did not matter how much the screaming Nazi officials might threaten me, I could not go against the teachings of my father's Bible. If I had understood the real danger I was in, I wonder what I would have done.

The group who still refused to say "Heil Hitler" were ushered into another corner, but it seemed with less menace. I was starting to feel more confident that this was just some strange German charade. They were carrying it out for their own unknowable reasons. Perhaps we might even be home for dinner.

An apparently kindly German gentleman asked us to sit down. He was dressed in civilian clothes, not the SS uniform with a sinister death's head on the hat. But then the penny dropped. If he was in plain clothes and working with the SS, he was from the Gestapo. If I trusted him, Ruth and me and possibly all of our family were dead.

"Good morning, young man and young lady. What are your names?" he began.

Somewhere inside me, a voice told me I was facing imminent danger of an unimaginable level.

"Your names?"

"Pawel. I mean Paul. My sister is called Ruth, sir."

"Quite so," said the man smiling at me in a most kindly fashion.

"Now Paul," he said drawing a little closer. "Who told you not to say 'Heil Hitler'?"

I knew I was in the most dreadful danger.

"Just tell me who told you. I am sure we can sort out any misunderstanding." He beamed at me showing every sign of friendliness. He was not threatening at all. Perhaps he just wanted to give me some friendly counselling or helpful advice.

But the image ran through my mind of that shiny hobnailed boot thudding with sickening force into my mother's leg. I knew the game was getting nastier but was uncertain what to say.

I summoned whatever inner strength I had and smiled at this apparent gentleman. "I don't know what is 'Heil Hitler,'" I beamed at them and talked in a sort of pidgin German.

As I smiled insanely at them, my face showed peace but somewhere deep inside my rib cage, my heart was thudding as if it was going to burst out and run home of its own accord, which is what I wanted to do. I was 13 and this had to be the performance of my life.

The Gestapo man looked at me quizzically.

"I know what is 'Guten Tag' or 'Guten Abend'." I smiled at him. *Thump! Thump!* He returned my smiled, waiting for me to say something. "... but I do not know what is 'Heil Hitler'." *Thump!*

He was so calm, so controlled, so nice. "So was it your mummy who told you not to say 'Heil Hitler'?" *Thump!* "Was it your daddy?" *Thump!* "Was it your pastor?"

"I not know what it mean." I smiled back while continuing to use my invented yokel-pidgin German.

He looked at me as though I was just a "Dummkopf"—an idiot. The room was quiet but I could hear the sounds of other children being asked similar questions in their corners.

"Abtreten! Dismissed!" He had believed my yokel story.

They sent Ruth and me into one of the school classes. And we were told that next Saturday we were to be here again—or face the consequences.

The class was soon over. It was so wonderful to leave the confines of the school and feel the fresh air on my face and see the clouds above us. The grey cloudy sky was so beautiful!

It must have been a huge adrenaline rush. We ran all the way home to the farm, where my mother was so relieved to see us that she burst into tears of joy.

But questions remained: Why had we been targeted? Could Mr L__ have reported our family? Could it have been Mr Hainig from school? Could it have been that we were Adventist and kept the Sabbath, when they wanted us to be at school? And then there was the threat of what might happen the next Sabbath. Would they come back for us again?

HOW I BECAME
A SHEPHERD

Early the next morning, my mother wiped away the tears and did that sort of half-smile, half-grimace that mothers do when they are trying to mask their distress from their children.

"You will have to go into hiding," she said.

My mother explained the danger of the situation. "You have to go, son," she concluded. "If they are after you, they will punish you."

As she spoke, she cut two slices of bread, wrapped them in paper and handed them to me.

"What about the rest of you, Mum?" I countered.

"Don't worry about us, we'll be OK," she tried to re-assure me. "We'll just tell them we haven't seen you and they will go away."

We both knew it was not that simple. If the SS came looking for me, the rest of my family were in immediate mortal danger.

It is normal for 13-year-old boys to believe in their own invincibility but, after the previous day's confrontation, I realised there were forces in the world that could threaten, harm and kill me. As ever, my mother was a long way ahead of me in understanding this.

"Now, what you have to do is this," my mother instructed. "Go to the Brenna mountains, it will take you about three hours on foot. There you will find a sheep farmer who is an old friend of mine. He is the richest farmer in the area and was even the mayor once. He is a rough, gruff old man but if you tell him who you are, he will accept you. You help him out on the farm and work hard and you'll be all right."

There was no time for formalities or niceties. I pulled together the few spare clothes I possessed and stuffed them into a small bag. I embraced my mother and younger siblings. Their embraces were so tight and so heartfelt that every instinct told me not to leave. But I knew I had to go. My heart was broken.

I had left home within half an hour of my mother's suggestion. Lost in thought and with only two pieces of hurriedly pocketed bread, I walked—as my mother told me—through the fields and forest of the Jarzebata Mountain.

I was walking slowly and dejectedly, often looking over my shoulder as if to fill my memory with as many images of my beloved home. I finally reached the summit of the mountain. I was very tired, physically and mentally, so I sat down on the rough mountain grass and looked homeward.

But I had to go on and continue to the sheep farm in the high country toward the Brenna Valley. As I walked, my cherished homeland of Wisła passed out of view.

The green hills were magnificent. The May sky was so utterly blue. We were experiencing the first warm days of spring. The squadrons of birds were all returning to nest for the summer. The bird song was so loud, especially the cuckoo. The bees were buzzing, counterpointed with the choir from all the other insects, hundreds of different varieties.

So many emotions raced through me: shock, denial, grief and—above all—fear of what the uncertain future might bring. At the same time, so many everyday but wonderful memories flooded my mind. I thought of the rattle of wooden cutlery as my mother made dinner, the comforting smell of the old barn or the trill of birds. I knew I would especially miss the spectacular views of the sunsets as the sun went down behind the mountains to the west of our farm. Would I ever see our beautiful farm again? When would I see my family again?

I thought again of the SS man who had kicked my mother so brutally. That memory would not leave my mind. It would be years before I would be able to erase that awful memory from my consciousness.

Grief and despair welled up inside me and I burst out crying like a child. I felt like an exile in my own country, in my own body. Tears of torment streamed down my face, as I unwillingly resumed my journey to the sheep farm at Brenna Mountain.

All the life I had known, my family and my childhood, disappeared from view with each step down the slope. In front of me were countless sheep and, in the distance, the sheep farmer's house with smoke curling up from the chimney.

* * *

"Hello, sir," I greeted the farmer. "I am Paweł Cieslar from Wisła." I didn't have to be "Paul" up here. I could be Polish again. Oddly enough, he was also Paweł Cieslar from Wisła. He owned the largest sheep farm in the district and, by reputation, was a clever man.

"My parents have sent me to ask if I can help out on your farm," I explained.

He wasn't a relative but he was a friend of my parents. Friendship was important and defined who you could trust your life to. That meant he would not give me away to the Nazis. My having appeared from nowhere may have seemed strange but labour on a farm is always short and farmers were always likely to accept any help offered.

"Well, come in, lad. Sit you down." He seemed welcoming.

"I really like working on farms," I replied, beaming at him with that mixture of enthusiasm and desperation known to anyone who has tried selling anything at a front door.

"But do you know anything about sheep?"

My family did not have any sheep and I knew nothing about looking after them. But if I said no, he might have sent me home.

"I love them," I said. I could not admit that I had only the most basic idea of what a shepherd actually did. "I find sheep such beautiful creatures," I enthused.

"Excellent," he said and went into the back room.

He emerged with a large sack of home-baked bread and said, "Come with me."

We walked a short distance and came upon his flock of some 300 sheep. There were also two wonderful dogs—Bury and Boce.

"All you have to do is make sure that they eat enough," the farmer explained. "And also that those ruffians from the forest don't come and steal them and that they don't get sick. You're happy to take this job on?"

"Oh yes!" I said brightly, even as my heart sank.

"Good, good," he said. "Oh, you might want to keep an eye out for wolves when the winter time comes."

Wolves? I thought. *Is he kidding?*

He wasn't. "The main thing is not to go out alone at night," he continued. "They howl a bit but if you stay indoors, you'll be safe enough."

At first, I wondered who was going to go out there with me. But I soon realised I was going to be alone. I was told the Estate Manager would pop in once a week to make sure I was all right. What he meant was that he would be checking that the sheep were all right!

"And here is your home," he said, puffing after we had walked some distance further up the mountainside.

He showed me what I thought was a small wooden tool shed. It had no heating but would keep the sleet off in the middle of the night. This was the shed where I was to live for the next year. The locals called it a *buda* or *kolyba*. Whatever they called it, it was a shed.

The farmer showed me a curious musical instrument. It was a trumpet some 2.5 metres (8 feet) long, made of pine wood and bound with cherry bark. It was called a tromba and was used in those parts as a communication device.

"Just blow this once every morning and I'll know you are still alive," the farmer said with a smile.

I knew how to blow a trumpet—but not anything like this! It was but one challenge of many I had to overcome.

On entering the buda, I found a wooden bench, which was to be my bed. There were no bedclothes but there was one old blanket, which I could pull over me. I would be warm enough, as long as I kept the fire going in the middle of the floor all night. If it went out in the middle of the night, the dreadful cold would haunt my dreams.

On the one hand, I had my hideout to dodge the SS. On the other hand, I was on my own up a mountain, with the real prospect of losing this kind farmer's sheep or perhaps freezing to death first, away from home for the first time.

* * *

When I awoke next morning, I had to remind myself that I was no longer in the bosom of the family but in an idyllic *pustka*—a Polish word describing a rural area not sullied by any human evil. The days lived up to this description. The nights most definitely did not.

At first it was terribly challenging. The sheep did not know me. I did not know them—or anything about them. It took the silly creatures a month to become comfortable with me. I lived in the tiny hut with little food and much responsibility for a young person. The sheep were dependent on me and the farmer was dependent on me as an employee in times of hardship, which increased by the day.

To my surprise, with time, I found that I could connect with the sheep and received lots of loving attention from them. I made friends with a small number of the leaders of the flock. They would nuzzle me and I would stroke them. Then when I gave a command for them to follow me, they would come and then the others would follow.

When the weather was fine and I was surrounded by the wonders of nature, it was a happy time. I love nature and flowers and the countryside. I love the stars at night, which in those mountain areas are sometimes so bright you could read by them—if there was anything to read. And the sunsets were often spectacular.

Looking after the sheep involved various battles against the forces of man and nature. I had to learn to be resourceful. My isolation certainly did that for me but the lessons were hard.

The major issue, of course, was that I had to look after the condition of the sheep. The pasture was poor and not sufficient for the sheep to thrive. They began to look undernourished, which was bad for them, bad for the owner and

My "buda" in the mountains. Here I was safe from the SS—almost.

bad for me. But I gradually learned how to use the dogs, how to keep the flock together and how to keep the sheep better nourished.

Still I was now a 14-year-old boy on my own all day and all night. We were about 3300 feet (1000 metres) above sea level, and cold rain and inclement weather could happen at almost any time. This was endlessly discouraging and utterly unbearable. I only had the clothes I had brought from home all those months ago. On my feet were the rough felt boots people wore in those parts. I seemed to spend more and more days soaking wet. I had nowhere to dry my clothes other than the fireplace, where I lit a fire in the evening. Often I would go to bed with wet socks and wake up in the morning with them equally wet.

I had 300 woolly charges, whose fleeces would have made me wonderfully warm clothes, but I was wet and freezing. Their meat would have made me positively fat and my condition was visibly declining. Moreover I developed a skin disease that came out as a painful red rash on my hands and legs, but with no doctor available, I just had to suffer through it.

Perhaps worst of all, during the long lonely days on the hillside, my mind replayed the way that the SS man had kicked my mother, as it would do for years afterward.

* * *

It must have been 11 o'clock at night. Milking the sheep had finished some time earlier. I was utterly exhausted, ready to lay down on my hard wooden bench and pull my single blanket over me. Suddenly, my two shepherd dogs— Bury and Boce—were making a lot of noise, clearly very agitated.

A cold chill of fear ran down my spine. I did not know what was going on but it certainly meant trouble. I looked outside but could not see anything. The dogs were running from the hut down to the edge of the forest and back again, barking and in a state of great excitement about something.

Then the dogs ran up the hill and out of sight. From the sound of their barking, they were on the top of an adjoining hill. It was odd behaviour; they normally stayed beside me, except when we were moving the sheep.

My mouth dried with fear and anticipation. My heart thumped so that I thought it would break out of my rib cage. Thoughts of tiredness and bed were replaced by thoughts of danger. My senses were heightened as I listened for any sound that might point to where the danger lay.

For a moment longer, I could not see or hearing anything except the barking of the dogs. Then—it sounded like voices. Was it voices or just the wind in the trees? No, it was definitely voices.

I was terrified to the core of my being. I wanted to scream but knew that, if I did, the voices would come to get me.

I was too tired and too afraid to think rationally. But an idea hit me. I slid off the bench and put my ear to the floor of the hut to try to hear any sound that might tell me what the danger was. Waiting allowed me to devise some plan to protect myself. Still I heard nothing.

I braced my leg against the door in a desperate attempt to stop anyone or anything coming in. Still I waited and waited. Nothing happened. The dogs seemed calmer and I wondered if the danger had passed.

Then there were footsteps outside—and voices close by. My terror was so great that I held back from screaming only with the greatest effort. I lay on the bed so that when they broke in they would beat my legs rather than my head.

The door burst open and my heart nearly burst in terror. I huddled under my blanket.

When I plucked up enough courage to come out, I saw that they were enormous men with big shaggy beards and massive Russian ushanka fur hats, with flaps that came down to cover their ears. The men pointed their machine guns at me and I saw the round magazines and threatening muzzles.

"It's a boy," said one of them in Polish.

"What have you got to eat?" another demanded.

I pointed to where I kept my bread and cheese. They kept me covered with their machine guns as they scoffed down my food for the next day.

"Any Germans around here?"

'No," I replied with a tremble in my voice.

"Right, well, what you are going

Me as a shepherd boy.

to do is to blow on that tromba and make it sound like an emergency. Go on, then!"

Their idea was to lure German troops up into the hills in the middle of the night and then ambush them.

I blew with all my might into the huge trumpet. I listened as the last echo died away in the darkness of the surrounding hills.

"Go on, boy, blow it again," they demanded.

I blew a second time and let the mournful sound die away on the breeze.

"Right—and one more time!"

I blew into the tromba for the third time and wondered what would happen next.

"Good lad," said one of them—and they disappeared into the darkness.

I waited for a German patrol to stumble into the ambush but none came.

* * *

Early the next morning, several farmers walked up from the valley.

"What was all that blowing for last night?" they asked. "Are you in trouble?"

I told him about the partisans.

Partisans were bad news for everyone. They went back down to their homes in the valley. Word had got around.

Blowing the shepherd's trumpet on a later visit to the mountains.

A few hours later, a German patrol came around looking for them. They asked me what had happened and what I had seen.

The patrol went off in the direction I had indicated. I did not see the patrol again or the partisans. They had simply melted into the night.

But every night I went to sleep not knowing if the two-o'clock knock would arrive and, if so, if it would be the last thing I was destined to hear. The event that triggered this fear and paranoia was one that I will never forget. It was my first encounter with the partisans but would not be my last.

THE WINTER OF MY DISCONTENT

My shepherd's life during the summer time was demanding but not unbearable. The mountains were lovely and the bird song in the trees was beautiful. But I had to ensure that my 300 sheep were well fed and that they were milked three times a day.

The estate manager would come up to my buda to help with this. I had to rise at 5 am and have a simple breakfast of bread and cheese washed down with pure mountain water. The first milking was at 5.30 am and would take about an hour to complete.

At 1 pm, I would have a simple lunch—again, bread and cheese—and we had to milk the sheep again at 2.30 pm. The third milking was at 8.30 pm, followed by a dinner of bread and milk. Of course, I did not have a watch but we learned to gauge the time fairly accurately from the position of the sun. The sun was also my alarm clock.

Between milkings, I had a range of duties. First, I had to heat up the milk and put it into a wooden container. Then I would add an amount of calf's rennet, which the farmer would bring up to me in a bottle. Then I would cover it and leave it to set.

On returning from herding the sheep, I had to shape the cheese into usable chunks. My homemade cheese was wonderful, the like of which could only be obtained today from expensive cheese shops. When my cheesemaking was done, I had to chop wood for the fire, which burned merrily on the floor of my buda.

* * *

Wintertime was not as pleasant. Across all of Europe, the winter of 1942 was especially inclement with thick snow, iced rivers and temperatures down to -40° Celsius (about -40° F). The vicious nature of the wind was actually frightening. It seemed to want to kill me. The trees in the forests bowed and creaked and groaned under abnormally heavy snow.

Late in the autumn, I had to move in with the estate manager, Jan Kawulok, and his wife who lived some half a kilometre away. They lived in a more substantial house that would actually support life in the middle of winter, which my buda would not. But this was only a partial escape from the weather.

As winter progressed, the snowdrifts nearly covered his house and the streams were frozen into an uncompromising solid mass. The nights were endless, black and terrifying as the wind howled outside like some monster trying to break into the house. Warmth was another country, of which I could remember little and knew less.

None of this excused me from my work. No matter how cold and bitter the days were, no matter how I suffered from colds or any other medical condition, I still had to carry out my shepherding duties.

Shepherd boy in the snow, painting by Katarzyna Mojak.

In these conditions, I had to feed the sheep the same three times a day with hay, which was piled up in the barn outside the house. During lambing time—from January to March—every two hours, both day and night, I was required to fight my way 100 yards down a lane, through the wind, to confirm that any newborn lambs were all right. If not, it was up to me to sort out the problem.

Sometimes the solution to a problem would be as simple as relocating the mother and lamb to prevent the newborn being trampled. Sometimes I would have to improvise a more complex solution. I may not have had a veterinary degree but I became an expert in sheep obstetrics.

That I did this every two hours meant that I suffered from chronic sleep deprivation. My life became a cocktail of biting cold, sleep deprivation, and the depression of the darkness and never-ending solitude.

"Mama, why did you bring me into this world?" I cried out into the freezing wind on more than one occasion. "Why was I born?"

On many occasion, I just sat down and cried. My faithful Bury and Boce were all that stood between me and utter despair. However, I soon learned that feeling sorry for myself was not going to achieve anything. I needed to find some kind of inner resilience and fortitude if I was going to survive.

When those harsh winters came, the wolves would come in from the east. They were starving and looking for food. A juicy lamb would fit the bill quite nicely, as would a scrawny shepherd boy. In the endless black winter nights, I could hear them calling. It was primeval, chilling and pitiless. Yet the presence of starving wolves was completely preferable to life under the Nazis.

My diet was limited to a chunk of bread that weighed some 11 pounds (5 kilograms) and had to last me for two weeks. It would actually last this long without going mouldy and I would eat it with sheep's cheese. The bread was like stone and I had to chew it and chew it to bring it to the point where I could actually swallow it.

Toothpaste was an unimaginable luxury but I would have to say that the stone-bread did a good job of keeping my teeth clean. Soap was another commodity that did not enter into my little closed-off world. On the other hand, it had the great advantage that my dogs knew with some certainty exactly where I was, even from considerable distance away.

* * *

Once winter had passed and I returned to my buda, life had fewer hardships. In my pustka, the forests were so beautiful with their fir and beech trees, their birds and, when the snows had gone, their wild flowers. I loved the quietness on sunny days. At night, the sky was like a beautiful black canopy dotted with a million glittering diamonds. Every so often, there would be a special treat: my eyes would track in fascination as a shooting star traversed the sky. I would lie on my back and marvel at it.

Bury and Boce snuffled around looking for small rodents to pick on or sometimes they just lay contentedly by my side. Sometimes the dogs would play with me. They were friendly and wonderful companions.

The silence was utter and complete. Occasionally, the dogs would make a sound. Sometimes there was the patter of some wild animal going about its business in the forest. Sometimes the sheep would make some small rustling sound. But otherwise the sound of silence lay like a blanket over the whole pustka.

It did not especially go through my mind but, at some time, the school would have noticed that I had disappeared. I was to discover later that the police had been around to ask what happened to me. My mother said that I had run away. They thought that I might be hiding in the neighbourhood and asked questions about me. The neighbours knew that I was in hiding somewhere, even if they did not know where I was. We were a tightly knit community and no-one gave me away to the Ordnungspolizei. After a while, the police decided that they had more pressing business.

Once a month, my boss, Paweł Cieslar, would walk from his house to my buda. Even though it was one of my rare human contacts, the focus was on business: about how well I was looking after the sheep and how I needed to work more diligently. More diligently? Already I was living on dry bread, deprived of sleep and freezing cold for months on end! He wanted me to care for his sheep to the ultimate extent of whatever capability I possessed. So the sheep were to be provided for—but who was going to look after me?

But I tried not to complain. In many ways, my isolated life was less than pleasant and I knew I was being deprived of my childhood but at least I was safe from bullets and bombs. Most Poles did not have this luxury in their lives.

My thoughts often focused on my family. They were only some 10 miles (16 kilometres) away but might as well have been in a different country. I often looked forward to that glorious day when I would have a reunion with them.

My religious convictions were very important, too, and I felt convinced that although I was alone, there was a God who knew about me and who cared.

But the other human contacts were much worse than the visits from the farmer—the ongoing visits from partisans. They were always in the area at night. Sometimes they would knock on my door in the middle of the night. These were desperate men—in the early days, they were Poles and later some Russians—and many times I would be rudely jolted from my slumbers by knocking on the door.

Three or four rough-looking men carrying firearms and festooned with hand-grenades would demand bread, cheese and the fattest sheep. Refusal was not an option. Oddly enough, I came to realise these men would not kill me, because I was worth more to them alive than dead.

VICTORY BEYOND BELIEF

One day my sister Marta came to visit me, and brought good news—my father was home! On receiving this news, I was given permission to visit my family, provided I returned the next day.

I left with a light heart to walk the 10 miles (16 kilometres) to our family home. I made sure that I was wearing the trilby hat that my father had sent me. I loved that hat and only ever took it off to sleep and I knew he would be pleased to see me wearing it.

When I arrived home, he was there—at our farmhouse! I rushed to embrace him. He rushed toward me and wrapped his arms around me. I hardly heard the words he spoke as he embraced me. I didn't need words. Our father was home. We were all so happy.

I was full of questions—most importantly, "Are you home for good or do you have to go back?"

"No, it's all over, son," he said. "No more Germany. I have an official release and I am home for good, praise God!"

I was puzzled. "Father, has anybody else been released from the labour camp? I haven't heard of anyone else coming home. How did you do it?"

My father smiled and said, "Well, sit down, son, and I will tell you all about it."

I sat, hugging my knees, expecting a good story.

When my father and the other Adventist men went to the Berlin labour camp in 1940, they told the firm representative that the Adventist group would not work on Saturdays, explaining their belief that it is the holy Sabbath day according to God's commandments. Amazingly, they were given Saturday free of work.

But three years later, in 1943, a new foreman told the Adventists they would have to work on Saturdays. He spoke to my father because he knew German. "Mr Cieslar!" the foreman said, "I strongly suggest that you Adventists do as you are told. From now on, you will work on Saturdays!"

The message was clear. If they did not conform, they would—as Volksdeutscher—be tried in court. Without any doubt, they would be heading for a concentration camp.

"No, sir!" my father replied. "You are aware that we are of the Adventist Christian faith and that we keep Saturdays holy according to God's commandments."

The foreman clenched his fists and said, "Cieslar, you and your group are working for the Reich. The Reich has no interest in your religious views. The Reich tells you what to do and you do it. That is reality. 'Befehl ist Befehl!' Orders are orders!"

The German way was always to obey orders no matter how unfair, disgusting or illegal the order may have been. The foreman leaned in close and continued, "There are 28 of you Adventist jokers playing up and you are making me look bad. Do you really think higher authority will tolerate that?"

In all probability, the foreman did not want to lose his best workers. The Adventists men were strong, willing and able. They earned respect for their work ethic and conscientiousness. They did not engage in any sabotage and, as such, were a highly prized commodity.

"You know the rules and I know the rules," the foreman said. Adventism was of no consequence to him. He hoped they would just buckle and not make his life any more difficult than it already was. The members of the Adventist group were classified as Polish and wore the dreaded "P" badges. If they did not do as they were told, they could expect to be sent to Sachsenhausen, the nearest major camp to Berlin, from which few came out alive. If my father disobeyed and was sent there, my mother and the rest of our family would never have known what happened to him.

"You are going to work on Saturdays!" the foreman insisted one last time before his patience and loss of face pushed him to the next stage.

My father and the other men knew the danger they faced. We found out years later that our father had written to our mother: "It is likely we will be sent to a concentration camp. If so, my intention is to escape and to hide in the woods or in a pile of farm straw outside Berlin. Should this happen, I expect I will die of starvation. If you do not hear from me again, this is what has happened. I love you all."

A short time after the confrontation with the foreman, two German policemen arrested the Adventist group. "You are under arrest for treason against Greater Germany," they said. "You are to accompany us."

They were taken to the local jail. The Third Reich did not dispense entirely with legal process but it did tend to work with great speed.

My father and a work colleague, Mr Jan Jelen from Cieszyn who also spoke German, decided to write a plea to the presiding magistrate:

> To the very honoured Judge,
> We the undersigned wish to make a statement.
> We are working in Greater Germany as willing labourers as we are required to do. We are not in any way in opposition to Greater Germany. As Volksdeutscher, we wish to assure you that we have no traitorous or unreasonable intention toward Greater Germany. We undertake the work to the best of our abilities. We also undertake to work the allotted number of hours in the service of the German government and to undertake all tasks allocated to us.
> We are, however, 28 men of the Adventist faith from Silesia. To us the Sabbath—Saturday—is sacred and our conscience does not allow us to labour on that holy day. This is an arrangement made by the Almighty God, not by men. We respectfully request your judgment to allow us to give the best of our labour but to grant us the great favour not to work on Saturday.
> In high esteem,
>
> Paul Cieslar, Jan Jelen

Soon it was their turn to stand before the magistrate.

"So Paul Cieslar, and Jan Jelen, you are refusing to work on Saturdays as required by your place of work."

"That is correct, sir," my father replied.

"I understand, from your letter, that you are very devout Christians?" the judge said.

"That is correct, sir."

"And you refuse to work on Saturdays?" the judge asked. "Why, precisely, is this, Mr Cieslar?"

"We are of the Adventist faith, sir," my father explained, "and we are asked by the Almighty God in His holy Bible to keep the Sabbath holy in accordance with His will. Our faith in God and commitment to His commandments does not allow us to work on the holy rest day."

At this point, my father and Jan Jelen had, in effect, signed their own death warrants. They now expected to be marched to prison and have their lives ended, one way or another.

Instead the judge spoke again, "So, Mr Cieslar and Mr Jelen, you are strong Christians and that is basis for your defence?"

"Yes," they replied. "We trust our almighty and omniscient God."

Then the judge asked them an unusual question: "Will Germany win this war or not?"

That was a loaded question. Within Hitler's Germany, to say Germany would not win the war was a treasonable offence and one that, alone, would buy them a one-way ticket to a concentration camp. But my father gave an answer the judge did not expect.

"We don't know," he said. "We are only simple human beings and cannot tell any future event. We cannot look into the future to say who will win this war. Only God knows the future."

My father and Mr Jelen knew they were playing with fire. Most judges would have condemned them for this alone. For whatever reason, this particular judge decided to hear them out.

"And who does your God say will win the war?" he asked.

My father gave him an honest and incredibly brave answer. "As a matter of fact," he said, "our God outlined 2600 years ago, in the prophetic book of Daniel, what will happen to the countries of Europe in this war."

"Really?" the judge asked, intrigued. "Can you show me this in the Bible?"

My father reached into his pocket and pulled out his small Bible. "Yes, sir."

The judge adjourned the proceedings. The court rose and the judge, together with my father and Mr Jelen, exited to his chambers behind the courtroom.

"Very well, Mr Cieslar, now show me the passage to which you referred," the judge said.

My father opened his Bible to chapter 2 of the book of Daniel. He pointed out the history of the nations from Babylon, to Medo-Persia, Greece, Rome and the division of Rome into 10 European countries and added that, according to this prophecy, Europe cannot be united until the day when the stone from outer space arrives. He explained that the stone is the second coming of Jesus Christ.

The judge quietly read Daniel 2 and considered it for himself. At that time, of course, Germany was successful in their military expansion. The German troops had fought their way to the gates of Moscow and into depths of the Caucasus. The confidence of the German nation was sky-high.

The judge laughed. He pointed to the open Bible and then to the two men standing before him. "Wünderbar!" he chortled. "I really like it! That is a good answer."

His laughter resolved into a decisive smile. "Case dismissed," he declared.

By the rules of the Third Reich, their refusal to work was treason. Their refusal to say that Germany would win the war was also treason. By letting them off, the judge was disobeying a direct order from Hitler and, if reported, could at least have been removed from the bench.

My father's refusal to work on Saturdays and his refusal to say that Germany would win the war was more than enough to have designated him as "asocial." A lucky result would have been to be handed over to the SS to be shot. It was more likely he would have been sent to Mauthausen concentration camp for extermination through hard labour.

But my father and the other Adventists found themselves walking down a Berlin street as free men. They went back to their huts and reassumed their duties. The foreman agreed, grudgingly, that the Adventists did not have to work on Saturdays.

Almost one and a half years later, the foreman again sent for my father. As my father entered the foreman's office, he realised there was no policeman or SS man waiting for him.

"You asked to see me, sir?"

"Yes," said the foreman. "This is your release paper. You can go home."

My father studied the piece of paper. It was issued by the magistrate court before which he had stood more than a year earlier. My father didn't ask any questions. He left the foreman's office. He said goodbye to everyone and left before any question could be asked of him. He went to the Berlin–Silesia station and boarded a train headed home.

His homecoming was joyous beyond belief. My father was convinced that God placed that judge in that court. He was the right man in the right place at the right time.

SHEEP ARE SURPRISINGLY BRIGHT

Next day, it was a 10-mile walk back up the mountain to the sheep. The sheep were still looking scraggy and underfed—and I was getting into trouble for it. To make matters worse, two of them had died. The estate manager had been telling the owner that I was not tending the sheep as well as I should.

I didn't know what to do. If I did nothing, the boss would come back and complain that the sheep were underfed. But the land was so poor and there was little for them to eat. It was all so frustrating.

However, a short distance away was a forestry plantation. Here the feed was good. The area grew thick with lush green grass, which my sheep would love. Some rather blood-curdling signs said that it was forbidden to enter the area, and neighbours had warned me that it was infested with partisans at night.

Fortunately, one dark night, I saw that a dreadful storm was brewing. Huge raindrops began to spatter on the stony ground. The bitter wind howled and beat me back to my hut for shelter. As the rain became worse, lashing the hillside like machine-gun bullets, the lightning flashed from one hill to another. The dogs recognised the danger and forced their way into the hut for shelter. I didn't have the heart to keep them out and, anyway, they helped keep me warm. On those bare hills, when the thunder crashed you could have read a book by it because the lightning was so bright.

For everyone else, this weather was a problem. For me, it was an opportunity. It was too horrible for partisans or informers to be out. The luscious fields were ours for the taking!

Braving the biting wind, the sharp pin pricks of the rain and the elemental cracks of the lightning, I took the sheep down to the point where the government land started. They had been huddled together against the terrible weather but I led them past the warning signs and ushered them down to the better feed. They knew my voice and trusted me, so they followed me.

The sheep ate their fill, despite the driving rain and vicious wind. I watched them from a sheltered point, under the branches of a large fir tree. I had hoped that the weather would maintain its appalling behaviour but had no reason to worry. If anything, it was getting worse. There were lightning strikes not far from us and some of the sheep were beginning to seem quite frightened.

I was starting to think that I had done a silly thing in bringing the sheep away from the protection of the sheepfold and into this lush but dangerous pasture.

Fortunately, the huge fir and beech trees offered some shelter. Even through the cold and the driving rain, it amused me that instead of standing under a fir tree as I had done, they would shelter under a beech tree. I even called them to me to come under the protective boughs of the fir trees. But not a single one of them would come to me. They knew my voice and trusted me but this time they refused. *What stupid animals!* I thought. With their denser leaves and branches, fir trees gave much better protection than beech trees.

BANG!

I had the sensation of being thrown into the air and landed with an undignified bump like a plane shot down by flak. I skidded across the muddy ground before coming to a halt. I had a few cuts and bruises but, fortunately, no broken bones. I must have lain unconscious for some minutes but then came to.

I looked groggily around. *What is that awful smell of burning all around me?* I thought. *What about the sheep? Are they dead or alive?*

Thankfully, the sheep were still under the nearby beech tree. The dogs were still at their posts. I had to get back in control of the situation. I tried to stand and discovered that I was still in one piece.

The fir tree, under which I had been standing, had been reduced to a smoking blackened stump in an instant. It had been hit by lightning! The sheep had sheltered under the beech trees because they knew, somehow, that lightning hits fir trees but does not hit beech trees. They also knew that when I was calling them to come that I was telling them to do something that they knew to be dangerous.

As I stood I became, aware of a vicious tinnitus—high-pitched whistling—in my ears, which would continue for a number of days. The rain was still battering and I was staggering. I called the sheep to me and told them to follow. Somehow, I led them across the meadow, over the small brook and back to their sheepfold.

I lay there that night thinking of all that had happened. I was lucky to be alive but at least the sheep had had a good meal! I decided I was not going to take my chances in the forestry land again.

After this experience, I acquired a new respect for my woolly charges. And, after a shaky start, I was gradually getting on top of this job.

* * *

Some weeks later, the farmer told me to go up to a particularly high pasture where the feed was better than at our home base. With the dogs, I set off but found our way barred by a wide river. While only about 2 feet (about 50 centimetres) deep but some 30 feet (10 metres) wide—and fast flowing.

This was definitely a job where I needed my skills with the herd leaders. So I found them, got them to the riverbank and, together with Bury and Boce, organised them to cross the river. But the sheep would not co-operate.

By this time, I had learned a few tricks—and I tried all of them. But it was to no avail. I was frustrated. Bury and Boce were frustrated. The sheep were frustrated because they did not want to risk life and limb in this swiftly flowing river.

I had one idea left to try. I knew that one of the herd leaders—a ewe—had a lamb with her. She trusted me to pick up the lamb, which I did, and I walked down to the riverbank. The ewe followed.

I forded the cold water of the river but I could feel the bottom with my feet. It was not too rocky so I was able to keep my footing. Behind me, through the roaring of the waters, I could hear the poor mother ewe complaining at the lamb being taken away.

I got to the other bank and walked out. The poor lamb was complaining at the enforced separation from its mother. As I staggered up the far riverbank,

I held the poor crying animal high so its mother could see it. It baa-ed and baa-ed, until the mother plunged into the river and swam across. The others followed.

After a couple of minutes, the entire flock had jumped in and had swum over. The dogs made sure that no sheep strayed or were lost. For the next hour, I lay in the sun to warm up and dry off my soaking clothes. The mother was reunited with its lamb and everyone was happy. Sometimes, it almost felt good to be alive.

Persuading the sheep to cross the river, painting by Katarzyna Mojak.

TOWARD THE WHIRLPOOLS OF DEATH

It had been a long, brutal and difficult winter. In the estate manager's cottage, I could not see out the window. The ice had been inches thick. At times, I had to be careful not to put my frozen feet too close to the stove or frostbite—and possible amputation—would have resulted.

In April, the fruit trees were normally in full bloom but this year we still had deep snow in the high country and that posed problems. I had run out of hay on which to feed the sheep, and they were facing starvation if I didn't figure out a way to feed them.

I heard from passing neighbours that in the Bystrzyca Valley—some 14 miles (23 kilometres) away, at a much lower altitude—farmers were already ploughing their fields and sowing seeds. My boss arranged for me to take the sheep down there. I enlisted the help of my younger brother Jerzy to move the flock down to a pasture where the snow had gone and the fields were covered in rich green grass on both sides of the swiftly flowing and beautiful River Olsa. It was a long way but I had to do something and I thanked God for my brother's help.

Jerzy and I duly got the sheep down to the valley, where the weather

My youngest brother Jerzy.

was actually warm and there was sunshine. I had forgotten how warm and beautiful sunshine could be. I saw the first blue skies I had seen for six weeks or longer. Not only that but the surroundings were breathtaking. The hill slopes were covered by wonderful fir trees and the air was exhilarating.

The pasture proved to be excellent and it was beginning to feel like a holiday. After the cold, ice and all-pervading dampness, it felt good to be alive. When the serious work of the day was done, I could talk and laugh with Jerzy and the farmer. The awful loneliness was behind me. I had never actually had a holiday but I imagined that if I were to have one, this is what it would feel like.

But, in those mountain regions, the weather can change suddenly from beautiful one minute to storm the next. The blue sky was dark grey within minutes. Dark clouds formed even as I looked at the sky. The warmth of the afternoon was driven away rapidly by a cold wind that wailed like the screams of dying animals. Even the simple act of walking forward felt like pushing through a curtain of rain.

As much as Jerzy and I could push forward, it pushed against us and even seemed to want to take us to some place we did not want to go. I had to hang on to my trilby hat. The rain lashed so hard that first of all it irritated me by pouring off the brim of my hat like a waterfall, dripping off the end of my chin and working its way down my shirt collar so that I had rivulets coursing down my back.

The sudden violent rain caused a rapid melting of snow in the hills above. After just an hour, the current in the River Olsa was flowing more quickly than usual and the snow-melt had whipped it into a torrent, which roared and threatened. Jerzy and I could not even consider taking shelter because the sheep were close to the river and, if one fell in, it would be swept away within seconds. We had to look after them.

We hoped the vile weather would pass quickly but it continued. The sheep were drenched, we were drenched and the river grew higher, faster and more deadly.

Despite the hazardous weather, Jerzy and I had noticed that the pasture on the far bank of the river was actually rather better than where we were. The weather was equally miserable on either side but the sheep would be better fed over there. We set out to take them over to the other side, which meant leading the sheep over two separate bridges: the first over the railway line and the second, some distance further, over the river. It did seem to pose something of a risk to the flock but the superior pasture seemed well worth it. We would just have to supervise the flock closely.

* * *

Just as we were driving the sheep onto the railway bridge, we heard a passenger train approaching rapidly. The hiss from the steam locomotive and the clattering and rumbling of the wheels upset the sheep, especially some of the younger lambs. Ten of them broke away from the flock and, for reasons best known to themselves, ran as fast as they could parallel to the train. They were panicking and out of control.

When the last carriage pulled away, the railway line was littered with the bodies of the lambs. It was a distressing sight. Some had legs severed. Some were cut in two. Some were dead but the ones who were still alive were even worse. It was terrible but we had to put them out of their misery. Not to kill them would have been an act of appalling cruelty. Making it worse for me was the knowledge that I would have to report to the boss that all of these animals had died in my care.

The sound of the train disappeared into the distance. Now all we could hear was the Olsa, which roared on, much higher, faster and more menacingly than usual.

We took the flock over the river as we had intended but neither Jerzy nor I spoke a word. We were devastated but could not dwell on this sad event. We still had to face the danger that more lambs could be lost in the river.

From my position, the roaring of the water sounded like a squadron of bombers taking off. If the sheep came too close to the riverbank, I shooed them away. Jerzy took up position on the other side of the pasture to protect the lambs from any traffic on the main road. Everything seemed under control.

Then a sudden gust blew my beloved trilby hat off my head and into the river. I could just not bear to lose that hat. Fortunately, it was not too far into the river. From a nearby bush, I broke the longest branch I could find. The water was carrying my hat away rapidly.

I thought seriously and consciously decided that I was not going to take any undue risks. But I stepped into the shallows of the river in my rubber boots and, holding the stick forward, attempted to retrieve my hat. I could reach the hat if I acted quickly. Just one more step should do it.

Then the ground beneath my feet disappeared and immediately I felt the shock of the roaring torrent. I felt the freezing cold of the melted snow. I also felt the fear of death—I had never learned to swim. The water was in my mouth and nose, and I spluttered to expel it.

I could not see where the river was taking me but I knew I was travelling quickly. As I came up in the water, I could see the bank speeding past and away from me. Then I was under the water again and being carried away from the sheep.

I tried to strike out for the riverbank. I went to shout but the cold, insistent, cruel water stifled my words and my breath. I knew it was unlikely Jerzy would have noticed me missing. I dipped under again.

Surfacing, I spluttered again to drive the freezing water out of my lungs. I was in a nightmare. Breath was a luxury. It seemed this was the end of me. The water played with me and threw me up and down, now through the air, now below the surface.

Debris of all types smashed into me. Boughs of trees thrashed me and submerged rocks crunched into my legs below the water. The water was driving me faster and faster.

My skull crunched onto the stones on the river bed and I realised I was going to drown. I thrashed out with the desperation of a boy who was going to die if he does not thrash out. I now knew I was probably not going to survive. I gave my arms and legs everything. I gasped as more icy water found its way into my lungs.

Through the air! Under the water! River bank speeding by! Gasp! More water in my lungs. I knew I had to frame my last words. Gasp! My last words were "Father in heaven, must I die so young? Save me, please."

I was now way down river and had reached the point where two tributaries joined the Olsa on the one side. The first tributary was the River Frydek and on the other the tributary was the River Mistek.

The river was wider and deeper now. It was faster but with less turbulence and I could keep myself afloat by thrashing wildly. This was not swimming—it was an act of a drowning boy using his arms like a crazed windmill in a forlorn hope that it might just save him.

But there was an even worse problem. Where the tributaries joined, the meeting of the waters caused whirlpools that could suck anyone down to the river bed. There would be no escape or second chance. To the locals, these waters were infamous for so many people having drowned in them. There was no time now for prayers or thought. I had to focus my entire being on keeping out of those whirlpools.

A large wave from one of the tributaries picked me up and dashed me against a rock. The thought went through my head that no-one could rescue me now. Thoughts of my parents, brothers and sisters flashed through my mind. I would never see them again. I was just too young to die!

The collision blasted all the air out of my lungs. I knew that the impact had done something to my legs, but the cold water had numbed any feeling. My hand searched with desperation for anything to grab on to. I found a cleft below the water line, grabbed it and held on for dear life. For the first time since I fell in, I was under control.

I now had time to collect my thoughts and I was conscious of being terrified. Before this, I had not even had time to think about it. I seemed to have been in the water for hours, but in reality it might have been 20 minutes.

Then came the third and most startling realisation: I was almost naked apart from my underwear in that freezing maelstrom! I had lost not only my hat but also my jacket, shirt and belt, and I had torn my trousers. The violence of the torrent had even ripped my boots off.

I spluttered to expel the water from my stomach and lungs. I did not have time to ask where all my clothes had disappeared to; I was too busy clinging to that rock with every ounce of strength in my young body.

I thanked God for the rock that saved my life! I then experienced with high-definition clarity the words of the beautiful hymn, taught to all of us by my parents: "Rock of Ages cleft for me./ Let me hide myself in Thee."

Never before or since has the double meaning of "The Rock" impressed itself so clearly on my consciousness. It made my heart pound so hard, that I felt it was going to pump out right there as I held tightly to that rock.

* * *

In the meantime, Jerzy had realised that something bad had happened and came running down the riverbank. He had been calling and whistling but we could not see each other. He had worked out that I had fallen into the river and was running along, trying to see me. He thought I must be drowned.

"Paweł! Paweł!" he shouted, bellowed and screamed. But there was no reply.

He became desperate. He ran along the riverbank but he could not catch sight of me. Then he saw something that resembled a ball floating on the water but not moving with the current. He ran along the bank as fast as he could. He realised it was a human head. He had found me.

"Paweł! Paweł!" he shouted again.

I could see him shout but could not hear him because of the roar of the river. He sprinted to a nearby farmhouse and soon the farmer came running with a rope, which they threw to me.

By this time, I was in shock and in a state of exhaustion. They threw the line in behind me so that the current carried it to me. I knew there was nothing else for it. I let go of the rock and grabbed the line, holding it more tightly than anything I have held on to in my life.

The current still battered me. Branches were flying down in the current

Hanging onto the rock, painting by Katarzyna Mojak.

and smashing into me. Suddenly I could feel the riverbed beneath me. I scrambled and scraped and grabbed with all I had—and then I was on dry land.

Almost naked, I was also battered and bruised. I was cut where sharp branches had lacerated my skin. But this was not a time for deliberations. I was freezing cold, so the farmer ran to get clothes and blankets to dry me off and dress me. Then I was helped to the house of the farmer, who gave me a hot drink and some food.

Meanwhile, the sheep were happily grazing on the riverbank under Jerzy's watchful eye. That was the thing with sheep. One minute they could act in an insane manner and, minutes later, they could be quietly nibbling as if they were living in some pastoral paradise.

Late the next day, I was recovering from the ordeal and was amazed when my father walked in through the door.

"Paweł!" he raised his voice and embraced me.

In his embrace, an awful thought went through my mind: I would have to confess that I had lost the wonderful hat he had given me.

"Father, what are you doing here?" I asked him. "What is the problem?"

"No," he said in a loving way, "I am asking you what the problem is with you."

I was amazed. How could he have known about the river rescue?

"How do you know?" I asked him. "Yes, it is true that I was almost dead—but how did you know?"

He told me that during the previous night he had been disturbed by a vivid dream. He said that the dream was of an orchestra. The orchestra was playing very well and I was playing in it. However, I was playing separately to the orchestra and was becoming detached from it.

"You tried to play your instrument and fit in with the orchestra but you couldn't," he said. "Everyone was looking at you and not very happy. The harder you tried, the worse it got. You were showing signs of extreme frustration."

His immediate instinct was that I was in grave danger. He awoke and told my mother that he was worried about me.

It was still dark. There were bandits and partisans to worry about but this did not deter him and he set off without hesitation. He did not have a car or any other transport. When he found me, he had walked more than 14 miles (22 kilometres). Judging by the time he arrived, he must have done it at a fast pace and almost without stopping.

NO HEIL HITLER!

As far as I recall, I don't think we mentioned the trilby hat—but we both thanked God for saving my life!

"MAMA, HELP ME!"

The summer brought with it a terrible drought. Away in the east, it created a problem for the German military in its gargantuan losing battle with the Russian Red Army. Closer to home, it caused problems for me and my sheep. I was responsible for finding green pasture on which they could feed but this was becoming increasingly difficult.

One particular day, the sun was hot again and I was relieved to accept the hospitality of even the most meagre shade at the edge of the forest. All the pastures around me were starting to dry up and the sheep were getting thinner. Out of desperation, I looked around and came up with an idea. Sheep look upon the leaves of ash trees as a delicacy, so why not climb up and get some?

I sharpened my large axe with a whetstone and hauled myself up an ash tree. Standing high in the tree, I swung my axe and it bit into a bough, festooned with lovely juicy ash leaves. After a couple more bites of the axe into the bough, it fell with a great crash. The sheep were slightly startled but then some of the brighter ones realised that this was a juicy snack. All the others then caught on and followed as sheep are wont to do.

This was the life! From my position up the tree, I had a great vantage point to see the lovely countryside. After a few more swings of the axe, a couple more boughs fell to earth and the sheep had a wonderful picnic on the leaves.

I adjusted my position and swung the axe again. The shining sharp blade hissed through the air, missed the branch completely and, instead of biting into hard ash wood, it bit into my left shin. I found myself flying through the air, falling 10 feet (3 metres) to the ground below and landing with a bone-jarring jolt. I entered a pain so vicious that my stomach turned and I thought I would vomit.

"Mama, help me!" She was not there but I was screaming with pain.

"Mama, save me or I am dead!" I screamed in my agony.

Only the sheep heard—and sheep involved in a picnic are not interested in cries of agony from shepherd boys. As I gathered my senses after the fall, I looked at my leg. It looked like meat on display in a butcher's shop window.

The blood was spurting in great globs. Through the pain and the nausea, I knew that if I did not stop the flow of blood I was going to bleed to death. The only item I had to bind my leg was my shirt. This had not been washed for some weeks but it was all I had.

I rolled up my trouser leg, by now dripping with fresh blood. The wound was deep and I could see the bone. The slightest movement of the leg was excruciatingly painful. Neighbours were too far away to hear my cries for help. Panic began to set in but I could not afford panic. I had to take a grip of my emotions and get on top of this awful situation.

I peeled my shirt off my body as fast as I could. I was whimpering like an animal in pain. I ripped the shirt into dirty bandages and bound them around my leg as tight as I could bear, in an attempt to stop the blood. It still seeped through. Words went through my mind like "septic poisoning" and even "gangrene." But the urgency of the pain told me to rip and bind, not think and ponder. The heavy throb of the pain continued agonisingly and mercilessly.

I bound another strip of my shirt around the wound and pulled it tight. At last the bleeding slowed. I panted hard and tried to bring my breathing under control. I did not dare to stand on it for fear of re-starting the bleeding. After a half hour or so, the pain was decreasing to some small extent and it seemed the blood had stopped. I tried to collect my thoughts.

Perhaps it was about an hour until the pain had subsided to the point where I could try to move myself. There were plenty of strong wooden sticks on the ground, so I selected a couple of the best ones to use as crutches. As I stood up, I devised a way of using the sticks and hobbling on one leg with the injured leg raised.

I prayed to heaven not to let the wound turn septic with the dirty pieces of shirt holding it together. Briefly I tried to walk on the right leg but the blood started again so I went back to hobbling. I made it back to my hut but the pain kept me awake all night.

* * *

The next afternoon my brother Jerzy and my sister Anna appeared in the distance. I was so glad to see them!

"Hello Paweł!" they greeted me. Then they noticed my injury. "What's wrong with your leg?"

I explained the situation and that I now had no shirt.

They explained that our mother had a presentiment the previous day that something was wrong with me. She had sent them up to the pasture with clean underclothes, some food and a clean shirt.

"Mum wants us to report back to her about how you are," my siblings explained.

They examined my injured shin. I did not have to tell them that I was not in a good condition. They set out quickly to walk home.

When they arrived, they told our mother about the accident. She did not wait for morning light but set out in the middle of the night to find me.

I was amazed when she arrived at my hut at first light. She had walked for about 10 miles (16 kilometres) in pitch black through partisan-infested woodlands. It was not a journey for the faint hearted.

She embraced me and kissed me. "Show me your leg, darling," she said with great tenderness.

The sight of the dark clotted blood around the gash must have filled her with horror, especially as it was held together with a filthy shirt. But she remained calm.

She peeled off the filthy rags, now caked with congealed blood. She gently washed the wound, removed as much of the mess and cleaned it as best she could. She then applied a natural healing remedy she had brought with her and bound it with a clean bandage. Even better, she gave me some home-cooked food to help build me up after the accident. I felt better already!

Apart from anything else, it was a treat just to have her company for a few precious hours. I got on well with both of my parents and her presence was a great source of enjoyment and afforded me the rare treat of a moment's relaxation.

She stayed at the hut for the rest of the day to care for me. As night settled, she said she had to return home to our farmhouse. This frightened me enormously. I knew the risks, which she had already taken on the previous night in walking to be with me. If she did it again, she was running the same risks again.

I had tears in my eyes as she prepared to leave. "Mum, you can't do it!," I begged. "It is too dangerous. Anything could happen to you. Anything!'

NO HEIL HITLER!

These were troubled times. A woman walking alone at night was in grave danger and her death would be just another one. And there were plenty of other dangers.

She breezily told me not to worry, that she would trust in God. "He will see me safely home," she assured me.

With that she headed home into the night, completing her total trip of 20 miles (32 kilometres) in that long day.

THE MYSTERY
WOMAN

I had been up there for nearly two years when I had my strangest experience. On a moonlit night, I heard a large plane fly from the east and circle around my fields.

Coming from the east, I assumed it must be Russian because the battle front was getting closer. I tried to see if it had black crosses on the wings or a red star. While the night was very bright, I could not see the markings. It struck me as odd.

The plane circled around my pasture two or three times, then went away. I had other duties and slipped into my normal nocturnal routine of tending the sheep, having my simple meal, then slipping into my makeshift bed covered only by my jacket and a blanket on a freezing night.

The next night, the same thing happened. The plane came from the east. Again it was a clear night and I could clearly see the large silhouette of the plane against the cold sky. Again it seemed to circle around my pasture, then straightened up and flew back the way it had come. Again I could not identify markings on the plane. It seemed increasingly strange.

The following night was cloudy and rain poured down. I had only had two meagre days free of the rain and it was back again. I was angry with the weather, with the world in general and with God. *At least the mysterious plane would not come!* I thought.

But it did. This time I could not see it but I could hear it approach and try to circle. But with the cloud cover so low, it could not find the point it wanted and it flew off again after only a couple of circuits. It all seemed very strange.

* * *

Next day, one of the neighbours, Jan Cieslar—not a relative—told me a most odd story. Another neighbour had been injured by someone who entered his house. At first, everyone assumed it was done by a trigger-happy German patrol pursuing "bandits."

The man and his wife lived some 3 miles (5 kilometres) from my sheep pasture in the high country. But it seemed that the theory of the trigger-happy German patrol could not have been more wrong. A couple of nights earlier, very late, he had been surprised to hear the dogs barking, followed by a knock at the door. He had been instantly on guard, although the knock was not that of the German army or SS. He was astonished to find a young, attractive woman on the doorstep.

This was odd. How could she have travelled in such an isolated place so late in the evening? The road was not good enough to allow a car up to the house. Only a military-tracked vehicle could have travelled up there but there was clearly no such vehicle there. She would have had to walk for miles—a woman alone—at night through partisan-infested woods. Nevertheless, she was Polish, according to her speech, and did not seem to pose any particular threat. He relaxed.

"Yes," said the man. "How can I help you?"

"I'm sorry to disturb you this late at night but I wondered if you could just tell me the way to Wisła," she responded.

This was absurd. She could only have found the farmhouse if she had gone out of her way to find it. However, the night was cold and he decided to invite her in. His wife had said "Good evening," then gone on to do some household chore.

The farmer explained the route to her, which was not complicated, but a couple of things occurred to him. To attempt to get to Wisła in that darkness was almost a suicide mission. She clearly had no vehicle. How could she possibly think of attempting it? She was youngish, maybe 35, attractive, presented well—and a complete mystery. His suspicions grew.

"I know it's a terrible imposition but would it be possible for you and your wife to put me up for the night?" the mysterious visitor asked. "I'm quite happy to pay you something."

The farmer was becoming alarmed, although as far as he could tell she had no accomplice and the dogs were not barking. Yet this mystery woman was beginning to worry him.

"I'm terribly sorry, Miss, but we are poor people and don't have any accommodation for guests," said the farmer. "I'm sorry but we cannot put you up."

He was totally unprepared for what happened next. In a second, she had a combat knife in her hand and it was coming toward him. He managed to evade the knife and shout a warning to his wife. This was in vain because the wife was out of earshot.

The mystery woman came at him again, and this time the look on her face clearly said that she intended to kill him. He did not have time to think about it. As she lunged at him, he ducked and grabbed her arm. The mystery woman was clearly trained to kill but her advantage of surprise was gone. Her arm was now in the grip of a burly Polish farmer and she was no match for him. He made her drop the knife and kicked it away on the floor.

Seeing that the immediate danger was passed, he dropped her arm and was about to throw her out. Then a small pistol appeared in her left hand and she fired, wounding his arm.

The mystery woman ran into the darkness and disappeared. The farmer's wife had not heard the struggle or the gunshots. But she came back into the house to find her husband bleeding and wounded. Screaming for help, she ran across the fields to the nearest neighbour, who sent his young son to the schoolhouse to telephone for an ambulance.

Getting an ambulance to that far-flung and isolated place was a feat in itself. Eventually, the ambulance men arrived on foot and led the wounded farmer to the nearest road, some distance away, where the ambulance was waiting. They took him to the hospital, where he was treated and made a good recovery.

This story sparked much speculation in this farming community. What could the motive have been? The mystery woman did not fit the mould of the average partisan. She was female and apparently quite refined. She was well presented and spoke in an educated manner. How had she received the training to kill? Neither the Russians nor the Germans used women in combat roles. So where had she come from? And where did she go?

Strange things happened in those late war years and we just assumed this was one of those. The whole area was shaken up as the word spread about the strange incident. Everyone was terrified that they might open the door and a young woman would be there to shoot them. This was worse than the SS! At least they wore a uniform and you could see them coming. Who could you trust? The answer was clear: no-one!

The episode was not yet ended. First, the Ordnungspolizei came up to the high country. They interviewed me and asked what I had seen. I told them about the strange plane coming from the east but I had nothing else to tell them. They thanked me and went away. Thankfully, they did not ask any questions about what I was doing up there, nor did they ask to see my papers, which would have shown them immediately that I was on the run!

The next day there were many soldiers swarming around the area. A troop of German Wehrmacht soldiers appeared and asked me the same questions. I gave them the same answers. They thanked me and went away.

It was all very odd but the mystery woman was certainly being taken seriously by the authorities. The soldiers combed the area for any clues but, after a day or so, the search was called off and I did not see them again.

THE END OF SHEPHERDING

Meanwhile, I seemed to be perpetually chilled. I was chilled in the rosy glow of morning. I was chilled in the afternoon. Worst of all, I was chilled in the night when it was dark and the inescapable cold and damp seemed to penetrate my flesh, my bones and my soul. Perhaps the psychological deprivation was even worse than the cold.

By this time, I was nearly 15. It was some months since I had had any human contact apart from the estate manager coming to check on me. In summer, I had also seen the farmer every month or two and, from time to time, family members had visited. But now there was no escape.

I was irretrievably cold and wet. The rash would get worse. The isolation was playing on my mind. I thought more about how that SS man had kicked my mother. Depression began to set in.

The weather got worse. The depression got worse. My thoughts got worse. The cold and the vicious biting wind returned. It seemed I could not escape it.

To make matters worse, partisans shot Bury. He was a lovely dog and was the braver of the two. It was getting dark on that awful night and I was walking in a forest clearing. Bury began to bark. I had heard the sound of snapping twigs in the forest, which warned me of partisans.

I told Bury to "stay!" but he disobeyed and ran into the forest after them. I heard him bark and then two sharp cracks: gunshots. I heard him scream. If I

My faithful dogs, Bury and Boce.

had gone after him, I would have been shot, too.

I went back to the hut with Boce but did not sleep all night. Was there any chance my faithful Bury was still alive and injured in the forest? I wanted to go and find him—and maybe help him. I also knew that if I went out there, it was unlikely I would be alive in the morning.

Eventually the light came over the hills. At the earliest possible moment, I went back to the place where I had heard the shots. There was no trace of him. Whoever the partisans were, they were professionals and left no clue that they had ever been there. I never found him. I cried and cried and cried at the loss of that poor faithful dog.

Two nights later, I was walking in a clearing with Boce, again late in the evening. He heard something and barked. I saw two muzzle flashes and Boce dropped. I ran across the clearing to him. He was still alive but had been shot in the head. His eyes were still open but I knew it was for the last time.

After a few minutes, they closed. "Boce! Boce!" I shouted and cradled his noble head. He died in my arms. I cried and cried for my dogs, for myself and for the stupid ridiculous world that I had been born into.

I brought a spade and dug a grave for him. I lowered him lovingly into it, as the tears streamed down my face. When the grave was filled, I built a fence around it with tree branches from forest so that if anyone came along they would not walk over his grave. I bent over his grave and said a simple child-like prayer for him. He deserved some peace, poor dog. Oh, how I cried and cried for him. I missed both of my dogs so much. I still grieve for them.

What wonderful animals they had been! What friends! In a corrupt world, they had been two beacons of decency. In a time when we were surrounded by evil, they had been the last bastions of what was good, loyal and helpful. The two dogs had been endlessly faithful and had discharged their duties to the best of their considerable abilities. Now they were no more.

My time as a shepherd was no more, either. I had been sleep-deprived, exposed to unendurable cold, isolated, nearly frozen to death, nearly drowned, terrorised by partisans, struck by lightning and nearly had my leg chopped off.

The only good point in the whole miserable experience had been the dogs—and now they were dead.

In a way, the loss of my dogs encapsulates what war is about. With just a muzzle flash, what you have loved is gone forever. There is no logic, no reprieve and no appeal. What has been alive is dead. That is what war is about. Those who glorify it are horrible.

My ability to proceed with the shepherding life died with the loss of my two best friends. It was clear that my "career" as a shepherd was drawing to an ignominious end. I bid the farmer a quick and not especially fond farewell and headed back down the mountain and the 10-mile (16-kilometre) walk to my parents' farm.

* * *

My mother and the rest of my family were overjoyed to see me. I was taller than when I had left but also quite sinewy. From my mother's point of view, I was terribly thin so she did what mothers always do in these sorts of situations. She fed me up with the best food in the house.

My brothers and sisters wanted to know all about my life as a shepherd. I wanted to know all about their news. Best of all, there had been no more visits from the SS to our house, although their constant patrols were a daily threat to the peace of the valley.

Rumours were circulating from those brave enough to listen to the Polish broadcasts from the BBC that the Russians were winning the war on the Eastern Front. The Germans were in orderly retreat but it was a retreat that was apparently never ending. We had to face the possibility that the retreat would pass through Upper Silesia and all the way to Berlin. You did not have to be a genius to deduce that the "fight-to-the-death" propaganda messages were softening everyone up for what was to come—a Russian invasion and another convulsion of fear and barbarity, with yet more strangers occupying our homeland.

My family's news was not entirely bad, however. Before my father's return, several of the local Wehrmacht soldiers had realised that my mother was having to cope with running the farm alone. They were farm boys themselves and knew the realities of life on a smallholding. They had offered her help without any thought of reward, just because it was the right thing to do.

We were grateful to these German lads for their offer. It was also an object lesson that even though their regime was septic and repulsive, there was still a thread of civilisation running through the German people. Made genuinely, my mother was tempted by the offer. But she also understood that an acceptance would have been dangerous.

Our family had retained our Polish identity and our integrity. To accept help from the Germans meant we might have been perceived as German. It was already clear that, in some months' time, the Third Reich would be no more. Accepting German help now might lead to something awful for our family later.

My mother politely declined the kind offer and managed as best she could. Unfortunately, Germans of another sort were making life more difficult for our family. At the time when I had left to go into the hills, it was not unusual for German officials to come to our home and requisition foodstuffs. They worked on a strict formula. They would tell the family how much food they needed to live. Needless to say, their assessment did not correspond to our hunger pangs. The rest was requisitioned without compensation.

On my return, the situation had changed. Everyone knew that the Eastern Front was a disaster for Germany. All families had been asked to donate socks, clothes, anything warm, to be given to the soldiers. The German army was also in danger of starving to death. Therefore, when the officials came on a requisitioning exercise, they no longer asked us to justify what we needed for ourselves. They simply took whatever they could find. My parents had six hungry children still living at home and the amount of food available was diminishing by the week.

One of the results of this scarcity of food was a new level of negativity in our family, which was never present before or since. Growing children get hungry. The shortages—and the hunger pangs they caused—were now leading to squabbles at the dinner table. It seemed that everyone felt they were not getting enough and all the others were getting too much. Even so, we would still try to share what we had with our mother.

"Come on, Mum," we would say. "I want you to have this last potato."

She would smile and say, "Don't be silly, Józef, I ate before you—I'm quite full."

But we knew she had not eaten that day and this realisation stopped the squabbles. We learned to accept what little we had to eat. The harmony of our home was restored.

Nevertheless, my mother was edging closer to breaking point. Often she would disappear into the fields for hours at a time. The absences became more common. When she returned, her face would be tear-stained.

"Mum, you've been crying," we children would say.

"No, no, the tears are just from the cold wind. I've just been across the fields to check on something."

We knew it was not true. We knew that behind her brave exterior she was being ground down by Adolf Hitler and his endless war. We children knew we had to rally around her and give as much help as we could.

THE BLACK WALL
—AND WORSE

S trange to say, there was yet another Paul Cieslar in this story. On the whole, I am glad I am this Paul Cieslar and not that one.

He was taken to Auschwitz. As the rumours about this place grew, our understanding was that you didn't get out except "through the chimney." *But he did get out.* There is a saying that it sometimes takes a crisis to show you who you really are—what you stand for and what you stand against. The other Paul was living proof of this dictum. I spoke with him a lot about his life-threatening experience and he wrote it out for me shortly before he died a few years ago.

By 1943, Oberschlesien was totally integrated into the Third Reich. It was part of Germany. We had to be German in word and deed—or at least give every outward impression that this was the case. Like all the rest of us "Germans," Paul had been summoned to the Wehrbezirk (the local military offices) to be registered for possible military service.

At 40 years old, his call-up status would be in the "low priority" category. His profession as mid-ranking public servant afforded no exemption. Nevertheless, there was no apparent problem in his being registered. The registrar proceeded to ask Paul some routine questions. But then the questioning went up a gear. "If called upon, would you give information about enemies of the Reich to the authorities and, if required, are you prepared to kill enemies of the Reich?" he was asked.

This other Paul gave a clear and unambiguous reply. "I do not want to kill any human being because I wish very fervently to keep the commandments of God," he explained.

The registrar looked at him earnestly and gravely. He put the same question to Paul three more times, each in a manner at once polite but with increasing menace.

Despite the steely glare, Paul continued to hold his position: "You may indeed take me for military service, as you are legally able to do. I am prepared to undertake any service and follow any order but I will never kill anyone."

The official clearly made a note to that effect on his personal file. He reached inside a drawer of his desk

The other Paul Cieslar.

and took out a small cloth badge with the letter "P" on it. This marked Paul as no longer German but Polish. That meant that he forfeited all the protection afforded to Germans.

In an instant, he was visibly marked as a man who could be taken for slave labour or used as a hostage and shot, if necessary. It marked him as a man who was racially inferior to the Volksdeutsch inhabitants of the area. He would have to step off the footpath and bow if he encountered a German official in uniform. Moreover, it marked him as a man with no rights, no privileges and little hope. Nevertheless, he was free to walk home and tell his family that they were now racial inferiors.

A few days later, his employment at the roads department was terminated without notice. The only job he could find was backbreaking work at the local quarry. He would have to work extremely long hours for little pay and in the harshest conditions. Protective clothing was unheard of. Machinery was unsafe. Work practices were geared to maximum extraction of stone and minimum care for the unfortunates who worked there. If he suffered injury or work-related illness, he would have no work at all and he and his family would be left in poverty. This is what happened to racial inferiors. It seemed that matters could not get worse. *But they did!*

Soon afterward, Paul Cieslar was arrested by the SS and was taken to the prison if the SS district office in Cieszyn. He was held in a dark, bug-ridden cell with dozens of other unfortunates. It was unlikely that anyone was going to charge them with a direct crime but they were in the gravest danger. It soon became clear that the raid in which the other prisoners had been picked up was part of a much larger action. Paul later recalled that there were some 65 people locked up in the overcrowded filthy cells.

* * *

The key grated in the ancient lock.

"Come on you lot, out!" said the SS man.

Paul and the others were packed into the van with armed soldiers before and behind. They were taken to another prison in Cieszyn and incarcerated in an even worse cell. He was left sitting on bare concrete in the darkness with minimal food and water for four days. Other prisoners were taken out for interrogation. There were no screams or sounds of torture but it was still a grave situation.

Eventually, some fellow prisoners were let out. Those who were on the Volksliste were let out first. Those who made promises of correct attitudes in the future were the next to go. Doubtlessly, those who had the right connections would have someone put in a word for them. As a wearer of the "P" badge, these remedies were not available to Paul. He was next to be summoned for interrogation.

The same set of questions came up again: "So, Mr Cieslar, we have some important questions for you. Will you promise to serve our Führer, Adolf Hitler? Will you promise to report any enemies of the German Reich? Will you promise to kill the enemies of the Reich if called upon to do so?" It was clear that they had access to his file and its record of his recalcitrant attitude.

"No, I will not kill anyone," he replied firmly. "It is against my religion and my conscience. Neither would I report any such person to the authorities who might kill them on my evidence."

Again, he was asked the same question three times by the investigating SS officer.

Finally Paul said with great clarity, "I am a Christian of the Seventh-day Adventist persuasion and I keep the commandments of God. Hence, I do not kill."

With that, he was sent back to the prison cell.

By this time, the original catch of prisoners had dwindled. Most of those remaining wore the "P" badge as he did. There was little point in talking and, anyway, the man you talked to could well be a Gestapo spy. All he could do was wait, although what he was waiting for was not clear.

He knew his wife Susi would be beside herself with fear that she would never see him again. The children would be missing their father. Their mother would comfort them but they would all know the truth: a week from now he might be dead. Susi and the children would pray for him. That was a comfort: they would pray for him as he prayed for them. He began to lose track of time.

Without any warning, the key grated again in the iron lock and the remaining prisoners were loaded onto a truck, again with armed SS men before and behind. No-one told them where they were going. They did not need to. After a journey of some 30 miles (50 kilometres), he saw the sign "Arbeit Macht Frei." His blood chilled.

He was at Auschwitz.

* * *

The camp to which he was sent was Auschwitz-Stammlager, the main camp. This was a place of horror, violence and murder but it did not have murder refined to an industrial process as happened at Auschwitz-Birkenau, a little more than a mile (2 kilometres) away. Auschwitz main camp was an old cavalry barracks with brick buildings, whose attractive architectural style fitted the comic opera style of the old empire but quite belied its current regime of terror.

The Nazis had rapidly turned it into a prisoner-of-war camp after the fall of Poland, then developed it into a place for terrorising political enemies and later into a huge slave-labour camp. Experiments on gassing were carried out there on Russian prisoners of war, as were experiments of sterilisation. It also provided vast numbers of slave labourers to local industry at the cost of 8 Reichsmarks per day. The commandant was the notorious war criminal Rudolf Hoss, who was later hanged after the Nuremberg trials. It was to this complex of camps that some six million people—including Jews from Russia,

Germany, Poland and all across Europe—were sent. Most of them were to perish here. This was where the other Paul Cieslar was sent.

I remember so clearly how he told me his story:

> Upon arriving at the camp at Auschwitz, I had my first sight of the conditions there. To say it was harsh was an understatement. We had heard that this place was a death camp and immediately you could see that this was true. I felt fantastic terrors, which I had not known existed. I had never looked horror in the face as I did at that moment.
>
> To tell you of only one aspect of it: there was a wall, painted black. That was where public executions happened on a daily basis. They made us watch them. Murder was an everyday event. When would it be my turn? How would I know? Would it be a random event or would it be a result of some charge?
>
> I was in tears. We all were. Everything around me said that the only way out was through some kind of divine intervention. My daily and nightly prayers were the sole driving force that helped me cherish the tiniest spark of hope. Even so, I knew that others, who had prayed no less fervently than I, were shot yesterday and today and would be shot tomorrow. I continued to pray each day but I have to admit that there were days when I felt utterly lost and hopeless. Being so far away from home, family and friends was like having my arm cut off. You have to be in that awful situation before you understand how it affects you.

* * *

Back in Wisła, his wife Susi had come straight to my father. The two men had been friends for a long time, but it was my father who was had been responsible for Paul's conversion to Christianity in general and Adventism in particular. As we all did, the other Paul had kept his profile low to disguise the fact that he had espoused Adventism. This was a necessary evil to minimise the dangers that this might pose to his family. The questioning of the Nazi officials had laid his faith bare. There was no hiding it now and the entire family were in the utmost peril.

Bitterly, Susi blamed my father for her husband's plight. "If you had never made him an Adventist, he would not now be going to die," she attacked. "Since you made him an Adventist, he has changed in a lot of ways and now he is going to die and it is all because of you."

Seeing the tears in her eyes, my poor father could not say anything to soften her terrible anguish.

Her face was a twisted mask of grief and sorrow and perhaps hatred for my father. "I've got two kids to look after and you and your church propaganda and your brainwashing have killed him and left me a widow," Susi said. "How are we going to live now?"

Matters were even worse than they appeared at first glance. My father was only too aware that this family had already lost two children in a house fire. Susi's rage and her pain hurt him deeply. It was so much the worse because he wanted to comfort her but he was the last person on earth from whom she would have accepted comfort at that moment.

To the Nazi consciousness, an initiative such as converting a person to Adventism was a serious crime against the notion of *Gleichschaltung*, loosely translated as "a fair go for everyone." In practice, it meant that everyone would conform to the norms laid down by the state and demonstrate, above all, obedience and subservience. The Nazi state had no toleration for religious minorities such as the Adventists. If Susi had said to the Nazi authorities what she had said openly to my father's face, our entire family would be at risk of death. She must have known she had this power over us. Fortunately, she was a decent person and chose not to use it, however angry she was with my father.

Besides our family, the entire Adventist community in Wisła prayed daily for Paul. His survival was beyond any reasonable hope but well within the realm of prayer. It was all we had to give us any hope of his survival. We prayed every morning and every night for him but he had disappeared from our neighbourhood and we knew what that meant.

As we prayed for him, we also prayed for ourselves. We knew that his wife was making accusations against us in the neighbourhood and that there were many collaborators in the area. If one of the loyal local Nazis told the local Blockleiter of my father's "guilt" in Paul's conversion to Adventism, we knew what to expect. We would be woken at 4 am to shouting, police whistles and barking dogs. We would be hustled into police cars and taken straightaway to Auschwitz to be worked to death until our final liberation "up the chimney."

The next day the authorities would have given our farm to a neighbour, possibly the one who reported us to the authorities. In a week, it would have been as if our family had never existed.

* * *

Meanwhile, the other Paul was discovering the realities of his position. He was now in the hands of the Totenkopfverband—the "Death's Head Units." This was the branch of the SS that operated the concentration camps. Their stock in trade was psychopathic cruelty to anyone who fell into their power. They were specially selected for their aptitude for viciousness, many of them released from prison or mental institutions after conviction for crimes of this type. For them, psychopathic fun was not only legal, they could earn a living from it.

As he entered the camp, Paul was issued with the standard blue-and-white striped uniform. The supervising guard told the new inmates, "For the first weeks you will not be working."

They had expected to work hard. Now, they would not be working. What would they be doing? The prospect chilled them. They had no idea what it meant, merely that it was going to be bad for them.

The regime was not too physically terrible for him but they were also there to see what disobedience could lead to. Gradually, the full horror of the truth dawned on Paul.

The first lesson was that death lay in permanent wait between Blocks 10 and 11 at the ominous edifice known as the Black Wall. This was a brick wall about 65 feet (about 20 metres) wide and 7 feet (2 metres) tall. It was pock marked with bullet holes. Those scheduled for death were usually made to stand against it as they were shot. If the victim was lucky, the shot would hit a vital organ and they would not even know it. If they were unlucky, they would be hit in the stomach and take hours to die. This latter would also serve as perverse entertainment for the guards.

The purpose of the Black Wall was to protect the brickwork behind it from being damaged by the countless rounds being fired into prisoners. Other prisoners were forced to watch, then take the bodies to the crematorium. The blood and other human remains that spattered the wall would be washed down to minimise the smell. New prisoners soon understood that this would be their fate if they disobeyed the slightest order or even looked at a guard in the wrong way. Not to wear your prison-issue hat could take you there. Or you could just be sent there as a random event to encourage the other people in your hut to work harder.

Each day there were deaths but this was no great problem for the men and women of the Totenkopfverbände. They would simply requisition a few hundred more bodies to be lifted from the streets.

Every few days, the prisoners would be summoned to assembly—or *Appell*—on the large parade ground. When this happened, the fear could be felt tangibly among the inmates. Paul had thought that nothing was worse than the Black Wall. He would find out there were things considerably worse.

The prisoners would stand in their white-and-blue striped uniforms in perfect rows, hats at exactly the right angle and at perfect attention. A group of camp guards would bring the prisoners to attention: "Haftlinge Stillstanden! Prisoners! Stand quietly!" The guards would then select perhaps six prisoners for special treatment. "You! Come here!" and "You—over there—come here!' They might then beat to death these prisoners with their bare hands, using whatever knuckledusters, knives or clubs they had with them. Or they might shoot the selected prisoners in some unusual and imaginative way. This would be met with great jocularity by all the guards. For good measure, they might get prisoners to agree how funny it was. On other occasions, the guards might set specially trained dogs on prisoners.

The work of the Totenkopfverbände in the camps was not just a matter of working people to death. It was also about psychological destruction of the survivors.

* * *

One morning, there was *Appell*. Paul had expected to be marched out to the parade ground for the purpose of roll call and terrorisation of some more unfortunate victims to the hooting amusement of the guards. But a guard of the Totenkopfverband came to the hut and called Paul and some others to him. This did not bode well. It usually meant some new and imaginative way of dying. The guard was apparently carrying a paper but Paul knew the rules. To look at what the guard was carrying could be deemed *eine Frechheit*—an impertinence—and the only possible punishment for impertinence was death.

"I wish to draw to your attention that some prisoners in this hut have more luck than wisdom!" the guard announced. He read out some names of inmates in that hut. Paul's name was included. "Mitkommen! Come with me!"

The prisoners knew how Auschwitz worked. They were to be killed in some extravagantly imaginative way. The selected prisoners were all in shock. In the background, they could still hear terrible things.

The guard marched them to the camp administrative office, where they were all given a bundle. Each man had their original clothes, contained in a bag with their names on.

"Get changed and follow me," the guard ordered. He led them outside the camp and a van drew up. "Get in."

Paul's initial impression was that it was a trick. It had to be. People who wore the "P" did not come out of Auschwitz alive. People who wore the "P" had no rights, no advocates and no hope. He waited for the bullet. He waited for the van to stop "for a toilet stop" that would be interrupted by the chatter of machine guns.

But the van did not stop. It took them to Cieszyn and stopped at the gates of the prison where he had spent the first four days of his imprisonment. He was surprised to realise that this was little more than three weeks earlier.

"Everybody out! OK, you are free to go wherever you want."

He walked toward the railway station and burst into tears of joy, of relief and of freedom. Paul said to me afterwards, "As I travelled back to my sweet home in beautiful Wisła, I considered myself the luckiest and happiest person in the world."

I was in another room of our farmhouse that day. I heard my father cry out with joy. Those of us children who were at home rushed to see what strange celebration our father was enjoying. We found him nearly passed out with astonishment.

It was the other Paul. He fell on my father's shoulders and they embraced each other. Paul gave out great uncontrollable sobs, which shook his whole body. My father brought him indoors and gave him something to eat and drink.

The story of his release was remarkable. Even then, we expected that the SS would come by his house and shoot him. But it never happened. The grown-ups talked about this singular episode for weeks. There was no obvious reason that he should have been let out. But we knew we had all been praying for him—and we do not have a better explanation. We praised God for Paul's safe return to us and his family.

JÓZEF
ESCAPES

My brother Józef was the handsomest, the tallest and perhaps the most charming of us all. Unfortunately, the Hitlerjugend—the Hitler Youth—also noticed him and realised that, as a 16 year old, he should have been in their ranks for two years already. Membership was compulsory. He duly received an "invitation" to join. The Hitlerjugend was a preparation for the German army, and apart from the songs, campfires and marching, there were also much Nazi propaganda and swearing of oaths to Adolf Hitler. It was a process of enforced Germanisation of our local Polish boys.

My parents were under no illusions about what would happen if they publicly backed Józef's decision not to join. A few days after the invitation, my mother was doing some chore outside our house when two Hitlerjugend boys appeared.

"Heil Hitler!" they said to my mother in a reasonably respectful manner.

"Guten Tag!" she replied charmingly.

"Heil Hitler!" they said more forcefully, clicking their heels in a perfect rendition of the approved greeting.

"Guten Tag!" she replied even more charmingly. They conceded the tactical setback.

"Where is Józef Cieslar?"

"No idea, boys," said my mother. "He went out, I think."

"Where did he go?"

"He didn't say," said my mother.

"When will he be back?"

"Absolutely no idea," she said.

"We'll be back," they promised, turning back toward the road.

It was becoming clear that civil disobedience was not going to work as a tactic. My parents sent Józef up into the mountains to hide him away, similar to my time spent as a mountain shepherd. It worked for a while.

The Hitlerjugend people kept coming back, asking the same questions, but my parents gave them the same answers. Eventually, he came back home. The Hitlerjugend web had traced him to his mountain hideaway. They were clearly on his trail and not giving up.

"There is no hope for me," he said one night. "I'd better go along."

But just when all seemed hopeless, a friend of my parents came up with an idea.

"Where is the last place they would look for him?" he asked.

My parents shrugged.

"Germany!" said the friend. "Send him to the Adventist Theological College at Friedensau—and he will totally disappear."

While the Adventist Church was suppressed in Silesia, it was allowed to carry on as normal in Germany. Arrangements were duly made for Józef and

Józef on horseback (centre) during his stay at Friedensau.

another friend Józef Holeksa to work on the large farm at the college that fed the students and also raised funds. In their spare time, the two Józefs also did some studies.

As hideouts go, this worked well. If Józef could ride out the storm, he might even stay there until the war finished, whenever that might be. There was a risky aspect to this. Because of his status as a Volksdeutscher, his Ausweis—his identity papers—would give him away to any official who chose to look, which would raise immediate questions as to what he was doing there.

The Adventist College at Friedensau is some 12 miles (20 kilometres) from Magdeburg. In the middle of thousands of acres of dense forest, it is isolated and a place of wonderful natural beauty. Józef must have felt secluded from the war and quite safe there. No-one was likely to question his "P" badge. There was every chance he would simply fall through the cracks in the system and become invisible.

At first he did not write home as a letter might give away his disappearance and our family's collaboration in this. The need for a low profile was brought home to us in a very practical way.

Some of our neighbours had incurred the suspicion of the local Gestapo. Another boy of military age had disappeared mysteriously, after receiving his call-up papers. A German collaborator had seen the family taking food into the forest. This led to a Gestapo car arriving at their door and taking the family away. No-one would tell them where the boy was. Later, the extended family were arrested also.

A couple of days later, the cars returned and all the members of the family who had been arrested were brought back to their home. Apparently the Gestapo had got nothing out of them—but this was not necessarily a good thing. The Gestapo pushed all of them into the house and pointed guns at the doors. They poured gasoline liberally around the rooms. They locked the doors and set the large wooden house on fire.

Józef in his RAD uniform.

We were awoken by the flames. The smoke went so high that it covered the eastern sky and dropped ash on the landscape for miles around. The house burned for hours. The Gestapo men stood outside all the while with firearms to ensure no-one escaped. There was one grandchild who was absent that day and who survived. The rest of the family perished in the flames.

I could write a hundred pages but could never adequately express the horror of that morning.

* * *

Before long, the college principal at Friedensau received a letter that Mr Józef Cieslar had to come to the civil administration offices in the nearby town of Burg and register his residence there. The authorities had traced him.

The principal spoke with Józef and was clearly alarmed. He was a decent man and clearly did not like the Nazi regime but his generosity to the two Józefs had gone as far as he dared. He asked Józef about the "P" badge.

"Cieslar, have you signed the Volksliste?" the principal asked.

"My father did it on my behalf, sir."

"Right, so you are not Polish, you are Volksdeutsch?"

"That is correct, sir," Józef said uneasily.

The principal did not hesitate. He ripped the badge off Józef's jacket.

"Do you understand what you have done?" the principal continued angrily. "You are a Volksdeutscher, running away from the army, and you are masquerading as a Pole."

Józef nodded.

"If the authorities come after you and find this, you are up against the wall in front of a firing squad. And this college is closed for harbouring deserters." He threw the "P" badge into the waste paper bin.

Józef nodded.

"As it is, Cieslar, they are giving you a chance to register. It could be worse."

Józef nodded again.

"Do not fail to do so. Do not ever think about running away," the principal continued. "You will bring suspicion that the college is harbouring deserters on the run. If you cause problems for the authorities, you will cause serious problems for us. You are aware what serious problems can lead to in Germany?" Józef nodded, bowed to the inevitable and duly registered.

He was now "in the system." Within 10 days, he received call-up papers to report to Hannover and be enrolled into the Arbeitsdienst and was put to work on various construction and maintenance projects. This was a step toward him being drafted into the German army.

Some time after his painful interview with the principal, Józef learned that the Adventist college had been requisitioned as a military hospital. This had nothing to do with harbouring deserters as far as anyone knew. It was just a further sign that Germany was losing the war and the demands to care for war-wounded were ascending to unimaginable heights.

* * *

At this time, Józef made a number of friends among the German boys called up with him. Such was the pervading atmosphere that even in the quasi-armed forces there were always some who reminded him that his status was merely that of a second-class Volksdeutsch and not a first-rate German. The problem appears to have been one that could be worked around rather than one that led to immediate danger or problems. It does, however, give a graphic illustration of the mindset against which people in the occupied territories had to battle on a daily basis.

After four months, he wrote that he had finished his period in the

Józef (left) with friends in Hannover shortly before his journey home.

Arbeitsdienst and was coming home on leave. He duly turned up at home with his smart uniform. We noticed that he wore a lemon-coloured armband on his left arm. It read "Deutsche Wehrmacht" in black gothic letters. He explained that his leave was prior to being assigned to some division of the Germany army and then, if he was unlucky, he would be sent eastwards. Very few German soldiers were coming back from the Eastern Front.

One young man did make it back from heavy fighting in Sevastopol. He told the sad story as to how he had had to leave another boy from our village behind. The lad had been shot by the Russians and needed medical attention. His comrades had to leave him.

"We could do nothing," said the lad who had returned. "The Russians were just behind us. If we had taken him, we would all have been killed. We had to leave him to the Russians. We could only hope that he had been finished off quickly."

Nonetheless, the boy's parents had to live with the sad news for the rest of their lives. But such occurrences were becoming commonplace.

After the war, the family was astonished to receive a letter with a Russian stamp. Russian soldiers had indeed found him. They had not finished him off but he died of the wounds he had received. They had buried him and must have found his address in his uniform. The letter was from one of the Russian soldiers who buried him. He must have carried the letter for some three years until the war ended, always with the intention of letting the boy's parents know where he was.

The Russian barbarity in that war is remembered six decades later. Nevertheless, among the evil, there was still some human decency. It applied to both sides.

* * *

On the second day of his leave, Józef cleaned his boots so they shone according to the Prussian parade-ground tradition. He pressed his trousers with a crease so sharp it seemed dangerous. He looked every inch the military man. He pulled on his tunic and said that he had to catch the train down to Cieszyn to register with the Wehrbezirkskommando, headquarters of the local military district.

A discussion started with my mother. It started quite low key, but escalated rapidly into an argument.

"Mother," Józef pleaded, "they will come here and stand me up against that wall and shoot me as a deserter. Then they will also shoot you and all your children for harbouring a deserter. We will all be gone!"

He knew what had happened to our neighbouring family.

But my mother was adamant. "You will not go to register!" she said decidedly. No Wehrmacht general ever gave such an imperious order.

This posed an immediate and urgent problem. The Cieslar boys and girls were brought up in a climate of total respect for parental authority.

It was clearly difficult for Józef to disobey such a command. However, this was a life-or-death situation. On the one hand, the Führer was calling him to the Eastern Front and, most probably, to a quick and early death. If he disobeyed the call, he would be shot anyway and without ceremony. On the other hand, he was faced with my mother's moral authority and absolute determination that he should not go back to the army. It is greatly to my mother's credit that she won. She was in no doubt that, if he had been caught going "absent without leave," not only would Józef be shot but the entire family would have been sent to a concentration camp or possibly been publicly hanged.

Józef did not register. He was now one of only two boys of military age still at home in the whole Wisła area. The other's freedom was due to a clerical error, but no-one bothered telling the Germans. It did mean though that Józef was unique in our area. He stood out. Rather than hide himself, however, he spent his time working on local farms and helping neighbours with their farm work as so many of the men had been called up and killed. This bothered those loyal to the Reich, not least the Blockleiter, whose job it was to pick up such anomalies and report them to the authorities.

Józef's continued presence in Wisła led to several suspicious comments. Several times we knew that Nazi informers came to our neighbours and asked about Józef. But we were saved by our neighbours—Protestants, Catholics and Adventist alike. They would say something to legitimise his presence.

"Oh, the Cieslar lad?" they would responded. "Is that the one with the gammy leg? He's lucky he can walk, that lad, with all those problems he's had with his legs. I doubt if the army would want him, tell you the truth. He could never do the goose step, he can hardly put one foot in front of the other."

Józef did actually have varicose veins in his left leg but it had not kept him out of the Arbeitsdienst.

Several people came to our house and warned us that informers were taking an interest and that all of us were in danger. These people were also risking being shot for covering up for him.

We waited for the "four-o'clock knock," which we fully expected. We had already seen how the Hitlerjugend people had tracked him down, not once but several times. We had seen how the Gestapo had exterminated almost an entire family over a similar incident. But Józef stayed at home and, at the time the Russians "liberated" us in May, 1945, the Nazi administration had never come for him.

THE WORST DAY
FOR OUR FAMILY

There were many close shaves for our family during Hitler's war. None was as close as when my eldest brother Jan had come home on leave from the labour camp in Berlin. Jan was as good a worker as my parents would have wanted. This led to the management's reward of a week's leave. It was still winter when he arrived home unexpectedly. Jan was concerned to find Józef at home, at permanent risk of arrest for desertion.

But the winter snow was too inviting.

"Let's make the most of this," said Jan. "The snow outside is wonderful, it's sunny, it's going to be one of the best days of the winter. You don't get many days like this. Let's go over to Istebna and do some serious skiing!"

Throwing caution to the wind, Józef agreed immediately, and they took off for the slopes.

It was a wonderful day. Our mother was glad to see Józef get outside the house, although she was ever mindful of the risks. They returned after a few hours, bubbling with the excitement of an afternoon's skiing. After a warming drink, they wanted to tell everyone about their adventures. It had been just what Józef needed. He had whooshed down the slopes with Jan and they were both on that high of excitement that skiing brings out in young people. But the joyful moment could not last.

"SS!" someone shouted. Two SS men were approaching the house on skis. They had rifles slung over their shoulders and were on alert for partisans. As we opened the door, the death's head motif on their caps struck immediate fear into all of us.

"Can we help you?" we asked.

"Two men came to this house on skis in the last hour or so. Which are they?"

After her two older sons were identified, our mother watched in horror as the SS men handcuffed Jan and Józef.

"Where are you taking my sons?" asked my mother fearfully.

"To Weichsel. Come on you two, get moving!"

The SS men now carried the skis over their shoulders and walked on each side of Jan and Józef. The SS men did not talk to them on the journey. With the SS you did not ask questions. All our two brothers could do was to walk along, not give any problems and hope that things would turn out alright. At SS headquarters, they were each put into a solitary cell. Bare and cold, each cell contained a bench with a blanket and nothing else.

* * *

Some time later, the door to Jan's cell opened and an SS man put his head around the door.

"Come with me," he ordered.

Jan was taken down the corridor and shown into an office where an Untersturmführer—a lieutenant—was awaiting him. Jan's mouth was dry. He knew that the SS were brutes and if they did not get what they wanted he could be injured or killed.

"Sit down, please. What is your name?"

"Jan Cieslar, sir."

"Where do you live?"

"Berlin, sir." Jan's heart was almost bursting out of its rib cage. Everyone knew the risks he was surrounded by.

The SS officer looked up in surprise. "Berlin?" he asked in an accusing manner. "What are you doing in Weichsel?"

"I am in work service, sir, and have a week's leave, so I am visiting my family."

"Papers?"

Jan's Ausweis—the vital identity document—showed that he was indeed in work service for the Reich. Not only was he a worker, he was a volunteer worker, with endorsements on the Ausweis for good conduct, as well as authenticating his claim of a week's leave. The SS officer was clearly surprised at this.

"You are a volunteer?" This was unusual because most people in work service were there by compulsion.

"Yes, sir."

Again there was a surprised silence. Jan hoped that the SS man would tell him why they had been arrested and what their charge was.

"Take him back to his cell."

"Jawohl, Herr Untersturmführer!"

An SS man took him back to the gloom, the cold and despair of the cell.

Józef was then taken to the officer. If the officer asked for his Ausweis, there would be a problem. The document was in the military office in Cieszyn, where he should have been registered. It would not be difficult for the officer to suspect him of desertion, which would inevitably lead to a firing squad early the next morning. Józef's heart was pounding as the questions began.

"Name?"

"Józef Cieslar, sir."

"Where do you live?"

"Weichsel, sir."

"What is your occupation?"

"Farmer, sir."

Józef waited for the question that would kill him and his family.

"Take him back," the officer ordered the attendant.

"Jawohl!"

The SS officer had not asked for his identification documents!

* * *

Back at our farm, we were all terrified. The issue was clear. Józef was a deserter. Our family was harbouring him. Our mother was terrified that he would be shot in public and the rest of the family would be disposed of in the woods around our farm. Some neighbours had seen how Jan and Józef were taken away and came to find out what had happened.

Our aunt made what was probably the most undiplomatic statement I have heard in all my days: "Well, Maria, it was you who insisted that Józef should not go back to the Wehrmacht. It was you who insisted he should stay at home."

If my mother was devastated before, now she was in an agony of fear. It meant that if her son was killed—as seemed very likely on that dreadful evening—it was my mother's fault.

Another person even said that my mother's faith had led her to be presumptuous. Tears flowed down my mother's face. I do not think that it occurred to us children that we, too, would be shot. But we were horrified at the effect of this terrible event on our mother.

She said some comforting words to us, finishing with "I am going to my bedroom to pray."

"Children," she said, "remember there is a saying that man's extremity is God's opportunity."

Later, she told us how she had wrestled in prayer for Józef's life on this most dangerous day.

* * *

Józef found himself back in his cell. He too was wondering what could be happening. None of this made any sense. He had clearly not been arrested as a deserter—but, then, why? The SS were capable of great evil but were not stupid. They knew they had a fearsome reputation and that anyone in their hands would be in fear of their lives.

Rather than torture them physically, the SS Untersturmführer left them without food or water in their cold, dark cells all night. The prisoners could torture themselves as they contemplated what might happen to them. Most prisoners came to the conclusion that it was better to cooperate and throw themselves on the mercy of the SS or they might place the blame on someone else. Not many would brave it out.

Several times during that long cold night they were brought out of their cells, each on his own, to be interrogated.

"Right, Cieslar, let's get down to business. You went to a cafe on the ski-slopes at Istebna and you robbed it, didn't you?"

"No, sir, if there was any robbery it was not us."

"Yes, you did. Do you think we are idiots?"

"No, sir, of course not, but we are quite innocent of any such charge."

After a half hour or so of this ordeal, the Untersturmführer would say, "Put him back."

And Jan and Józef were taken back for some more sleepless, terrifying hours of solitary confinement. Unbelievably, the SS men had still not asked for Józef's identification papers.

* * *

Back at our farm, no-one slept at all that night. We prayed again and again for our two brothers. We knew that by the time the sun went down the next evening, every member of our family could be dead. We had to do something but did not know what.

Early in the morning, my sister Marta volunteered to go to the SS headquarters to try to see them. "I will take them some food and see what I can find out," she said.

"No!" my mother replied. "It is much too dangerous!"

It was dangerous; for our family, it was a final roll of the dice. But it was the only thing we could think of that might yield any result at all. Marta was very courageous—and we had no better ideas.

Marta walked the hour-and-a-half into Weichsel. She entered the SS headquarters quaking with fear and trepidation but she summoned up all of her courage.

"Heil Hitler!" she said to the SS man on the desk. To say "Guten Tag" in that terrible place was tantamount to treason.

"I've brought some breakfast for my brothers—they're called Cieslar—and they are in here somewhere. Can I give them their breakfast, please?" she asked politely.

"No, it is not possible to see them," said the man on the front desk. On his uniform cap was that death's head, the symbol of total power over life and death.

Marta is an outgoing person with a vivacious personality. If anyone could get to see them she could. "I brought them something to eat so that you don't need to cook for them," she persisteded.

"All right, Fraulein," he relented. "If you give me the breakfasts, I will take it down to them."

So she knew they were still alive and in the cells. At least she could report something back home.

* * *

Both Jan and Józef were tired and terrified beyond words. The interrogations had gone on all night but the SS could not obtain the confession they were expecting. Both brothers knew that the rough stuff would start at some point but so far they were still in one piece. The whole situation seemed strange.

At one point, they heard the clump of boots coming up the corridor. Was this when the knuckledusters and the rubber truncheons came out?

"Your sister brought this for you," the officer said, delivering Marta's breakfast.

Then, at about 11 o'clock that morning, something even stranger happened.

Again they heard the staccato sound of jackboots in the corridor approaching their cells. There were other footsteps as well. The grill to each of the cells was opened.

"Is this one of the men?" they heard a voice ask.

There was a pause. "That is definitely not them" was the eventual reply.

Both Jan and Józef recognised those voices from somewhere: the people speaking were the owners of the cafe.

"OK, you two, out you go," the officer said gruffly, unlocking their cell doors in turn.

They were free. They didn't wait around long but, before they left, they got the story as to what had happened. The cafe at Istebna had been robbed by two men, suspected of being partisans, which is why the SS were involved rather than the civil police.

Jan and Józef had been identified as "not from these parts"—Istebna is about 6 miles (10 kilometres) from our house—so they had come under suspicion. The cafe owners had reported the theft to the SS, who had followed the ski-tracks back to our farm.

It is likely the SS had doubts from the start. Partisans did not live on farms; they lived rough. Jan's Ausweis showed he was a bona fide member of the work service. Jan and Józef would have looked like farmers, not partisans. Marta's appearance would have confirmed that they were what they said: partisans do not have charming 16-year-old girls delivering breakfast.

It probably came as no surprise to the SS that Jan and Józef were innocent. For our family, that was not an issue. If Józef's deserter status was discovered, we all would have been killed. Around lunchtime, my brothers were back home and our family breathed a sigh of relief, which must have been heard all around our neighbourhood. What a thanksgiving prayer we had!

THE MYSTERY TRAIN

To an adolescent boy, the railways in the days of steam were a romantic, never-ending opera. The railway workers seemed to belong to an esoteric cast of people with their ornate uniforms, their impenetrable jargon, and the obvious and heart-warming camaraderie. Stations were places of exciting secrets with telegraph offices, rooms where oil lamps were filled with paraffin, and the large communal rooms where workers kept their long official coats, lunch boxes and exotic equipment. The prima donnas of the operatic performance were the locomotives themselves and the men who drove them.

The locomotives we used to see were astonishing huge beasts huffing out great plumes of black smoke and white steam. As they passed by with a great roar, the whiff of hot oil was sweet. The boilers were encrusted with all manner of contraptions for undertaking one or other of the hundreds of vital roles in keeping these behemoths working efficiently. They were painted black but with red bits here and there, which made them look grand, even works of art.

I especially used to like the trains when I was watching the cows in the fields around our farm. My father would say, "At 11.30, you can bring the cows to the byre." We had no wristwatches, so the train from Wisła was our timekeeper, as it had been on that first morning of the war. At 9.30, I would take a break from my duties to watch it disappear down the single track to Glebce and know that the next train would signal it was time for me to take the cows back up to our farm.

I had to make several trips to surrounding towns at this time to visit friends and also for studying purposes. On this particular afternoon, I was sitting at the station at Goleszow, waiting for my connection that would take me back home to Wisła. A train approached the station in the time-honoured manner.

I watched the train approach with a pleasant feeling of one who looks admiringly at a work of engineering. It brought back pleasant memories of my recently departed childhood. This train chuffed its way into the station. It was a train of cattle trucks but my attention was caught by the length of this train. I had never seen such a long train of cattle trucks.

Normally, a freight train would have passed straight through and proceeded north to Bielsko. However, the signals were against it. This was a normal procedure when a train in the opposite direction was approaching. The signalman had to hold one train back to allow the other to pass. There was a grinding of brakes.

The cattle trucks behind it clanked into each other as they bunched up, followed by a hiss of steam. I heard a baby crying, but there was no baby on the platform. It appeared to be inside the cattle truck. I looked around to see where the crying was really coming from. No, it was coming from inside the cattle truck.

From inside the cattle truck, I could also hear adult voices speaking. The tones were hushed, but there were several of them. There was a man's voice, then a girl's voice and that baby crying again. At first I thought I was imagining it or that somehow noises had been scrambled in the hurly burly of a busy railway station. But I could definitely hear voices from inside the nearest cattle truck.

A couple of times in our house, I had heard my father have hushed conversations with my uncles. We children only knew that they had discussed "certain trains." They clearly did not wish us to know what they were discussing. On the subject of the trains, they were always very circumspect and careful that we did not hear. It seemed these mystery trains were active in Upper Silesia and moved surreptitiously in the dead of night

My blood chilled. This must be one of those same mystery trains!

I looked at the side of the truck to see if I could get any clue as to what was going on. Sometimes on the side of a freight wagon there might be a chalked sign saying "Chorzow", "Warszawa" or "Lublin" that would give a clue as to the ultimate destination. There was no such sign. There were windows high up in the side of the truck but too high for me to see inside. The windows were covered with barbed wire. Nevertheless I could still clearly hear voices inside.

I walked along the platform, trying to look like just another bored traveller awaiting a connection but with my ears trying to pick up any clues. At the same time, I tried to take in what I could. Was there any indication of the destination? Was there any detail that might hint at what the purpose of this train was? It seemed there was nothing.

The rumours were that some people had seen trains like this. There were various theories about where they might be going or who might be in them. No-one seemed to know for certain. But when people talked of the mystery trains, it was only ever with trusted family members or friends, people who would not give you away to the SS.

In the previous few months, the rumours had changed. Initially the rumours had been that the trains were going to "the factory," although no-one had any idea where that might be. More recently the rumours had been of "the death factory." That sounded like yet another crackpot rumour of the sort that abounded in Nazi-occupied Poland. In any event, people seemed to know they should not talk openly about these trains. I tried to look nonchalant, while taking in what I could of the train.

The train on the other line came in and disgorged its passengers. The signal went "off" for the mystery train. The fireman checked back along the length of the train to ensure there were no encumbrances. "Right away!" he shouted to the driver. The massive wheels began to roll and the valve gear on the sides of the huge wheels gyrated in its own unfathomable mystery.

The baby was still crying. As other cattle trucks passed, I could hear other babies crying as well. The train gathered speed and was going quite quickly as the last truck sped past me. I watched the red paraffin lamps on the back of the last wagon disappear down the line toward Bielsko. I also did a check of self-preservation to be sure that no policeman or other railway official was taking an interest in me. I seemed safe. But a shiver of relief tinged with horror went through me. I knew I was in the presence of evil but did not know of what kind.

When I returned home, the sense of utmost evil would not leave me. I walked to the peak of the Mountain of Kozince, which formed part of my parents' farm. I stopped from time to time to look at the natural beauty around me, perhaps I wanted it as an antidote. I sat down and had the beautiful view of the whole Wisła Valley in front of me. I wanted to be alone with my thoughts.

Contemplating the mass transport of innocent women, children and civilians, possibly to some kind of death factory, added to my other experiences of the war. In my mind's eye was the sick vision of police dogs and SS troops with their death's head badges. It plunged me into a sad mood, one of depression and confusion.

I asked myself about the meaning of human life. Why can human beings act in such an inhuman manner? Could there ever be a beautiful dawn to herald a safe, happy and meaningful life?

I could not erase those questions from my mind, even as I wrestled with them for a long time and could not find any satisfactory answers. But I was clear that I wanted something better than the perpetual evil of Hitler's Reich.

In the next few days, I mentioned to trusted friends that I had seen one of the mystery trains at close quarters.

"Was it going eastward?" they asked.

"Yes," I said.

"They all are," was their response. "Where could they be going?"

All I knew—somehow—was that I had been in the presence of an unutterable evil.

THE AXMANN COMETH

November 4, 1944, found me with my family. It was actually a happy time, despite the many threats around us. The Germans had requisitioned almost all our potatoes, corn and wool without any payment. This had plunged us into destitution but we were still happy to be reunited.

Away in the distance, we could hear the thunder of the Russians already approaching Bielsko city. It had been evident on my arrival back home that the Jewish residents of the area had all disappeared. The Jewish businesses were still there and the houses in which they had lived. But the Jewish people themselves had disappeared and no-one knew where they had gone.

They had not been the only ones to suffer. We had seen many German civilians and sympathisers, who knew their days were numbered and that something awful would befall them if they did not get away from the advancing Russians. Since July, the roads had been clogged with thousands of refugees trying to move westward to escape the Russians, and the barbarity and destruction that came with their brand of liberation. The atmosphere was one of gloom. Whether in uniform or not, everyone looked forward with trepidation and uncertainty.

The lucky refugees had handcarts or even horses and carts. None had vehicles because there was no fuel to be had. The faces of the adults showed a humanity that had been vanquished. Much worse were the cries of the children. Often we heard the refugees' children rather than saw them. The children would be covered with blankets to protect them from the ravages of the oncoming winter.

The Third Reich was now playing out its last scene on the stage of world history. They had set the world in flames and they were perishing in their own flames. The raucous-voiced corporal whose words "Deutschland über Alles in der Welt" had been heard over the wavelengths of the world for a dozen years was now trembling in his bunker in Berlin. The Nazis had had their day of arrogance. Now the day had dawned when their bill would be paid in full.

* * *

I had returned from the life of a shepherd at Brenna. The hardships had made me tough, confident and resourceful, albeit with a nasty skin disease that had developed from the constant rain, the biting cold and lack of proper food. I had become so miserable that I felt I would rather be dead at home than living in those primitive conditions. But my mother fed me as well as she could and, with her care, I was starting to recover the condition that was normal for a 15-year-old boy.

My father saw me as a man now, rather than the child who had gone off some two years earlier. My brothers and sisters were also seeing a change in their brother and were happy for me. I would imagine that my parents felt a certain quiet pride.

At any rate, our family were chatting together. We enjoyed our company so much and my mother especially loved it when the family were together, laughing and talking together, our smiling faces warmed in the flickering of the kerosene lamp.

BANG! BANG! BANG! Conversation froze. We looked at each other. Our relaxed mood suddenly iced into fright. We knew that knock and knew it spelled danger. My father opened the door. A uniformed policeman pushed his way inside without being invited. He produced a warrant that authorised him to take boys aged 15 to 16 with him for some unstated purpose. He singled me out immediately. "Paul Cieslar, get your things together and come with me!" he ordered.

There was no room for negotiation and no explanation. After five years of Nazi domination, we all knew that disobedience meant punishment beyond reason, beyond sanity and most likely beyond survival.

I went upstairs and packed a small suitcase. My heart was beating loudly. I had no idea what this was about. I was reasonably certain that I could not be suspected of anything. My parents had seen to it that I had been out of circulation and invisible to the Third Reich. But somehow or other they had found me.

"Hurry up and come on!" shouted the German agent.

I did not cry. It went through my mind that I was a man now. But the nagging feeling in my stomach felt like a bright burning flare of desperation.

"Komm mit!" he said. "Come with me!"

As the man bundled me out the door, my mother gave me a Bible to read. I will never forget the words my parents said as the policeman pushed me down the road that led to Wisła-Głebce station.

"Son, remember our prayers will go with you everywhere," they called after me.

I knew they meant it from the bottom of their very existence. I also knew that whatever the power of prayer, I needed all of it. It took the edge off that flame in my stomach but I knew I was in danger, whatever the situation was.

We walked through the gathering gloom of the late afternoon. In the distance, we could hear the clattering of heavy machine guns, cannon fire and the whoosh of the Katyusha rockets as they dealt destruction to the remaining forces of the Third Reich and to anyone else who happened to be in the way.

A mere boy did not question a figure of authority such as a policeman. Such impertinence would not receive the requested information but could well earn a broken nose or some other injury. But I was terrified, confused, dejected— and we kept on walking and walking toward Wisła-Głebce station.

We arrived after 40 minutes of walking to find the whole area blacked out. Royal Air Force night raids had been pushing further and further east and the Americans had been running raids from their airfields in Italy. A strict blackout was enforced.

To my relief, we stopped at the railway station. This was not good but it seemed better than the police station and its unknown horrors. Evening had settled over the town and there were few people standing in the darkening gloom of the platform. A solitary railway locomotive was steaming and wheezing as it stood sulking in the station yard.

"Wait there!" commanded the German policeman. He spoke to the driver on the footplate. There was a questioning tone from the driver. There was the sharp rebuke of authority from the policeman. He went to the signal box, climbed up the stairs and returned a minute or so later.

"Climb up," said the policeman.

"What?"

"Don't question orders. Get up onto the locomotive!"

I had to comply. My terror was subsiding a little but was replaced with a feeling of confusion.

"Come on, lad," said the driver, "just stand over there." He motioned me to a corner of the tender where I would not be in the way of the driver or the fireman who was feeding this monster with coal.

I could feel the coal-dust grinding under my feet. I heard the roar of the firebox and saw the crew's faces lit with the orange glow. The hiss of steam from the safety valves was deafening.

The fireman looked out of his window and called, "Right away!"

The driver pulled the regulator lever and a massive blast came out of the funnel at the front. I saw Wisła-Glebce station sliding behind me. Mercifully, the horrible noise from the safety valves stopped.

I realised I was being kidnapped—if that was the correct term to describe what was happening to me.

We lurched forward and travelled on and on through blacked-out stations and towns with no glimmer of light. The driver and fireman largely ignored me. The fireman kept shovelling glittering black coal into the firebox. It was quite impressive how they knew precisely where all the signals were. It was also impressive how all of the signals were waiting for us. The policeman must have organised that when he went to the signal box.

"Just look out of the way, lad," said the fireman, in a not-unkindly way.

I was starting to find the whole procedure of operating a steam locomotive fascinating with its levers, gauges, hand-wheels and the ever-present roar from the yellow-glowing firebox. But I was getting in his way a little bit as I tried to follow what was going on.

We clattered through more dark stations for an hour or so before we gradually slowed to a stop.

"Off you get," said the driver.

The station name said "Cieszyn". This was further than I had ever been in my life. So many questions swirled through my mind.

A man was waiting for me on the platform. "Komm mit," he said.

I swung down from the engine with my case and he led me into a large hall, somewhere outside the station.

"Stay there!" he instructed and he left. I heard a key turn in a lock. It echoed around in the darkness. His footsteps ebbed away into the distance and the darkness—and I never saw him again.

The room appeared to be a disused waiting room. I tried to sleep on some ancient bench seats but, tired as I was, sleep would not come. I was hungry and thirsty and just wanted to go home. I also knew that, in the nightmare that was the Third Reich, what you wanted to do with your life was of no importance to anyone.

* * *

In the morning, the door opened and yet another unknown man said "Komm mit!" We walked across the bridge from the Polish side of town to the Czech side. I was left to wait in a waiting room

A couple of boys of my age were brought in. They were as bewildered as I was. From their accents, I could tell they were also Silesian. They had no idea where we were going.

Then the door was unlocked again and more boys came in, then more. By early afternoon, there were dozens of us. By late afternoon, the hall was almost filled with more than 100 boys, carrying small suitcases and clearly worried about what this was all about.

"Paul, what are you doing here?" a voice asked.

It was Andrzej Polok from Wisła. He was a good lad, strong of arm and a welcome sight in this strange adventure I had been thrust into. I was just so pleased to see a familiar face in the middle of these strange and bewildering goings on. We both had someone to trust now. We struck an immediate friendship. He and I would be allies. At the time, we had no idea to what extent that alliance would be tested.

As a group of boys, we were mainly strangers to each other but, being young people, we quickly made friends and the first topic of conversation was "What are we here for?" There were several intelligent guesses but it was clear that no-one knew.

Through the window, we saw a train pull into the platform beside our waiting room. The locomotive was the oldest piece of working equipment I have ever seen. It leaked white steam and gave off putrid black smoke. It seemed this train was for us.

Looking back, what this meant was the Russians were coming westward at great speed. Trains were being lost to the Russian onslaught or were being used to take troops to the front line. What was left had been obsolete when my father was a boy.

Loaded onto this ageing train, we made slow progress through the pretty countryside. It seemed that every half hour we would be shunted into a siding to allow a train of higher importance to the war effort to pass clunking by.

I was fighting back the tears as I looked out of the train window and thought about my parents, my family and my beautiful farmhouse home. They were all now far behind me. It seemed to me that I had been taken so far away from my home in Wisła that I would never be able to return.

Then someone thought what a good idea it would be to open the window. We hung out our heads, watching the countryside flashing past. The cool wind in my face made me forget my pain for a moment.

We could see a bridge approaching. It would be fascinating to see what happened as we passed underneath. We plunged from the gray November daylight into the sudden blackness of the long dark tunnel. The first thing was that it was black. The second thing was that the noise was unbearable. The third was that the carriage filled with acrid black smoke and we coughed and coughed.

"Will you get that window up?" shouted someone.

We closed the windows as quickly as we could, still gasping for breath. When we saw each other, we laughed. Our faces were completely black with soot. We all giggled at the silliness of it and, for a moment, forgot about the cruel uprooting from our families.

The train eventually slowed down. It was drawing into an extremely pretty town. The sign on the platform said "Sternberg." The train stopped. Andrzej and I looked at each other. This was it.

"Alle raus!" boomed a voice from the platform. "Everybody out."

A rather unpleasant man directed us to form ranks on the platform.

"My name is Oberfeldwebel Weiss!" he announced.

* * *

What we did not know was that we had been taken away from our families at the behest of one Artur Axmann, the leader of the Hitlerjugend and fanatically loyal to Hitler. Had we known the reason for our mass kidnapping, every one of us would have run for our lives, because that would have been the only rational thing to do. But, for the moment, we did not know.

IN THE SERVICE OF THE FÜHRER

Oberfeldwebel (Warrant Officer) Weiss marched us through the town. It was a strange and dreamlike experience. It was a lovely, 18th-century town with a beautiful old castle on the hill, dating back to the times of the Holy Roman Empire. The buildings were of the Austro-Hungarian Empire, fairy-tale-like and painted in pastel colours. In happier times, this town would attract thousands of tourists.

We were still dressed in our ordinary working clothes and we did not make a stirring sight. In particular, the women in the street pointed at us and laughed out loud. "Slovakian boots!" they shouted as they noticed our homemade boots, similar to those peasants wore in Slovakia.

We were in Moravia and the people had pretensions to be more Germanic, more advanced and more civilised. In particular, they wore shoes, which to us were an unimaginable luxury. Although they were effectively calling us bumpkins, the mood was light and their laughter quite pleasant.

It did, however, seem that Oberfeldwebel Weiss had no sense of humour. He marched us with military severity to an old school building on the outskirts of town. Then he drew us up into ranks again.

"You are now in a Hitlerjugend formation," he barked. "It is my job to train you. Training will begin tomorrow morning. You are not allowed out of camp without a permit signed by me. You will follow all orders to the exact letter. Now, you will get out of your civilian clothes and put on your uniforms."

NO HEIL HITLER!

One odd thing about our time at Sternberg was that no-one ever told us what the unit name was. In an army, regimental identity is a vital part of training. But we were simply an amorphous Hitlerjugend group.

Our uniforms were black paramilitary uniforms with an intriguing armband. It was of red and white hoops with a Swastika in a diamond. A black forage cap finished off the ensemble. I definitely liked the black leather boots, as these were the first pair of proper footwear I had owned.

It slowly dawned on us what was going on. We had been called up into a Hitler Youth Kampfgruppe—fighting unit—and were to be trained as soldiers to fight the Russians—or "accursed Bolsheviks," as Weiss was wont to call them.

There was a small detail here that only occurred to me much later. When we took off our civilian clothes, they were taken away. We did not receive any receipt confirming ownership of a given parcel of clothes. Looking back, this now makes sense. The people who ran the Sternberg camp did not expect us to receive our clothes back. They expected all the boys to be killed.

As we formed up in our new uniforms on the *Appelplatz*—the parade ground—it became obvious that our intake from Oberschlesien was but one part of a much bigger picture. There were about 700 boys in our unit.

We had given the standard "Heil Hitler" salute. I knew my father's ban on the salute would have meant my death and knew also that he would not want that. So I did it but hated every moment I was performing it.

"Heil Hitler!" I shouted as enthusiastically as I could manage.

The option not to say "Heil Hitler" was an interesting one. From the first invasion in 1939, not to do so had been an offence, which could lead to a one-way trip to a concentration camp. But now there was an extra twist. After the attempt on Hitler's life some months previously, Heinrich Himmler had brought in the new "sippenhaft" or extended family law. This meant that, if I did not say "Heil Hitler," I would certainly go to a concentration camp but so might my father, mother, brothers, sisters, aunts and uncles. There was no trial, no appeal, no hope of coming out. As a result of this, we all said "Heil Hitler" when we really had to, but only with great reluctance.

Perhaps this book should be called "No Heil Hitler—Most of the Time."

* * *

The Oberfeldwebel screamed an exceptionally dirty word at us and his face turning a shade of beetroot. Perhaps 50 years old, he was a strange-looking man. He had a long face with tinges of red that would turn to a dark red when he became angry, which was on a regular basis. In the more extreme rages the dark red hue could develop interesting tinges of purple and navy blue.

The officer was very lively and energetic in his movements, and genuinely devoted to the cause of Germany in general and Adolf Hitler in particular. He stood ramrod straight like a real Prussian. The most striking feature of his appearance was that his left eye was glass. Possibly this was as a result of a war wound in World War I. He believed strongly in *Kameradschaft*—comradeship in arms—and to that end we had to sing lusty marching songs everywhere we went. Ultimately, he believed with overwhelming passion in the honour of death for the fatherland and for Adolf Hitler.

He screamed the same oath again. It seemed that when we shot our arms forward in the standard salute our fingertips were trembling a little bit and our heel clicks were not exactly coordinated in the approved manner. We practiced it over and over. Eventually, he let us off the Appelplatz and back to barracks.

On that first evening, we all fell into the deep sleep of the utterly exhausted. It seemed that we had only been asleep for some minutes when we were woken by Weiss. He took special pride in opening the dormitory door without warning and shouting, "Nicht schlafen! Aufstehen!—No sleeping! Get up!"

The bond between Andrzej and I deepened rapidly in this new and alien situation. But there was another advantage to our friendship. The Hitlerjugend was an organisation in which bullies thrived and were even encouraged. I was slight of frame and quiet by nature. The world of the Hitlerjugend had bestowed on me the status of "victim." Andrzej, however, was at the other extreme of the strength scale. He was tall, thick of arm and leg, and immensely powerful. In those early days, other boys challenged him to a wrestling match. Andrzej always won with ease. This was not due to any subtle technique but to his unusual strength. After a while, the challenges stopped, as it became clear that no-one could match him.

Our training began immediately. There was a wet day early in our time at Sternberg when the Oberfeldwebel showed just how things worked. He ordered us into a marching formation and took us through the town. "Eins, zwei, drei, vier—one, two, three, four," he barked to keep us in step. '"Sing, Hitlerjugend, sing!"

We dutifully obliged with one of the hundreds of marching songs with which the German military was armed. Then we came to the muddy riverbank.

"Ford the stream!" the Oberfeldwebel demanded.

The boys looked at the mud and the swiftly flowing river. They paused.

Weiss came up to the boys in the first rank. "Adolf Hitler would be ashamed of you," he screamed, his face purple.

I wondered if his glass eye would explode out of its socket and, if so, how far it would travel.

"The Hitlerjugend is his special youth organisation," he continued to berate us. "You should be proud! But you are not proud. You are afraid to get your feet wet. The Führer would be ashamed if he were to see what I am looking at now."

He was a terrifying man but we did not move a muscle.

"REMEMBER! You are the youth of Hitler! HITLER! Eins—zwei—drei—vier"—and into the muddy river we went.

The cold, the mud, the chance of being swept away suddenly seemed less terrifying than the thought of incurring the Oberfeldwebel's wrath.

* * *

Oddly enough, the evenings at Sternberg were very enjoyable. One of the Hitlerjugend boys, Peter, had a rich tenor voice and an endless repertoire of songs. Some were the Nazi military songs, which the Oberfeldwebel loved. Some were traditional German folk songs. Some were even love songs. Every night the Oberfeldwebel would tell Peter to come out in front of the boys and lead us in singing.

Sometimes Peter might sing a traditional song such as the "Loreley." Sometimes he would lead us in a rendition of "Schlesierland." This song reminded me of Freulein Teuber at school. It also reminded me of the hills and streams around our farm—and my family. When we sang it, I would often have to fight back tears of nostalgia for my home. Any visible tears would have confirmed me as "victim," if any of the convinced Nazis had spotted them.

Peter's valuable role in helping with morale meant that he was given special privileges, including sitting with the Oberfeldwebel at meal times. This meant he got better food and freedom from being picked on. He also got to associate with the "herd leaders" among the boys. They were loyal to Hitler and they got the special privileges of carrying the banners when we marched.

As training progressed, we learned how to shoot rifles, as well as how to prime and throw a German "potato masher" hand grenade.

One day, Weiss brought a series of dummies onto the parade ground and taught us how to use a bayonet.

"Boys, let me show you what you do if you walking through the forest and you come across a bandit," he barked. "You cannot shoot him or you will bring his comrades down on you. You can only bayonet him."

He looked around grimly for effect. "There is no point stabbing someone in the back with a bayonet," Weiss continued. "You have to dig the blade into the entrails and twist like this and like this and . . . like this." He demonstrated this horrifying action. "Then Ivan will still be alive but he will be writhing in pain and not able to do anything to you." He smiled his horrible smile. "Now you try."

He demanded that we meet his high standards of sadism and butchery.

"Nein, nein, nein! He is still alive! Stick it further in! Rip his guts out, go on! You cannot do it that way. You have to be the first and quickest!" Some of the boys were a little too slow, and he screamed and shouted at them.

While I went through the prescribed motions, I was absolutely trembling.

I wondered how one human being could do that to another. There was little doubt that Weiss at some point had done it in reality and somehow had found it an exhilarating experience. This was a different sort of human being to those I had met at home. If I were to pick out a single word to describe him it would be "brutal."

All of this abattoir training deepened my friendship with Andrzej. In such a place as the Sternberg training establishment, with boys who would do anything for the Oberfeldwebel's approval, you really needed someone to trust. Boys would inform on others just for a little extra food or to be allowed to carry the Nazi banners. Andrzej proved to be a stalwart and a true friend. We stayed together as much as possible.

Weiss' singularity was perhaps never more evident than in a bizarre training session that we undertook one day when the weather was particularly terrible. He brought us into a long corridor inside the main administration building. We were mightily relieved that we would not have to exercise in the downpour outside. We had to line up in perfect formation along the corridor for a session of drill. As usual three of the more "politically reliable" boys were selected to carry the Nazi banners, which they did with great pomp and ceremony.

"Eyes right! Eyes left! Eyes forward! One step forward! About turn!"

While this was not an unusual drill, we did wonder if all of the screaming, the sprays of spittle and the slaps were really necessary. If your drill was not perfect, Weiss would just walk up to you and slap you across the face, making your brains rattle as you staggered backwards from the blow. If he was in a bad mood, he might just stop you having your lunch and then give you heavy drill all afternoon.

Then we had to fall out of the line and march directly to him. "Links, rechts, links, rechts! Stillstanden!" We had to be totally perfect and the march had to be exactly according to the rule book of whichever Kaiser's army Weiss had been indoctrinated into.

That day he kept us going for hours and we all had pains in the neck from standing to attention for such a long time.

* * *

Before we had left home, many of our neighbours had listened secretly to the BBC or Radio Free Europe broadcasts. They would quietly pass information on to us. Despite the endless propaganda of Goebbels' radio stations, we knew the Russians were advancing steadily. The vast German army was being over-run by the even vaster Russian army.

We did not know but guessed that the casualties were colossal. This proved to be the case as dozens of complete divisions of as many as 15,000 men were disappearing without a single survivor to tell the story of what had happened. It seemed the Third Reich was unravelling on all fronts. If they were relying on boys of our age to protect them—I was still only 15—then it meant they were desperate.

As teenagers, we did not focus too much on the broader aspects of the war. Somewhere over the next range of hills we could hear the ever-present rumble of artillery. But in the style of teenage boys everywhere, some of the boys thought there might be opportunity to go into town and chat up the local girls. It was not to be. The Oberfeldwebel would only allow us out of camp in groups and even then a "reliable" group leader was appointed who had to account for our actions.

THOSE WHO SHALL BE DAMNED

The morning began with the usual shout, "Nicht schlafen! Aufstehen!"—and we all piled out of bed, trying to look as enthusiastic as possible in our exhausted state. But this day was different. He told us that we had other duties. We were marched, singing the appropriate marching song, to a large nearby building.

"This is the field hospital and they need some help," the Oberfeldwebel explained. "You will work as orderlies, moving men from the station to the hospital. It's only a short distance. A doctor or a nurse will tell you what to do. It is quite simple."

Naturally, Andrzej and I formed a two-man team to do as ordered. It was simple work but that task will haunt me forever.

At Sternberg station, there were hundreds of them, recently left there by a hospital train. There were men with simple wounds, such as bullet wounds in the arms and legs. Many had amputated arms and legs. Some had been shot in the eye and their bandages were crusted with black blood. Some had stomach wounds and their entrails only held in with bandages. Some had their faces totally swathed in bandages—fortunately, we could not see those wounds.

The medical staff worked furiously but clearly could not cope with the sheer numbers. We soon noticed that only the least wounded were being treated. If a man were lightly wounded, we would place him in a queue to see a doctor. A bullet wound would be dressed and the man told to dress, then sent back to the station. The walking wounded were clearly returning to the front.

Those with more severe wounds were taken to wards, in which they were made as comfortable as possible until they could be seen or they died. The most severe cases were given morphine and left to die. The lucky ones might have had a nurse to hold their hand in their last moments but most did not. They simply went out of existence. They were carried out by some of us and another soldier brought in while the bed was still warm—and often still stained.

Some beds were covered in blood. Some were covered in excrement and urine. Some were covered in bodily fluids from some indescribable slimy internal organ. Some had smears of flesh from the burns patients. Were we in a field hospital or a slaughterhouse?

The screaming never stopped. As soon as one was given morphine, another started. Many men screamed to be "finished off" and put out of their misery. I am sure some were given fatal doses of morphine to stop the agony, the senseless prolongation of life and the sheer nerve-splitting row.

Some of the sufferers cursed Russia and all the "hordes of filthy Mongols" invading their civilisation. Others cursed the Nazis for taking them away and having them killed. Some cursed Germany for taking them away from their mothers and girlfriends. In the death agonies, many cursed Hitler. Millions of others would have agreed.

For me, this duty was doubly difficult as I had a phobia about blood. This slaughterhouse was utterly nauseating. When we were carrying the stretchers, I always tried to organise Andrzej go at the back so I would not see what we were carrying. I really did not wish to incur the Oberfeldwebel's wrath by vomiting on the floor, although it was possible no-one would have noticed if I did. There were plenty of puddles of it already.

One experience at that field hospital touched the depth of my heart. As a young boy, I stood face to face with a young soldier, who was in convulsive pain. His head and been bandaged and his arm had been blasted off.

Andrzej and I gently lay the soldier on a mattress on the floor. The man's face was bathed in sweat, his eyes glazed with pain or sedation, but he managed to speak slowly.

"I am going to die," he said helplessly, almost in a whisper. "You will put me in a grave. But please tell my mother what happened to me—and that I love her."

I tried to say something in response, but couldn't. I had to go outside to pull myself together. I felt anger and disbelief but also overwhelmed by the love for our mothers we each held onto equally. It was an emotional experience that haunted me for a long time.

From these experiences, I gained a deeper understanding of what is meant by "war." It starts with a politician talking about rights, destiny and glory. It progresses to flags, marches, wonderful singing, uniforms that impress every girl in sight and troop trains festooned with brave young men waving farewell. It ends in a hospital ward with filthy frightened men missing body parts and leaking bodily fluids into pools on the floor, screaming for morphine or a bullet to end the whole "glorious" experience. In his stirring and well-rehearsed speeches, Adolf Hitler had forgotten to mention this.

Thankfully, we were taken off hospital duties after a short time. Seeing the terrible wounds made us wonder what was happening to our families. We had heard the thunder of the guns before we left home. We knew that they could be caught in crossfire or even shot by the advancing Bolsheviks. The heaviness of that worry was with us every day.

TRAINING BECOMES MORE SERIOUS

It was not long until we proceeded to more advanced training: how to proceed unobserved by the enemy, how to knock out a Russian tank. We were about to learn the true agenda of our stay at Sternberg. It all started according to the by-now normal routine. So there we were one morning marching along and singing the appropriate song, to a farm just outside of Sternberg.

Looking at those rolling green hills and the pleasant woods reminded me so much of home. An odd thought went through my mind. I had read somewhere of a Swiss soldier who had been in a foreign country, far from home. He heard the sound of cowbells. The singing and the trumpets and the sight of the hills reminded him of the music and sights of home. It made him want to rip off his uniform, throw away his weapons and just go home as quickly as possible. So it was with me. I felt an irrepressible longing for my Silesian homeland, the green hills and—more than anything—my family. But my lovely daydream was soon shattered.

"Right, then, you horrible lot!" shouted Weiss. "I am going to the top of that hill. You are to approach me without being seen. I do not want to see any one of you, is that clear?"

"Ja, Herr Oberfeldwebel."

He ran out of sight, presumably to the top of a small hillock.

"How are we supposed to get up there unobserved?" asked someone.

"Up that track," suggested another boy, full of enthusiasm.

He pointed to a shallow gully that had been worn away by centuries of ox-drawn cart wheels.

"It's full of mud, you daft beggar," someone responded as the enthusiasm abated.

Some boys crouched down and slid into the bottom of the gully. "Oh yuck! This is absolutely filthy," complained one of the boys.

Water had collected in the gully from the cold winter rains. The bottom of the gully was filled with slimy black ooze, at least a foot deep and mixed into an unholy goulash with the manure of oxen, horses and probably other unnameable but fetid beasts.

I was not going to wallow like a pig through that for hundreds of yards! I climbed up the side of the gully, which I thought was out of sight, and edged along on the grass. This at least let me remain slightly clean and also dodge the mud and puddles.

Without any warning, Weiss appeared from around a corner. He ran at me and screamed, "I said, 'Out of sight,' you horrible little man!"

I froze, looking at him in terror.

"Stand up, Cieslar!" he bellowed.

I stood up and he went to give me a heavy kick behind. Instinctively, I tried to dodge but his boot caught me in the lower back.

Stars danced in front of my eyes, as pain shot up my back. My legs suddenly felt numb and collapsed beneath me. I fell to the ground.

This was not a playful kick that might hurt pride but little else. This was a savage, brutal kick. I burst into tears with the pain that exploded down my back and all the way down my legs. I could not walk. I could not get up. I could not even crawl.

"Get up, you malingering little pansy," he screamed.

I writhed in agony. The boys looked at me. They looked at Weiss and wondered what would happen next.

Even Weiss could see that I was in severe pain. He stood up. I was still obviously in agony. He muttered something, which I did not hear but a couple of boys said, "Ja, Herr Oberfeldwebel," and disappeared back toward the barracks.

"Stay there, Cieslar!" he shouted, as if I would have gone anywhere else in that condition.

As the rest of the group carried on with whatever delights the Oberfeldwebel had in store for them, the two boys returned from the barracks with a stretcher. But I did not notice what they were doing. My world was one of pain.

When the exercise was over, four boys had to carry me back to the barracks, through the town. Of course, everyone had to sing a joyful song, covered in sticky, stinking mud, even me in pain on my stretcher. It was very musical and jolly being in the Hitlerjugend!

Back at the barracks, Weiss shouted at me again: "Get up!"

It was clear to the boys that I was in considerable pain, but it seemed not to the Oberfeldwebel. What he did next seems to defy any kind of logic. He pushed his finger deep down inside my throat, making me vomit all of the pumpernickel and cheese from my breakfast on the grass.

I was 15 and they wanted me to have the physical capabilities of a grown man—a grown man's speed, reactions and ruthlessness. At our stage of immaturity, we were quite incapable of performing some of the things Weiss demanded of us. Moreover, I had been brought up to value human life. Hitler's world was a total negation of everything I knew to be right and decent. The hatred and killing that were so much a part of the Nazi world was a disgrace to humanity—and they were trying to persuade us that brutality and inhumanity were the right thing for Germany.

* * *

After a couple of days lying flat on my back, my damaged vertebrae worked their way back to where they were supposed to be. Our training then took a rather bizarre twist but one that we enjoyed immensely. This is a great example of how wonderful it is to be 15 and to enjoy what is in front of your eyes without thinking about what is behind the scenes.

"Today," said the Oberfeldwebel, "I will teach you the Panzerfaust." He produced a bulbous rocket-looking thing.

"This is a Panzerfaust. Now, watch this." He dropped the small rocket into a hollow tube, put it on his shoulder and pointed it at a target that had been set up some 250 feet (75 metres) away.

"Is everybody watching?"

"Ja, Herr Oberfeldwebel," we chorused. He had our attention.

He pulled a trigger. A flame shot out of the back of the tube and the rocket flashed through the air. Less than a second later, it had demolished the target. We all gasped at the power of the thing.

"Now it's your turn."

He asked for volunteers and showed them how to hold the launching tube, how to load it, how to point it and how to use the trigger.

"Do not pull the trigger until I say! This thing will take out a tank! If you hit one of the Bolsheviks' T-34s, this will puncture the armour, explode inside and turn Ivan into so much Gehacktes Fleisch"—a German dish made of raw mince, which might sound awful but they told us was quite delicious.

Our first few attempts were awful. Fortunately, the targets had been set up so that even if we missed, we would not destroy the parish church, the town hall or the wonderful medieval castle. Eventually, however, our marksmanship improved. For us as teenage boys, firing and watching the other boys fire the Panzerfausts was great fun.

"This is getting better," said Weiss. "Now, in order to make sure you get the revolting little yellow Mongol bogeymen, this is what we have to do." He got down on the ground and inched his way forward on his elbows. Memories of that awful crawl through the mud came back to me.

"Now, if you are 300 feet [100 metres] from Ivan you will possibly get him. If you are 150 feet [50 metres] from Ivan, you will probably get him. If you are 60 feet [20 metres] from Ivan, you will definitely get him. And don't forget: if Ivan is hit with one of these, he is not going to jump out of his tank and come and get you. You will have presented him a one-way ticket to the great Kremlin in the sky."

I noticed how taken a lot of the boys, especially the younger ones, were with the whole notion and the sheer flamboyant drama of it.

But it was not a game. A few days later, we noticed a strange silence on the parade ground.

"What's up?" asked Andrzej of some of the others.

A boy had been resting his chin on a Panzerfaust, touched the trigger by mistake and blown his head off instantly. The blood had spattered for a significant distance. Many of the boys had seen it.

* * *

At the same time our training was ramping up in other ways. The Oberfeldwebel would crash into our dormitory at 1.30 in the morning.

"Nicht schlafen! Aufstehen!"

He would give us five minutes to dress in full kit and line up on the Appell ground for inspection. He would put us through some drill and then shout, "Dismissed!"—and we would all troop off, boggy eyed, back to bed.

At 4 am, the same would happen again. "Nicht schlafen! Aufstehen!—Do not sleep! Get up!"

We would do another half hour's drill in the darkest, coldest hours of the night. Fortunately, my time as a shepherd had toughened me to this kind of challenge and I coped with it better than most. Some of the boys were almost dropping asleep all day.

After we had mastered the Panzerfaust, we were assembled for Appell one day to find bicycles—lots of them—on the parade ground.

"Pick yourselves a bike!" Weiss shouted. "Today we have a special drill."

The drill was great fun! The goal was to ride around the countryside, spot a tank, dismount and take cover and then, when the tank was only 60 feet (20 metres) away, hit it hard and fast! Then the plan was to ride back to base to get more Panzerfausts.

We were actually quite good at this and would doubtlessly knock out a large number of T-34s. The question was how many of the Hitlerjugend boy soldiers would survive. The obvious answer was very few.

At this point, it dawned on me why more than 700 boys had been called up in a perfunctory manner and brought to Sternberg.

Weiss was training us for a suicide mission. And it seemed our training would soon be completed.

THE DAY OF GLORY HAS ARRIVED!

I remember the date with crystal clarity: April 5, 1945. The Russian guns were moving inexorably westward toward Berlin. They had moved some 125 miles (200 kilometres) westward since we had been kidnapped. That meant our homes might now be in Russian hands but we had no way of knowing if our families were alive or what the "barbaric Bolsheviks" had done to them.

We assembled for morning Appell as normal but there was someone with Weiss. He wore the compelling but sinister black dress uniform of the Waffen SS, the fighting branch of the SS organisation. They were brutal and ruthless but included some of the finest military units in history.

This man was a perfect example. With its silver death's head, the hat was a perfect angle. On his chest were shiny medals with resplendent ribbons. On his collar were the silver Sigrunes of the SS. At his waist was the familiar SS black belt with the SS crest and the motto "Mein Ehre Heißt Treue"—"My honour is loyalty." His boots shone like liquorice. He was every inch the Wagnerian hero.

Without any further ado, he jumped from a standing start up onto a table. That impressed us immediately.

I believe his rank was Obersturmführer or First Lieutenant. He told his name—which I do not remember—and began to sing in a powerful Wagnerian baritone, "Deutschland, Deutschland über alles."

"Jungen mitsingen!" he ordered. "Sing it with me, boys!"

Now he had our full attention.

"Sieg!" he shouted. Out shot his right hand in a perfect salute.

"Heil!" we replied with an equally perfect rendition of shooting out our right hands and clicking our heels.

"Ausgezeichnet," he said. "Excellent!"

"Adolfhitlerjugend," he addressed us. "I have come to tell you some important things." He looked around at us with a strange mixture of menace and benevolence. "You have heard the rumours that our Führer—Adolf Hitler—is dead."

No-one actually dared to nod because this could start an investigation as to who was listening to foreign radio and would therefore face the death penalty. The Obersturmführer appeared distraught at the notion that the beloved Führer might no longer be with us. He raised his arms as a token of honesty.

"But I am authorised to tell you that our Führer is alive and well." He paused to let the wonderful news sink in before continuing. "And at this moment, he is organising the overthrow of the enemies of our Reich."

A ripple went through the ranks. Hitler had not been heard of for months, probably not since the last attempt on his life in July the previous year.

"Boys, do you remember what happened at the gates of Vienna?" the Obersturmführer continued.

"Ja!" we chorused. "The Turks were turned back."

He let it sink in. "They were indeed," he agreed, with a smile. "And I am also authorised to tell you about certain new wonder weapons."

He looked around and saw that all were keen to hear.

"You know about the V1 and V2 rockets that are making life difficult for Mr Churchill, the English warmonger?"

"Ja," we chorused.

"Well, there is now a V3, which is a gun so massive that it can fire from the cliffs of Calais and hit London."

Another ripple of interest ran through the ranks.

"We have new jet fighter planes, the Me262s, which are twice as fast as the poxy British Spitfire."

The ripple grew louder.

"We have rocket planes, the Me163s, which are so fast and so deadly that no enemy fighter or bomber can withstand them, or even get a shot at them."

He looked around once more for effect and then, with a conspiratorial air, added, "And there are other weapons, which are about to come into service and which are so secret that I am not even authorised to talk about them."

He paused. "But I can tell you that our enemies will get a terrible shock when they see what has hit them."

His body language eased into that of a man who was totally confident. He was a very convincing speaker and most of the boys were clearly moved by his gifts of oratory. Andrzej and I were not moved. We did not trust him.

"The events at the Gates of Vienna will be nothing compared to what is going to happen to the Russians, to Tommy and to the Amerikaner." He paused again for effect. "I can now tell you that Adolf Hitler is ready! He is ready to unleash these miracle weapons that will bring our enemies to an inglorious and humiliating defeat."

He beamed down at us from his position on the table.

"As soon as the Führer gives his command to unleash these weapons, victory will be ours. It will only be a few days now."

Could this man possibly be wrong? He seemed so utterly convinced of what he was saying.

"Now, the question I have for you is this . . ."

We seemed to hold our breath as we waited.

"Do you German boys of the Hitlerjugend want to fight for the Fatherland and play a role in this historic victory for our beloved Führer? Do you want revenge against the barbaric Russians?"

This latter was, in truth, developing a certain attraction.

"Do you want to share in this, the greatest victory of the German Reich?"

He was so good at his job. His delivery was word perfect and he seemed strong, bright and humorous. I imagined that the decorations on his tunic were for conspicuous gallantry.

"Hoorah! Hoorah!" most of us shouted.

Most of the lads were genuinely enthused by this glittering opportunity. Others of us knew that not to look enthusiastic was itself life-threatening.

But Andrzej and I and a few others knew he was lying, deluded or both. My instincts told me beyond any reasonable doubt that we could not believe the Obersturmführer.

Back in the real world, the Russians were just over the horizon from where we stood. The guns never stopped firing. The British and Americans were advancing at a similar rate in the west. Nothing was stopping the enemies of Hitler's regime and the collapse of his German Herrenvolk could be seen in all directions. Germany was going to lose the war. The really burning issue of the day seemed to be not whether the war could be won but whether you could surrender to the civilised British and Americans in preference to the "uncivilised" Russians.

"Excellent, boys, excellent!" purred the Obersturmführer. Most basked in his approval as he motivated them for the great adventure to come.

As far as I was concerned, it was clear that we were being given a sugar-coated death sentence.

"Well, boys, I am glad to tell you that you can take part in a famous victory for our German Reich! You will tell your grandchildren about these famous events and they will wish they had been there with you."

These boys were not going to have grandchildren. We would be lucky to be still breathing a couple of weeks from now.

But the Obersturmführer was coming to the point. "Tomorrow, we will go to the railway station. A special train will take you to the capital of the Reich— Berlin. Your mission is to fight against the accursed Russians. You only need to hold on for a few days. The Führer is almost ready to unleash his new and powerful weapons against the enemies of our country. When he does so, those enemies will understand the power of Germany. They will wish they had never been brought into this world.

"Are you with me?"

Now dawned a different perspective. We had carried the wounded soldiers from the train to the makeshift hospital and could guess what kind of slaughterhouse the front must be. The cheers became muted.

Now the response involved thoughts such as, *We are on bikes and they are in tanks.* It raised the spectre of *We should still be in school and they are putting us against a load of uncivilised Mongolian savages.* Most of all, perhaps, it raised thoughts like, *The war is lost and I would prefer not to die for a lost cause.* It also raised questions of whether the Nazi cause was one you would want to die for, anyway.

However, most of the boys were still enthusiastic, especially the ones to whom the Oberfeldwebel had given special privileges, extra food and allowed them to carry the Hitlerjugend banners. But on that lovely spring morning in the picturesque town of Sternberg in the Reichsprotektorät of Mähren, there was a chill in the air.

* * *

The chill was also inside me as I contemplated death in Berlin. I looked around. Boys were in groups discussing the wonderful presentation we had just witnessed. They were so enthused. What the Obersturmführer had just outlined was better than chatting up the local girls. It was better than bayoneting a straw-filled pillowcase. It was better than firing a Panzerfaust into a brick wall. The boys seemed wonderfully innocent of the fact that they were being taken away to die.

I have sometimes wondered if it was my time as a shepherd that saved my life. That life had been hard, but it had taught me self-reliance, resourcefulness and self-confidence at an age when most children are still worrying about school lessons. The challenges and the loneliness had meant that I had to go from child to man in days rather than years. If I had not built instincts for survival and the capability to react quickly, I would have lost my sheep and possibly my life. The instinct was kicking in again now.

It was as if God was saying, "Get out right now or else you are going to die." They had not told us that the Russians were advancing virtually unchecked across eastern Germany, held back not by German bullets but by the length and efficiency of their supply chain. They had not told us—but we could hear those big guns and they were coming closer by the day.

"Andrzej, can we go somewhere and talk?"

He knew what I wanted to talk about immediately. He also knew it was dangerous. We had to think fast and act even faster. Some of the other boys were already striking poses of military enthusiasm. Some were talking about taking 20 Russians with them. Some of the brighter ones just looked subdued and resigned to their fate. At any rate, we knew that our furtive conversation, if heard, would lead to death.

We slid furtively into a bathroom cubicle. Even so, we had to make sure no-one was in the next stall.

"Andrzej! We've got to think now. Do you think we should go to Berlin?" I began.

He was silent. He knew what it meant. Desertion was treason and treason meant death. We had heard that the Feldgendarmerie—the military police—were hanging deserters from trees.

"I'm afraid, Paweł," he said. "I'm so afraid."

If Andrzej was afraid, I was utterly terrified. It was a question of which was more terrifying: certain death in front of a Russian tank or the possibility of death by hanging from a tree in a foreign country.

"So what do you think we have to do?"

"I really don't know."

"Andrzej, this SS man is telling us that Germany is going to win the war, right?"

"Yes."

"So, is that thunder we can hear in the distance?"

"No. It's Russian artillery."

"Andrzej, if we go to Berlin we will die. There is little time. We have to escape immediately or we are on that train. It will be a one-way journey."

He looked terrified. But I expect I looked terrified as well. He nodded.

I do not know how the plan came to me. I just know that, at that moment, a plan formed in my mind that gave us a small hope of possible survival. We knew it was small but we also knew that there would be no return trip from Berlin.

"Have you got any money, Andrzej?"

"Yes, I haven't spent a pfennig since I've been here."

I had not spent any money either, the ban on going into town had seen to that. The few Reichsmarks we possessed might just come in handy.

"Well, first thing is to go to the kitchen and get hold of as much bread as you can. Hide it in your uniform. We will need it desperately. Get all of your money but leave everything else just as it is. We don't want to arouse suspicions that we have left."

Andrzej nodded and went off toward the kitchens. I prayed inwardly that no-one would challenge him there. I did not know if he could withstand it.

Meanwhile, I walked down the corridor to the Oberfeldwebel's office.

"Herein!" he responded to my knock. "Come in!"

"Heil Hitler, Herr Oberfeldwebel!"

"Ja?" Oberfeldwebel Weiss raised a quizzical eyebrow. I had to look as if I were keen to go to Berlin.

"Herr Oberfeldwebel, I would appreciate it if you would kindly give us permission to go swimming, please?"

"Why?' he grunted.

I had to persuade Weiss, somehow, of my enthusiasm to go and shoot up dozens of Russian tanks on my second-hand bicycle.

"Polok and I, Herr Oberfeldwebel, we want to be cleaned up before we go out to fight the Bolsheviks. We need to go now because there will not be time to get clean in the morning."

I was aware of the risk I was taking. We had often gone swimming but only in organised groups of 40 boys, supervised by a senior boy and all correctly singing the marching song of the day. During all our time in Sternberg, neither we nor any other boy had ever been outside just one or two together. The reason was obvious. The Hitlerjugend did not want any absconders. Everybody had an inborn obligation to die for Hitler.

Weiss looked at me as if his one functioning eye was some sort of woodworking tool, which was designed to probe, rip and violate. He seemed to see into my soul. I knew that if my gaze wavered then all was lost, for both Andrzej and me. I had to concentrate on knocking out dozens of Russian tanks and the swimming bath.

He turned to his desk and pulled out a pad of papers. My heart leaped with joy. But I knew it was critical to keep my stern soldier-face. I hoped my eyes would not give me away.

"How much time?"

"One hour, Herr Oberfeldwebel."

He scribbled, ripped the sheet off the pad, stamped it with the appropriate stamp and handed it to me.

"You will return at 1500 hours."

"Danke schon, Herr Oberfeldwebel! Heil Hitler!"

"Bitte schon—Thank you very much—Cieslar. Heil Hitler!"

I clicked my heels in the prescribed manner, knowing I was giving him the "Heil Hitler" salute for the last time. I spun on my heel and went purposefully to pick up Andrzej.

'Have you got the bread?'

He showed me. It was not a feast but it would help us for a day or so.

"Good! Let's get moving."

I looked at the leave pass. It was our passport to—what? Not to freedom, possibly to a hanging from a tree, possibly to a firing squad, but absconding was the best option available to us. At any rate, it took us away from an appointment with "Ivan" and his brutal friends. It was dated today and was valid until 3 pm, which meant we had a couple of hours' start. They would not know of our disappearance until, perhaps, 3.30. By that time, we would have 5 miles (8 kilometres) start.

We walked nonchalantly down to the sentries on the gate and showed them our pass, being careful to show that we were carrying swimming costumes.

"Heil Hitler!" shouted the sentry.

"Heil Hitler!" we shouted back.

We walked through the town and down to the swimming baths, where we left our swimming costumes—and kept going. Then we ran and ran until we felt we could run no more.

In that moment, we were actually thankful to the Oberfeldwebel for making us very fit. We ran and walked and ran and walked until we were clear of the town and into the surrounding foothills. But we had crossed the line. Now things were getting serious.

PUT NOT THY TRUST IN OXEN!

We set off in our Hitlerjugend uniforms, marching along as fast as we thought we could sustain. However, the land rises sharply east of Sternberg, and we were soon into the very hilly territory of the Jesenik Mountains. We had climbed to a considerable altitude.

The Moravian countryside was green and pleasant. The aspect of the rolling hills and trilling streams was wonderful for our spirits after the grim warlike aspect of the Oberfeldwebel's care. We kept on climbing. We found that we had reached the last of the winter snows. This was good. It meant that we were putting distance between the Oberfeldwebel and possible pursuers.

We rationed our meagre bread but it soon went. Our strength was diminishing, too. We knew we had to ask for food at farms. We reasoned that if we watched a farm for a half hour or so we would be able to see if there were any men around. We reasoned that men would be more likely to turn us in as deserters. On the other hand, women seemed more likely to take a more maternal view, perhaps take pity on our youthfulness and give us some scraps.

We realised we were using the skills we had learned in training. That first night we slept under the fir trees. The sky was clear. There was no rain. We wanted to avoid farmhouses as much as possible as these represented a risk of being given away. We did not know exactly where we were but we knew which way was southeast and could navigate using the sun.

From time to time, we heard the thunder of Russian guns in the distance. As long as we headed toward them, we were heading roughly toward home. This had the unfortunate snag that, on a cloudy day when the artillery was silent, we could go in the wrong direction. And we did so a few times. We could not follow road signs because they had been taken down so as not to give help to the Russians.

We knocked on several doors and almost all of them gave us something. Only one farmhouse was so clearly suspicious of us that we just took to our heels and ran. Farmhouses did not possess telephones in those days so running a short distance was sufficient to buy a reasonable chance of liberty.

* * *

After two days, we came to a large, isolated farmhouse, high in the hills. The old farmer was standing outside. We plucked up our courage. Hunger was by now growing into pains in our stomachs. It weakened our resolve to avoid males. We had to talk to him. We had to eat. Hunger is a powerful motivator.

"Good afternoon, sir," we said in our most ingratiating tones. "We wonder if you would be so kind as to spare us a little bread?"

He was old enough and smart enough to realise we were on the run.

"Well, lads," he said with a glint in his eye, "on my farm, nothing is free." He looked at us purposefully.

"I'll give you something to eat, but you'll need to do some jobs for me first."

We were probably not the first deserters he had exploited but we were in no position to negotiate terms.

"Yes, just tell us what you want done and we'll do it."

"Well, what I want you to do is this . . ." He took two large hayforks from a hook on the wall. "Now, you see in that open field there is a pile of straw?"

"Yes," we said, as our hearts sank. It was huge! This man was really taking advantage of our desperate situation.

"All you have to do is to go up there and bring down straw enough for my 50 cows to lie down on comfortably in the byre."

We obediently went into the field with the hayforks and brought down the first load. Again, we were thankful for our weeks of training, which had made us fit. But the meagre amount of food we had eaten in the previous two days had made us weak. We were almost passing out with hunger. It was going to take at least 20 trips and we could not have done it without fainting from hunger. It was beyond our physical capability.

Then an idea hit me. On the far side of the barnyard, eight oxen were lying comfortably and chewing the cud. We were up against it and they had nothing better to do.

I ran my idea past Andrzej. He seemed underwhelmed but could see no better solution.

"Right," I said. "So all we have to do is to get the brutes hitched up to this cart."

I was used to working on a farm. I was used to horses but I had not handled oxen. Still, it seemed a perfect plan. One trip up the hill with the oxen on the cart, one trip back down with a cart full of straw—and the job was done. The old farmer would be pleased and we would get some desperately needed food.

Our first and immediate revelation was that oxen are not willing beasts of burden. We tried to get two of them to stand up so we could hitch them to the cart. But they refused to move.

Andrzej and I each took up a large and stout stick. After a couple of hefty whacks, they stood up but let us know they were not happy and they continued to be stubborn. Even when we had them in roughly the right position to hitch to the cart, they still refused to move. We pushed them, shoved them, cajoled them and shouted at them—in a number of languages. We even kicked them but they would not let us hitch them. After some minutes, we were sweating with exertion but somehow we had achieved the objective of having them harnessed side by side to the cart.

Despite our sense of achievement, we were still a long way from completing our assigned task—and the oxen were still not cooperative. If we tried to go right, they would go left. If we tried to go left, they would go straight ahead. If we wanted to go straight ahead, the oxen could go off in random directions.

Instead of driving from behind, I went in front and stood between the two beasts. They were big! Our idea was that Andrzej would drive from behind and I would steer using the chains that tethered the oxen to the cart shaft. In order to drive them, I had to stand between them, grab the chains, walk forward and pull them in the direction I wanted to go. If they veered off course or went too fast or too slow, I would hit them across the neck with my stick.

It seemed this was beginning to work. The cart was moving at just the right speed. They were going in a straight line. They were not veering off. They sped up a little but by now I had the control procedure well rehearsed and gave them a sound whack. I waited for them to slow down but they started to go faster . . . and faster.

"Paweł!" shouted Andrzej. "Watch out for those trees."

I was starting to lose control and turned to see a clump of oak trees approaching at a fast rate. I decided to jump for it. But the oxen were going faster and I realised I could not jump. If I had gone underneath them, I would have been trampled and the cart would have run over me.

By now the oxen were furious with the beating and it seemed they were looking for revenge. They were ignoring my commands, heading directly for a large oak tree. I braced myself for the impact.

One ox went to the right; one ox went to the left. I was in the middle and the chain between them pinned me to the tree.

With the impact on the tree, I hoped they would slacken off but they continued to press the chain forward with me inside it. Blood spurted from my nose as they crushed me against the tree.

I was staring death in the face and, in desperation, screamed, "Jesus! Save me!"

At this moment, something extraordinary happened—the chain broke with a loud twang and released my lungs.

I was freed from the tree and fell to the ground, gasping for every painful breath. At least I could now breathe, even if every breath was accompanied

This is how the oxen pinned me to the tree, drawn for me by a friend.

by a spatter of blood and a wheezing sound like that ancient train that had taken me to Sternberg. Each breath racked my lungs and caused me to wince in pain.

At once, Andrzej, who had been trying to pull the oxen off me, was joined by the farmer who had looked out of a window to see how we were getting on.

"Boy, thank goodness you are still alive," said the farmer with a worried look on his face. He and Andrzej carried me to the farmhouse and gave me some basic medical help.

Once he had extricated me from the oxen, the old farmer turned out to be a decent man. He looked after me as well as he was able to in his poor farmhouse, letting me lie on a straw mattress on the farmhouse floor to recuperate. After some hours, the immediate pain had subsided and I appeared to be suffering from nothing worse than bruised ribs.

The farmer generously shared a simple meal with us, for which we were grateful. He let us stay the night but we knew he was taking a fearful risk in helping two deserters on the run. As soon as it was light the next morning, we thanked him profusely and left his lonely farm.

But as this new day dawned, I also thanked God for saving my life.

ON
THE RUN

W e were fortified with the food the old farmer had given us and were soon making good progress. On the outskirts of a small town, we passed a playground where some children were studying something intently.

"Hi, kids!" we said. They looked up at us. "Is this the right road for Ostrava?"

They turned out to be a school group, who happened to be studying a map of the area.

"Tell you what, lads, if you like, we'll buy that map off you. Really, we'll give you some money for it."

The amount of cash we had was small but, in our dire situation, a map was something we would pay for. The map was probably the most valuable thing we could wish for.

"We can't give you this map because we are doing school work and we need it," one of the boys explained. "But my dad is just in that house over there and I know that he has a spare one. I'll just go home and pick it up. Wait here."

"OK," we said nonchalantly. We were surprised that life and farm work and school work just went on as normal with the Russians such a short distance away.

The boy started out for home. But the sixth sense of the fugitive kicked in immediately and without warning.

"Andrzej," I said quietly, "this is dangerous. Don't ask questions, just run for it. Now!" We set off as fast as we could.

The boy saw us running and we heard him shout, "Vati, Vati, Spionen! Daddy, Daddy, spies!"

We sprinted into a small wood and out of sight. Soon, my bruised ribs were hurting so bitterly that I find it difficult to describe the pain but our preservation instinct told us to run as fast and far as we could. After some minutes, we realised that no-one was following us. We stopped and gasped for breath.

"Andrzej," I said, panting like a racehorse after a big race.

"Yes, Pawel?"

"We have to consider that they might come after us."

He looked at me, clearly fearing the possibility but also realising that it could well happen.

If the man reported us, I knew what it might mean. I had seen the German army in manhunts when I was a shepherd. It would involve police, possibly soldiers and definitely dogs. It was a dreadful prospect.

We had become good at telling direction by noting where the sun was in the morning, where it was at midday and where it was in the evening. It kept us travelling eastwards. In the present emergency, we decided to head westwards. That would make it difficult for any manhunt.

We had some rainy overcast days where we could not see the sun at all. In that case, the chosen direction became more of a leap of faith. More than once, we found that we had walked in a large circle and come back to somewhere we had been earlier.

We were soon without food again. Our uniforms were worn and tattered. Our faces were haggard for lack of sleep. Our eyes were sunken and our demeanour had now changed from that of the proud race, inculcated into us by the Oberfeldwebel, to more like that of a pair of hunted, hungry foxes.

* * *

One afternoon, we were faced with a rapidly flowing River Odra. It might have been 35 feet (10 metres) wide and appeared deep. With the melting springtime snows feeding it from the higher pastures and mountains, the water was high and there was no way across by stepping on boulders.

We decided to walk upstream, where it might be narrower. Eventually, we came to a point in the river where a large amount of wood, branches and tree stumps had collected.

"That is our way over," I said to Andrzej.

He did not look convinced. I did not feel convinced but there seemed to be no other options.

"How do we get over that?" he asked.

I explained that if we could work our way through the water onto the woodpile it would give us a half-way staging point across the river.

"What happens when we get there?" he rightly asked.

I did not know but said something like "Oh, we can work it out when we have made it that far."

We duly waded through the swift water. At this point, it occurred to me that it really would have been useful if I had learned to swim. The water came over my feet, up my legs. And it was so very cold. A few days previously, this water would have been snow on the high pastures. It certainly felt like that. But when you are on the run, comfort is a luxury soon forgotten. Survival is all that counts and, if we got over this river and kept going, we might just survive.

We climbed onto the pile of wood and pulled ourselves clear of the water. From this vantage point, we realised that the first section was the easy part. We were now faced with a raging torrent twice as wide as that we had come across, with no way to know how deep it was. I knew all about being swept away by a river in flood and did not want a repetition. But we just had to press on.

On the second leg of the crossing, the water came over our feet as before, then it came up to our waists. We could not stop now. The water came up to our chests, nearly up to our throats, and the water was icy cold and running so quickly that it nearly took us off our feet. If we lost our footing, we would be lost.

Then we realised the water was not getting deeper. We exchanged glances. The cold had made it too difficult to talk. We kept going. The water was now around our chest, then around our waist, around our thighs—and we were out. Our teeth were chattering and we were shivering with the cold.

We flopped on the riverbank and looked back at the bubbling, swirling torrent. I do not know what Andrzej was thinking but I thought we were crazy to have even tried it. But we were over and we were on dry land. There was just one small snag that we now had to face. It was dusk, it was cold, and we were soaking wet and freezing cold. If we did not dry our uniforms, we were going to be in trouble. There was no other option: we just kept going westward, cold and freezing, until we were sure no-one was following us and then turned eastward—or what we hoped was eastward—again.

* * *

Just beyond the River Odra was a steep mountain. Nearing the top, we approached a small wooden house. As usual, we carried out our reconnaissance: Was there a man there? Was there a woman there? Was it safe? We knocked on the door, our instincts were finely tuned for any small clue that might tell us to run for our lives.

A woman answered the door and was surprised to find two extremely scruffy and soaking wet Hitlerjugend boys. She would have known, of course, that we were deserters but that probably endeared us to her.

"Yes, boys?"

"Good evening, madam. We wondered if you could help us by giving us a little spare bread and perhaps some matches."

Happily she did this and we at least had something to put into our stomachs. We could not ask her to give us somewhere to sleep, which would have endangered her life. We were very grateful for what she had given us. As night fell, the temperature was dropping and we were still soaking wet.

We went deep into the forest, hopefully out of sight of any malevolent authority. We gathered firewood and built a good-sized bonfire. We were far enough out in the countryside that we were probably safe from German patrols. We could only hope that our fire would not attract any unwanted attention. We were too cold and wet, and knew that if we did not dry off it would be very bad for us. We did not have any choice. The fire flared and gradually settled down into red embers. We sat as close as we could to it to dry off our uniforms.

Soon, our wet uniforms began to steam. Maybe it was this that encouraged us just a bit too much. We moved closer to help the drying process. The steaming increased, which was just what we wanted, and my trousers were soon dry. I tried to get a little closer so that my jacket would dry as well.

But I slipped awkwardly and my leg slid into the burning embers. My already-warm uniform trousers began to steam and singe and I let out an involuntary gasp. Andrzej did not know what to do. I had no time to think. I just rolled over and over on the damp ground and, fortunately, my trousers cooled a little. I sat there dazed—my top half still wet and cold, while my bottom half was a ragged mess of charred and smoking trousers.

When we awoke to the astringent greyness of the next Moravian dawn, I found that my trousers were burned into ribbons, which hung down and flapped around my legs. I looked like a scarecrow. Anyone seeing me would know that I was a vagrant of some kind and the tattered Hitlerjugend uniform would confirm me as a deserter. It seemed we were pushing our luck too far.

We continued to head east. Now we tried to avoid seeing anyone. We could not trust anyone but this meant that we were receiving no food. We could drink from mountain streams, which were all right as long as you did not find a maggoty dead sheep higher up in the stream. The cold, the furtive nature of our journey, the lack of sleep and the absence of food were adding to a growing sense of hopelessness. We had no doubt that deserting from the Hitlerjugend suicide squad was the right thing to do. We had given it our best. But we were at the point of thinking that our best might not have been good enough.

MORE LEAPS
OF FAITH

O i! You two!"
Our blood froze.

"Come over here."

Another farmer had seen us. We did not have the energy to run away any more.

"Yes, sir," we stammered as he came closer to us. "What can we do for you?"

"Well, it looks as though you lads need some help, doesn't it?"

We nodded in sullen agreement, almost to the point of resignation.

"Come on, come with me."

Andrzej and I looked at each other. Our stamina was running out and we now had little to lose. We were glad that we did: he proved to be quite kind to us. Perhaps he had relatives in a similar situation and wanted to help us as he would want someone else to help his family.

First, he gave us something to eat. It was a simple meal with bread but it tasted wonderful. Somehow we had found a man with the best-tasting bread in the world. Our spirits rose. He also gave us a warm drink.

"Right, you can stay here the night," the kind farmer offered. "Here's the address of a relative of mine in Ostrava. He will give you some food, some new clothes and maybe a bed for the night. It is too dangerous to stay here, so you have to be off in the morning, but I will give you the directions to Ostrava."

This sounded wonderful. Ostrava was a major milestone on our way to the Polish border.

But as we walked through the outskirts of Ostrava in our scruffy state, we might as well have been carrying a large flag with the word "deserters." We were still in our Hitlerjugend uniforms but my dirty trousers were flapping around my legs, making me look like a refugee from a circus. Everyone in the street would know we were on the run but we somehow managed not to be seen by any police or SS. We asked the way to the address we had been given and received some strange looks from people who, nevertheless, helped us.

Despite our positive experiences in the country, we were still wary and we discussed whether it was safe to go to the house. "Will it be a trap?" we wondered out loud.

Our discussion continued something like this: "He didn't have to help us. He could just have called the police or SS and had us arrested."

"But maybe it's a German policeman or SS man that he has sent us to?"

"Did he look like someone who would have a relative who was a German policeman?"

"He looked more like one of our people from Wisła."

It did not immediately look like a trap. The address turned out to be a restaurant, so we decided to make the leap of faith. If we were wrong, we were sure the Feldgendarmerie were adept at stringing people up quickly and efficiently. Our parents would never have known what had happened to us, but that was a not unusual in the time of Adolf Hitler.

We decided that maybe our latest leap of faith had a half-way stage. Fortunately, the building had a small park opposite. We decided to lurk in the bushes for a while and watch who went to the restaurant. If police or SS went there, we would think again. We could not stay too long as my appearance was a complete giveaway and would certainly attract any official eyes who might look our way. The clientele seemed innocuous, looking like labourers or farmers. They were too old to be out on the front line, so there were no uniforms to be afraid of. My own uniform was the only one to be afraid of. We could not hang around the park much longer without drawing attention.

"Shall we do it?" I asked quietly.

Andrzej nodded. There were no other viable options.

We found the proprietor presiding over his shop. We did not, of course, know the name of the man who had sent us but we explained the situation.

"Come in, boys," said the owner. He took us quickly around the back. "You need help don't you?"

We nodded a nod of desperation.

He gave us something to eat. Yet again something plain and basic tasted utterly wonderful.

"How far is it to Cieszyn?" we asked him as we ate.

"About 20 miles [about 30 kilometres]," he replied. "I can give you food for the journey and a change of trousers, but you will need to leave tomorrow morning. It is dangerous to stay here. You might be able to take a train there. The Reds are not far from Cieszyn but as far as I know the trains were running all right yesterday."

It was a great step forward. Just to pull on some civilian clothes again would help us blend in with the outside world. Our small amount of money was enough to purchase two tickets. In the normal manner, the man did not ask our names and we did not ask his.

We thanked this unknown man from the bottom of our hearts. For the moment at least, things were going our way.

* * *

The railway station was quite close and we found that the trains were still running. A passenger train pulled in, full of German troops going to the front line. We noticed the soldiers were old enough to be our fathers. That meant that the young men were either already at the front or already dead. Few of these people would be alive a month from now. What a world we were living in!

Our journey lasted an hour. We did not engage anyone in conversation or speak to each other. We just tried to be as invisible as possible.

As the train jolted forward, I knew what Andrzej was thinking and he knew what I was thinking. How were we going to get past customs at Cieszyn? We knew that if we were pulled up on the train, our Ausweis would give us away as Hitlerjugend on the run. There was a bridge we had to cross over the River Olsa. It was impossible to gain access to the bridge without going through the customs hall. But we had come this far and we could not stop now.

The train rattled on until it was coming through the marshalling yards at the outskirts of Cieszyn. We were going to have to work out some form of ... what? Subterfuge? Slipping across while no-one was looking? This was our biggest challenge since we had left Sternberg five days earlier.

We hung around near the entrance to the bridge, trying not to draw attention to ourselves as our eyes sought in vain for any clue as to how we might get across. We considered a number of scenarios but there seemed no easy way. We were not going to take any undue chances now. Over the River Olsa was Poland. We tried to blend in with the local people.

Then the air-raid siren went! This was close enough to the front line for shells, bombs and bullets to be flying. A train clattered into the station with undue haste, came to an indecent stop with a screaming of breaks and hiss of steam. The engine driver and fireman were first out of their cab and they ran for shelter, leaving their train to its own devices. The railway officials ran after them. The carriage doors opened suddenly and the entire trainload of people ran for cover. No-one bothered about ticket collection, checking Ausweis or looking for deserters.

For everyone on the platform, the sirens meant an air raid was on the way. That meant death and destruction. The bombs were no respecter of person or property. If you were not sheltered, you were in the gravest danger. The station emptied of people in seconds as the sirens went on. Andrzej and I now had the station to ourselves.

But we could hear planes approaching in the distance. The engines were deep-throated, menacing and loud. They were American bombers and there were many of them. The station was empty. The streets were empty. The bombers were closer.

We ran to the customs hall, which was now also deserted. We walked through and onto the bridge. It seemed we were the only people still above ground in the entire town. The bombers were nearly overhead now and the roar of the engines made the station shiver.

For all we knew, the bombers might have been targeting the bridge—but this was our chance! We sprinted across the bridge as the bombers appeared overhead. We could not hear ourselves think as the sound of the low-flying planes shook the whole town.

But no bombs fell. The bomber force passed by and began to recede into the distance. Cieszyn was not the target this time. We were nearly onto the Polish side and sprinted to get across the bridge before anyone appeared at the Polish customs point.

We clattered through the customs hall on the Polish side as the all-clear was just starting to sound. By the time people had re-appeared in the street, we were well clear of the railway installations and were in the street, panting and laughing. We had just crossed back into Poland!

* * *

The road home was one we knew well. It brought us the 12 miles (about 20 kilometres) home, through familiar forests and mountains. We knew the back tracks, too remote for the Feldgendarmerie to patrol. We knew which streams we could drink in and which we could not.

I could begin to think about what it would be like for my parents when I walked in through the door. They had no idea we were coming and our return would be a surprise for everyone. The kind man of Ostrava had given us some bread to eat and that kept us going.

Some eight exhausting hours later, we walked into our farmyard.

To the end of my days, I will remember how my mother's face lit up. "Paweł, you have come from heaven!" she cried.

My father and my brothers and sisters came running. We embraced and kissed. While my mother gave us something to eat, my father, brothers and sisters wanted to know what had happened since I had been taken away. It dawned on me that they were expecting Andrzej and I back in one piece.

"You were expecting us, weren't you?" I asked my parents.

They laughed and nodded. Then they explained what happened.

Of the several letters I had written, one had been delivered. So they had known that I was in Sternberg. My parents had prevailed on a neighbour, Jan Huta, to go to Sternberg to find Andrzej and me, and bring us home safely.

"But why him?" I asked. "I thought he had lost a leg."

"That's the whole point," my father explained. "As a possessor of the War Wound Badge, he was in a great position to intercede for you."

First, all he had to do was to show the badge and he could travel free on the railways, insofar as the trains were still running. Then, when he got to Sternberg, his possession of the military honour would gain him immediate access to the officer in charge. The Germans held their war wounded in high regard and possession of such a badge could open doors.

"Anyway," my father continued, "he got to Sternberg and found the barracks and he got to see an Oberfeldwebel."

Inside, I would have liked to have fallen through the floor rather than hear this story. Did this contact mean Oberfeldwebel Weiss knew where we were and that we would be found and arrested?

"Jan asked him to confirm if you were at the barracks and . . ."

"We weren't," I continued.

"No," said my father with a grin. I got the distinct impression that our desertion at a time of national crisis did not worry him at all.

"That is what the Oberfeldwebel said, 'They disappeared last night!' He was not amused." Jan had told him that search parties had been sent out for us. Apparently the Oberfeldwebel made a number of colourful threats about what he would do to us if he could get his hands on us. My father actually laughed, while sharing this report.

Our formation came under the SS, meaning we would be shot if caught after deserting. Jan also reported that some other boys had followed our lead and had disappeared into the hills. We all hoped that they had been as fortunate as we had been.

"Do you think they will come after us, Dad?" I asked with genuine concern.

"The whole place is falling to pieces," he said. "If they can't deliver a letter, I doubt if they will worry about two young absconders."

But there was more to Jan's report. Just as he was leaving to come home, Jan told my father, the boys were taken to a large square by the station. I realised he had missed us by only a few hours. He told my father that the boys were drawn up into columns for an oath ceremony, in preparation for embarking on the waiting special trains.

If Andrzej and I had not absconded, we would have had to take a solemn oath to Adolf Hitler personally that we would lay down our lives for him. I was thankful we had avoided that.

After a long time of telling our own story, I fell into bed and slept for many hours. I had actually made it home! I wondered afterwards what would have happened if I had been faced with taking an oath of loyalty to Hitler. Would I have refused it and risked my life? Would my parents have wanted me to do so? I am glad that I do not know.

* * *

We were to learn later that our fate would have been similar to what happened at the Pichelsdorf Bridge in Berlin on April 23. Here, 5000 boys stood by with rifles and Panzerfausts ready to oppose the Russian Army. Within five days of battle, 4500 had been killed or wounded. The mission was to hold the bridge for General Wenck's army coming from the south to relieve the troops in Berlin. What the boys would learn was that Wenck's army had been destroyed in its entirety. Hitler was moving phantom armies to save the encirclement of Berlin. In the five-day battle, thousands of Hitlerjugend boys—and they were only boys—were killed. Many committed suicide rather than be taken alive by the Russians. Anyone who did not stand and fight to the death was shot or hanged by SS executioners, who patrolled the streets looking for anyone who might be a deserter.

Approximately, 58,000 Hitlerjugend boys were involved in the final fighting around Berlin. Of these, 55,000 are believed to have died.

Many years later, a friend visited the Waldfriedhof Cemetery in Berlin where many of them lie. I gave him the names of some of the boys I knew. He told me there are rows and rows and rows of them. He did not find any of the names I gave him. Most gravestones bear a simple word: "Unbekannt" meaning "Unknown".

This book is probably the only record that several hundred young boys were trained, indoctrinated and sent to their deaths from the training camp at Sternberg. It is unlikely that any other boys survived.

NERVES
OF ROPE

We had arrived home to discover that Wisła was still "Weichsel" and was still in German-held territory—but only just. The thunder of the guns could be heard like a threatening toothache that never went away. Unfortunately for us, the front was only a short distance from us and we could even see it from our farm. Gradually, the sound of thunder came closer and closer.

The sounds of battle were loud, with heavy fighting happening only 2 miles (3 kilometres) away. At night, we went to sleep with the sound of battle in our ears and when we woke up it was still there. Occasionally, a stray shell would cause an explosion near our property and would wake us all in the middle of the night.

"Everyone OK?" my dad would shout through the house.

"Yes, it was two fields away," one of my siblings would answer back through the darkness. And we would go back to sleep.

We were fortunate that "our" Russians were of the more civilised variety. They were regular soldiers with discipline that kept them from raping, stealing or vandalising. Despite the awful barbarism of many of the Russian soldiers, we viewed "our" Russians as liberators.

* * *

Once I had settled back at home among joyous scenes, my family told me of an incident that had happened only a month earlier.

Józef had been the man of the house at the time, being on permanent absconders' leave from the army. My father had been away somewhere at the time. Józef went out one afternoon to visit one of his friends.

As he was on his way back home, Józef heard a plane come over from the east. As he neared our farm, he peered through the fading winter light and saw black specks moving low against the snow.

By this stage of the war, all his instincts could sense danger instantly. He looked more carefully. Could it be some dogs from our neighbourhood? No, these were human figures. He realised they were folding parachutes to be hidden in the nearby forest. They were Russians!

One of them noticed Józef and pointed a rifle at him. He put up his hands immediately. One or two were for shooting him "just to be on the safe side." But one of their number was Polish and soon realised Józef was Polish too.

"Tell the officer that we will not give them away to the Germans," Józef said to him. "We don't like them either."

"It's OK, lads," the Polish partisan assured his colleagues. "You don't have to kill him—he's Polish, not German. He's more use to us alive than dead."

The officer thought this was a good idea. "Tell him to take us to his house," he ordered. "If he plays us false, he's going to get a bullet. Make sure he understands."

We were to find out later that the Polish partisan's entire family had been sent to Auschwitz and he had been the only one who managed to escape to Russia. While there, he volunteered to return with the Russian partisans to exact whatever revenge he could. We never knew his name.

Later that night, my mother heard Józef arriving home as she had expected. She was going to scold him for coming back so late and making her worry. What she had not expected was that he would come with 16 nervous but belligerent Russian partisans. They wore huge ushanka fur hats with the red star prominently displayed on the front. They were in heavy black winter uniforms that made them look especially huge. They were heavily armed with rifles, machine guns and pistols. Grenades swung from attachments to their uniforms. They were festooned with ammunition belts filled with deadly bullets.

"It's OK, Mum," Józef tried to sound reassuring. "They just want to stay for a bit."

Under his breath, he whispered, "I actually don't think we are in a position to tell them to go away."

My mother saw the logic and, terrified though she was, she agreed that they could come in. They thanked her and immediately began to check their weapons, making sure they were clean, oiled and—especially—loaded.

The Polish partisan then did something quite unexpected. He produced a fur hat and a woollen scarf, which he had brought from Russia, and gave them both to my mother as gesture of appreciation.

Mother was stunned. She had never had such a hat in her life.

The Russian partisans stayed in our home for a couple of hours, then went back to the nearby forest.

* * *

Some time later, one partisan came back to our farm and, with the knowledge of my parents, was hiding in the upper barn where we kept the hay for our cattle. But early one morning, the dogs were barking on the neighbour's farm. Everyone in our house was living on nerves at this time, with the front

My mother was amazed to find Józef and some very threating Russians at the door, painting by Katarzyna Mojak.

line moving closer all the time. My mother looked through the front window and saw a frightening sight. A German patrol was coming toward our farm.

A few minutes later, a Feldwebel—a sergeant—of the Wehrmacht knocked at the door. Behind him were a few armed German soldiers, looking a little bored. They were not expecting an imminent confrontation with Russians.

In order to distract the German soldiers from searching our farm as they usually did, she met them at the front door.

"Augenblick!" shouted my mother. "One moment!"

She opened the door. "Yes, what can I do for you?"

"Sorry to bother you, Ma'am, but we're just out looking for any bandits or partisans that might be in the area."

"Oh, that's fine," my mother responded with forced cheeriness. "Are you and your boys feeling hungry at all? I could offer you a hot drink and a bite to eat if you like."

With Russians hiding in the upper barn with loaded weapons, she actually invited them into our kitchen.

"That's very kind, madam," the Feldwebel replied. "Men! Over here, this lady will give us something to warm us up."

"Willkommen, willkommen, Deutsche Soldaten. Kommen Sie mal 'rein," my mother fussed. "Welcome, welcome, German soldiers, come in."

"Thank you, kind lady," said the soldiers as they clumped into the house with their hobnail boots and gleaming firearms.

"It's alright, lads. This lady's one of us—echt deutsch [real German]," the Feldwebel said, although how they could have called my mother this with her broken German remains a mystery.

My mother's heart was beating like a drum, nearly bursting out of her chest. She made them a warm drink of Bauerntee, a black tea that was common among farmers in central Europe. She prepared them a simple meal of homemade bread and butter. As they ate, Mother could only imagine what the tension was like in the upper barn among the Russians.

"That was lovely, Madam. Thank you very much," said the Feldwebel as they finished eating.

"Not a problem, sir. We all have to do our bit," said Mother. "Now here are some eggs for you to take home, because you all need to eat to keep your strength up."

They thanked her profusely for this rare treat. They finished the plate of bread and were soon ready to continue their patrol.

"Come on, men. This won't win the war!" said the Feldwebel. "Thanks very much for that, kind Frau. We really needed it. If you see any bandits, will you let us know? We've got reports of several sightings around here and we want to get them before they get you."

Because of my mother's hospitality, they did not search the house—this time.

"Thank you," said my mother, her feeling of relief beginning to grow.

The Wehrmacht soldiers clumped out again, gave her a final wave of thanks and went on into the woods. My mother waited until the dogs on the next farm had stopped barking before she told the Russians that the Germans were gone.

They went their own way, thanking my mother profusely for avoiding a murderous fight.

Looking back, I wonder how my mother had the mental strength to do that. She must have had nerves of rope—as the expression goes in Polish.

* * *

The Polish partisan with the Russians did quite a favour for our family in the next day or so. He showed Józef exactly where their parachutes had been hidden.

"They'll make lovely shirts," he said helpfully.

Józef gathered them up and delivered them to my mother to work her magic as a seamstress.

"Just one thing, though," she said, "you can only wear these when the Germans have gone or else we'll have the SS around asking where we got the nice white parachute silk from. But there should not be too long to wait now."

Despite my mothers hopefulness, we soon realised that there was still more drama to come.

A couple of days later, the Russian partisans were on a patrol in the woods and encountered a man also in Russian uniform. He had the letters "US" painted crudely on his uniform. He told them he had been a Russian prisoner of war.

"Hello, comrades!" he shouted.

The Russian partisans surrounded him and they all shook hands.

"I was in the Red Army and taken prisoner but I escaped," the fugitive explained.

He joined them and stayed with them on patrol for some hours. Eventually, he took them to a small house near the forest.

"You'll be all right here," he assured them. "I'll be on my way, so good luck! Have a good trip to Berlin."

They thanked him for his help and the man left.

Only a few minutes later, the Russians discovered the house was surrounded by German troops. The man had been an agent provocateur sent to lure them to their death.

The Russian partisans run upstairs and shot from the windows, threw hand grenades and raked the surrounding Germans with machine gun bullets. Soon the house was on fire.

One by one, the Russians were killed. The last one was inside the roof cavity as the fire licked up toward him and the bullets still whizzed as they fired through the building. In an act of desperation, he climbed out onto the roof, expecting the Germans to shoot at him. He discovered that he was on the back of the roof but all the German soldiers were at the front of the building and could not see him. He jumped down to the ground, landing as quietly as he could, and ran away into the forest.

The Germans must have thought all the Russians were dead because they were not following him, nor were they looking around to make sure none of the soldiers got away. He came back to our farm to hide and stayed with us for several months.

BRAVERY OF
THE NIGHT

A s I settled back into life at home, I met the one remaining Russian partisan, although we saw little of him. He hid out on the farm somewhere and only rarely came to the house. We also began noticing other changes around our area. The whole Nazi paraphernalia and—especially the greetings of "Heil Hitler!"—was beginning to disappear. We knew that the Third Reich was disintegrating rapidly and thought that, if we could just sit out the next few weeks, it was unlikely that the Feldgendarmerie were going to be active in looking for deserters. However, our assumptions proved tragically mistaken.

Ever the practical man, my father got me organised into doing some useful work. Most of the farm horses had been requisitioned by the Wehrmacht, who throughout the war continued to utilise large numbers of horses. This meant the motive power for the farms was largely absent. There were few tractors available and, even if we had them, fuel was almost impossible to obtain. The requisitioning of the farm horses was yet another indicator that the Reich was in increasingly desperate straits.

The local farmers made a deputation to the senior-ranking German officer. They asked whether, in the absence of farm horses, it would be possible for the Wehrmacht to loan back some horses to allow farmers to carry on with their vital tasks. The senior German officer supported this idea and also offered to call for volunteers among the soldiers as help for the farmers. This produced a large labour force who worked as volunteers on the local farms.

Some of the soldiers came from urban areas and had never ploughed a furrow in their lives but they seemed enthusiastic.

I was allocated the job of supervising some of these less skilled soldiers working on neighbouring farms, helping them be useful farm workers. All the while, the front was only a few miles away and we could hear the artillery and the sharp rat-tat of heavy machine guns in the distance.

At the bottom of the hill, there was a farmhouse. Some of us knew a Russian partisan was hiding in the barn up the hill near us. Even more, we knew he was hiding under a heap of hay. This meant, of course, that if he was found, there would be a roundup of local people—including us—and there would be reprisals. People would be put against a wall and shot, and some would be sent to Auschwitz.

Suddenly, a patrol appeared. They wore grey-green uniforms and the death's head insignia of an SS counterinsurgency unit. Their appearance chilled us. We knew they would shoot us without compunction if they suspected anything untoward.

After marching up the hill, the SS unit sat down by the farmer's barn, only a hundred yards or so from where I was working. Their dog was restive, trying to get into the barn. It scraped and scrabbled, very intent on something. And the SS men began to take an interest in the dog's behaviour.

We knew the partisan would have his machine gun and hand grenades ready and if he shot at the SS men, he might overshoot and hit us. But we could not show any reaction because that would bring suspicion on us. All we could do was hope that something would happen to distract the dog.

Suddenly, a hare jumped out of the bushes and the dog ran after it as fast as possible.

"Here, boy," the handler shouted. But the dog had the hapless animal in its sights and it was focussed on the hunt.

The dog ran, the handler ran, all the SS men ran and those of us watching nervously, now laughed as they disappeared down the hill. It was yet another close call.

* * *

A few days later, a more typically sad occurrence took place. This event demonstrated what my fate would have been had I been caught absconding from the Hitlerjugend.

Late in the evening, we heard a frantic knocking at the door. This could bode ill. It might be the German army. It might be partisans. It might be the SS. It might even be the Russians come to rape all the women and hurt the men.

"Who's there?" whispered my father through the door.

"We're lost, please help us," said a voice.

My father opened the door to find three wild-eyed, filthy, desperate Wehrmacht soldiers in decrepit German Feldgrau uniforms. From their accents, we figured they were from Germany itself. From his experience in World War I, my father noticed immediately that they had no weapons. He recognised them as deserters.

They were from the German army and, therefore, they were the enemy. But at the same time, they were just three young men caught up in the horrors of war and not particularly guilty of anything. My father took pity on them in much the same way as people had taken pity on Andrzej and me when we were on the run.

My father invited them in and offered them dinner. They warmed themselves by the fire. It was late evening, just about the time when we were about to have our evening prayer meeting. We prayed together and my father decided we would sing a hymn in the German language so that the three German soldiers could understand it. It is called "Hoch auf dem Meer Unter Gottes Geleit"— "High on the Seas Escorted by God." We invited them to sing with us.

> High on the sea escorted by God
> We're pulling for home, pulling for home.
> Heavily beset by storm, cross and sorrow,
> We're pulling for home, pulling for home.
> The Lord prepares those as promised,
> We're pulling for home, pulling for home
> Far from the safe haven of peace,
> We sail bravely to our homes!

The effect on the three soldiers was surprising. They burst into tears and cried like children. They were particularly affected by the words "Wir ziehen heim"—"We are pulling for home." Our evening hymn had inadvertently touched a nerve. They had seen enough of death and destruction. All they wanted was to be at home with their families.

They confessed to us that they were deserters. Our family looked at them with pity, sympathy and dread in equal proportions. We knew that if they were caught, they were dead men. They knew it also but flight gave them a chance of survival. To fight against the Russian hordes meant death at best.

They pulled themselves together and adopted a more soldierly bearing. One of them told us their story.

"In 1938, we went to a rally," said the soldier. "We saw Adolf Hitler speak and fell under his spell. He told us when we were 16 years old that he would make Germany great and that tomorrow belonged to us. We volunteered for the army to take part in the great glory of the new Germany. We fell for all the rubbish he talked and we believed every word he said. He deceived us. Now look at what is happening: it's all lost.

"We threw away our guns and grenades. We have had enough. We just want to go home. We would be grateful if you could just show us the tracks that will take us to Moravia. Can you show us the way?"

My father nodded with understanding. "Yes, of course I can," he said quietly.

He would help them to find the safest way through the forest and on mountain trails.

"All you can do is to try it," my father advised.

My father understood what would have happened to Andrzej and me if we had been caught. Strangers had helped his son and perhaps my father felt he wanted to help someone else's son.

"Get some sleep," my father instructed. "I'll call you when it's time to go."

"Thank you so very much, sir," they replied.

My father woke the three soldiers at 4 am. He took them over a couple of hills near the village of Kubulonka and pointed to the border between Silesia and Moravia. At a crossroads, he showed them a narrow track that led to the border.

"Carry on that way and you will come through Ostrava, Praha and then back home to Germany." The route they were looking for was close to the one that Andrzej and I had travelled in coming home.

They thanked him profusely, shook his hand and left. My father arrived home at around 6 in the morning and went back to bed. But he was very anxious about the risks the three German boys were running.

* * *

That afternoon, my father returned from a short visit to Wisła-Centrum and was dreadfully upset. He had seen the three Germans marched through town under escort by the Feldgendarmerie. We later learned that they had been brought to the cemetery where they had been shot and buried. They were about

25 years old, the rumbling of the guns was still audible and the war was almost over. But the killing just went on.

It seemed they were decent young men and they did not tell the Feldgendarmerie that we had helped them. If they had, we would have been shot as well. They had respected my father's conspicuous bravery in showing them through the fields in the dead of night, risking his own life and family. It was a pity that such boys had to die in those last death throes of Hitler's evil regime. Their families would not have known what happened. They would have hoped for their return one day to Bremen, Frankfurt or wherever they came from.

When the last of the German prisoners from Russia arrived back some 10 years later, their families at some point would have admitted sadly that their sons were not coming home The three families could only wonder at what had happened.

This event still touches my heart today.

THE FINAL CASUALTIES OF A SENSELESS WAR

I kept on working in the fields with the German soldiers but I was surprised no-one ever bothered to ask why I was not in uniform. While the war was all but over, yet more men were being called up. In the previous week, the Wehrmacht had begun compulsorily drafting boys as young as 14 and men up to 60 years old into a new formation called the Volkssturm—"the people's militia." A current joke had it that two SS men were going through a cemetery. A passerby asked them what they were doing and they replied, "Looking for more volunteers for the Volkssturm."

It was an exercise in mass suicide. The few who had uniforms wore those they had been given in World War I—if they still fitted. Their weapons, if they had any, were rough and ready. Some of them—and I saw this myself—were on walking sticks.

My father actually received call-up papers into the Volksturm but managed to be diagnosed with some "life-threatening" sickness. Whatever he was suffering from was less life threatening than a trip to the Russian Front!

But even as time ran out for the German Reich, brutal killings and the terror they brought continued to haunt our community.

* * *

Kalisz the Postman.

The first concerned our Postman Kalisz. He was married to my second cousin and I had known him since he had delivered letters to my school. He would chat with us children when he delivered letters to the school. He was a popular man around the village. But he made no secret of his distaste for the Nazis and all of their works. Behind closed doors, he would say to his relatives, "This is a government that will come to an end."

By the end of the war—for it was only a couple of weeks away—most people agreed with him but were prudent enough not to say so. Late heavy snow was still with us in April. On one of those snowy days, Postman Kalisz was missing. He had not reported for work.

Someone reported they had seen two SS men on a horse-drawn sleigh pick him up the previous evening from the post office, where he was working late. The scene was almost like a Christmas card, but this one had a deadly feel about it. They pointed to the direction in which the sleigh had gone. The villagers went to the woods but the sleigh tracks were obliterated by fresh snow. The search party could find no trace of him.

As the weather warmed, his body appeared from beneath the melting snow.

At the funeral—immediately after the war had ended—the priest told the story of his terrible death. His fingers had been broken like sticks, with his nails pulled out. His body was broken from a tremendous beating with a heavy object like an iron bar. His skull was cracked. There were deep knife wounds slashed across his body.

There was no motive that would further the cause of the expiring Third Reich. They were not after information. There was no political, military or administrative gain. It was the work of disturbed and sick men. There were hundreds at the funeral and almost the entire congregation was in tears.

Some weeks later, rumours began to circulate that someone close to Kalisz had betrayed him but these questions were never resolved. Having clearly lost the war, it seems the SS men decided to have a little robust "fun" before they pulled out of the area and went on the run themselves to dodge the avenging Russians. As the war closed, SS men were often shot out of hand, both on the Eastern and the Western fronts.

* * *

Jan Szalbot.

The second funeral was of a family friend who had been called up into the Wehrmacht. Jan Szalbot was home on leave, even though the front line was only a little more than a mile away, where the fighting carried on for three months with neither side obtaining a clear advantage. Despite the tide running against them, the German army did quite a job of maintaining discipline, military procedures and obeying the rules right up until the war's end.

Jan decided to go "absent without leave" and not return to his unit. There was a reasonable chance the Russians would break through and our area would be liberated. His mother had asked him to go home but Jan felt it was too dangerous, both for himself and for all his family. Hiding in the forest, he was unlucky enough to run into a German patrol.

He decided he would try to fool them. "Hello there! I am lost," he said. "Can you tell me how to get back to my unit?"

"No problem," they said. "Just come with us to the local command centre and we'll sort it out."

He recognised that they were about to arrest him for desertion.

"You're not taking me anywhere," he said as he lashed out at the first soldier who tried to grab him. Jan was a large, strong man and quickly laid the first soldier out. He grabbed a second soldier and nearly overpowered him but a third soldier hit him on the back of the head with a rifle butt, knocking him out cold. They shot him without further ado.

As soon as the Wehrmacht withdrew—only a few days later—we had another sad funeral. "If only he had stayed at home," his mother said to me as she broke down in tears, "there would have been no funeral."

* * *

It went on and on. Another friend of the family was called up into the Wehrmacht: Jerzy Pilch. He was stationed in Bielsko. He asked for a two-day pass to visit his wife, who lived not far from us. When he came home, there was a knock on his door. It was a group of partisans.

"Come with us, Jerzy Pilch!" was the invitation that signalled that his life was over.

They took him into the forest and made him dig his grave. Then they shot him.

Another case related to a single woman who lived in the town. One sunny afternoon an informer noticed men's underwear hanging on her washing line. The SS knocked on her door and found she was hiding a concentration camp escapee. They were both shot immediately. Rumours were rife as to who had alerted the SS.

Amid this kind of brutality, our family recognised how fortunate we were that such a person did not alert the authorities about Józef. We lived in perpetual fear of such a thing happening to us. It seemed the slaughter would never end.

* * *

Jerzy Pilch (left) with my brother Jan.

Around this time, another two Russian parachutists arrived at our home one evening.

"Good evening," they greeted my father. "We want you to show us where Mr L___, the Blockleiter, lives."

Their purpose was clear. They were well organised and evidently knew who my father was. They especially knew who Mr L___ was and his track record as a Blockleiter. They were a two-man death squad, sent to "liquidate" a number of people before their main force arrived in the area. They had with them a list of some 30 people who were targeted for death.

Thankfully, my father was not on the list but, if he did not cooperate, they would not hesitate to shoot him as well. Nevertheless, cold-blooded murder could not be condoned and might be dangerous for the rest of the neighbourhood.

My father pleaded with the Russians. He explained that the Germans were still in the area and there would be terrible reprisals if they shot this man. My father possessed the persuasiveness of desperation and the paratroopers relented.

As a compromise, they kicked their way into Mr L___'s house, sprayed his house with machine gun bullets and reduced Mr L___ and his wife to shaking with terror. They showed him a hand-grenade. "If you continue to be a naughty boy, this could go off in your house," they warned. "It would make a nasty, nasty mess."

Suitably chastened, Mr L___ kept a low profile for the next few weeks.

The fighting in the Wisła-Malinka area went on for week after week.

One day, the Russians were pouring artillery fire—round after round—into the German positions in the battered remnants of a village. Eventually, a Polish local went to the Russian Kommandanteur and pointed out that the German positions they were shelling were empty. The Wehrmacht had pulled out during the previous night.

Then the front crashed forward like a giant wave and we were left behind in Russian-occupied territory. The bulk of the Red Army were only in our area for a day or so, then they moved forward into Lower Silesia and Germany proper, leaving a small number of troops to undertake mopping up operations and clear out the last of the Nazis.

Mr L___ survived the war. He was put into jail for four years by the Communist government. This must have been a terrible ordeal and he died shortly after release. More than 60 years later, he is still spoken of negatively in the region.

* * *

But not all stories involve human perfidy and nasty characters.

Another strange story was that of Jan Swider. He had been taken by the Germans to a slave-labour camp. In early 1944, the Russians had overrun wherever he was, which must have been in the east of Poland. Liberation was a relative term and did not include sending him home, which was still on the other side of a nasty front line.

Jan Swider spoke Russian, from his time as a prisoner of war in Russia in World War I. So his strategy was to make himself useful to the Russians in the field kitchens and to travel with them as they pushed inexorably westward.

In the first few weeks of 1945, he found himself on a hilltop outside Wisła. It was familiar territory. He borrowed a pair of binoculars from a Russian soldier and scanned the hillside opposite. There was his house. His wife was hanging out the washing as his children played in the yard. He wanted more than anything to cross the valley and be reunited with them. But the German front line was between him and his family. The German army was well dug in and fighting a slowly losing battle.

It took days—that must have seemed like years—to dislodge the last vestiges of the Third Reich but at last the Wehrmacht pulled back and the Russians prepared to move forward. As he was not actually in the Russian army, he was not under any form of military orders so he just charged down the valley and ran up the other side.

His wife and children were astonished and perhaps a little frightened to see this scruffy man running toward their farmhouse. But the wild man seemed to know the wife's name—he shouted it as he ran. And he seemed to know the children's names.

It would have been a wonderful thing to freeze that moment in time when the Swider family realised for the first time that their father was home. For two years, they would not have known if he was alive or dead or had met any other fate.

* * *

About this time, my brothers and I climbed a nearby hill to watch the front line in action in the valley of Malinka, more than a mile (about 2 kilometres) away. We could see every detail of the front line set out like a panorama before us. To our right were the Germans with their heavy artillery and heavy machine guns. Away to our left were the Russians with their equally heavy artillery, their T-34 tanks and, most memorable of all, their Katyusha rockets. Guns went "bang" and machine guns rattled but the "whoosh" of the Katyushas was the most terrifying of all.

We sat up there on the high hill for some hours. A German artillery piece would boom and we could watch the shell explode in a spectacular upheaval of earth and stone. Sometimes we saw a shell hit a farmhouse that would splinter as if it were paper. When the cascading fragments came back to earth and the smoke cleared, another family's dwelling place was gone. Half a second and a sheet of yellow flame were all it took.

This was dreadful! We knew the people who lived in these houses and we wondered how they could survive. We were to discover later that the people had taken shelter in their cellars and there were, in fact, few casualties.

In the background was the perpetual rattle of the machine guns from both sides and the acrid smell of smoke from the explosions.

When the Russians came to advance, one of their tanks might put a shell into a house to clear the way for it to rumble forward. As often as not, the tank driver would just run the tank through the house. Most were made of wood and fell to pieces quite easily.

Down on the battlefield, men were dying by the dozens but the scene was a fascinating spectacle to the eyes of teenage boys. The battle line in Wisła had remained static for some weeks. Neither side could get the breakthrough they needed. But it was clear that the Russians had to win in the end. They were not as clever as the Germans but had many more men and seemed not to mind if they lost thousands as long as there were no Germans left.

Eventually, the Wehrmacht gunners spotted us on the hillside. They did not know who we were. We did not have the same uniforms as them and that was enough for them to know. They started to fire artillery shells at us. We ran for it and the shells exploded harmlessly somewhere behind us. We did not look back.

THE DAY THE RUSSIANS CAME

"**H**ey! Your comrades are here!" I called out as I entered the barn.

It was a cold spring day late in April, 1945. I was speaking to the one Russian paratrooper who had come to our farm and who had survived. My mother told me to go and tell him that he could come out now.

He had been with us for a number of months by this time. In the normal manner of special forces, he did not give us his name. He was hiding under the hay in our barn.

The main body of the Russian Army had gone through Oberschlesien and, as a fairly remote area, we were the last to be mopped up. But the Germans had officially withdrawn from the area and there was not a single German left.

The news came from Wisła-Centrum like lightning: "The Germans have run away!" Although it was an hour's walk away, we could hear the commotion in Wisła. The whole town was clearly going crazy. This was the sound of mad, deranged joy.

And I had expected the Russian partisan to be overjoyed but his manner was suspicious.

"Look here!" he said and showed me his service revolver. "Here are two bullets. If you are playing me false, the first one is for you and the second is for me. Do you understand?" He looked at me piercingly and earnestly. He was quite serious.

I smiled at him "You don't need to worry; everyone is saying that there are Russian trucks and tanks in town. The Germans have gone, you will see!"

"You will come with me."

"Sure!"

He seemed a little less suspicious.

As we walked into Wisła-Centrum—as of that day, no longer "Weichsel"—there was enough activity to persuade him I was not deceiving him.

The news had exploded.

The Germans had gone. The war was over!

People jumped up and down for sheer joy. They embraced each other in the street. They banged pots and pans together. They danced to the sound of an unheard orchestra. Total strangers embraced and kissed each other. They screamed and shouted.

The trappings of Nazidom—the flags and loudspeakers and pictures of Hitler—were ripped down with great enthusiasm but without ceremony. Every flag was torn down. Every banner was ripped into a thousand shreds. Every picture of Hitler was taken into the street and trampled with joy and gusto under foot.

It was wonderful. Reichsmarks were gone, replaced with our own złoty. Postage stamps with Hitler's lugubrious head were gone. There were to be no more signs in the main square telling us to be good Volksdeutscher. The people were Polish again and spoke Polish. Speaking the German language was a memory. The SS and their ghastly regime was a memory. It was over!

Perhaps best of all, there was no "Heil Hitler" anymore!

A number of people who had disappeared years earlier suddenly re-appeared that morning. They were in a terrible state and had clearly been living rough for years.

It is difficult to describe how relieved we were that Hitler's thugs had gone. We did not have to worry any more that someone could come to our door at 4 am and take us to a concentration camp. We did not have to worry that someone had denounced us for not saying "Heil Hitler" with enough gusto. We did not have to worry that we might encounter an SS bully with his silver death's head and that he might beat us up for fun.

We were free! It was a wonderful cleansing, liberating moment. The old world of Adolf Hitler had gone and now we were stepping into a brave new world.

"Paweł," said the paratrooper, "I have some errands to attend to and you can come with me."

That suited me well. I was happy that the Germans had gone and curious to see what the new occupying army would be like. I noticed immediately that, unlike the disciplined German military, the Russians were much more scruffy, unkempt and menacing. They were worse than the shepherds from the forest. It came as no surprise later when they also proved capable of a serious level of barbarism.

But the first battalions of front-line Russian troops who passed through Wisła were well disciplined and no crimes were perpetrated by them. They were professional and focussed. They were extremely vigilant and on the lookout for any sign of German counter-attacks or any other military action. The officers were organising the troops to go after the retreating Germans.

The paratrooper did not belong to any army unit. But, to my amazement, after being parachuted in, he knew exactly where to go: to the newly established Russian military headquarters in the middle of the Russian camp. Moreover, he was apparently expected there and was readily accepted as a member of the headquarters team. He went to make whatever report he had to make and I waited for him.

Nearby, a group of senior Russian officers with resplendent shoulder-boards were talking with a young woman, who seemed about 35 years of age. I could not follow the conversation as it was all in Russian but they seemed to be laughing in a light-hearted way and were rather enjoying their conversation.

After a few minutes, the paratrooper returned and told me the most curious story.

"You see that woman there?" He nodded toward the woman who seemed to be the centre of attention.

"Yes," I said.

"Let me tell you about her."

Whether she was Russian or Polish or German, I do not remember. What I do remember is that he told me she had become a cook for the German officers. She had used her proximity to senior Wehrmacht officers to look at files, listen in to conversations and pick up what information she could. She had passed on a lot of German operational planning details to the Russians.

"And shall I tell you something else?"

"Yes, what?" I asked eagerly.

"She was looking for the shepherd boy: you, Paweł."

"For me? Why me?"

216

"Because you were the shepherd boy up in the high country all on your own…"

My blood chilled. The strange aeroplane from the east, making strange circuits around my pasture! This was the mystery woman who tried to kill the man on the mountain, where I had worked a shepherd. I remembered the searches for her.

Her mission was to infiltrate the German high command and, of course, it made total sense that after she had parachuted in, anyone who she saw would have to die. She could not leave anyone alive who had seen her in the first 24 hours of her arrival and who might have described her to the SS.

If the third night had not been so foggy, she would have parachuted onto my pasture, asked me questions about local German activity, then she might have "liquidated" me—as the Russians charmingly put it.

The Russian paratrooper smiled and nodded. His role must have been in intelligence because he clearly knew all about it, which included the fact that I was the target.

* * *

Things changed quickly in our community. Overnight, "Volksdeutsch" became bad and "Polak" became good, especially if you spoke Polish as a first language. My family went through a willing and immediate metamorphosis back to Polish without any problems. We saw ourselves as Polish and all of our friends and neighbours saw themselves as such. We simply reverted to being Polish and I reverted to being Paweł.

Thankfully, our farm had little that anyone would want to steal. During the front-line fighting, the Russians had established the reputation in other places that they would steal anything not bolted to the floor.

Under the constant threat of rape, it was no longer safe for a woman to walk anywhere in the town. Later we learned with utter dismay that a friend of ours in a village near Bielsko had been forced to watch while many Russian soldiers raped his wife, one after another. If he had said one word they would have shot him. The Russian officers did not interfere in this sort of behaviour. People soon became very wary of the Russian "liberators."

Just as the Nazis had their hit-list for moving in, so did the Russians. Again, many people in Wisła disappeared. We never saw them again and often had no idea as to their fate. Some were imprisoned and did return but not until many years later. It also became clear that any Pole who had any connection with the

Polish government in London was destined for serious trouble with the new Communist government.

There was also a trickle back into the area of those Jews who had survived the holocaust. By this time, people had heard about the mass killings and had learned of the fate of the millions who were not going to come back. The people I knew were moved by their plight and did what they could to help them.

In other parts of Poland, returning Jews were not so fortunate. Having survived the SS and Nazi concentration camps, they were killed by Polish civilians on their return.

* * *

In the aftermath of all of these sad events came a strange but wonderful occasion, which happened at a local wedding. A family friend was to marry a girl named Katerina. My parents had met her several times and were impressed by her. We were all glad to have her come to live with us in Wisła.

My parents were at the wedding but I was not. Immediately afterward, they came home excited and told us the most amazing tale.

Perhaps the emotion of the occasion loosened Katerina's tongue, but she began to talk about things better not talked about at such a happy event. My parents were amazed when she told them that she had worked in the local military administration in Cieszyn. With anti-Nazi feeling still high, collaborators were keeping a low profile but Katerina did not seem to worry about this at all. My parents were totally taken aback that she knew about Józef's case.

"Now, Mrs Cieslar," she chattered happily, "I will tell you how your son was saved."

How could this Katerina possibly know who Józef was, let alone how he was "saved"? We simply did not know why he had got away with desertion. Naturally, my parents were anxious to hear her story.

"So the Nazis never came for Józef?" she asked with a twinkle in her eye.

"No, and we never knew why," my mother replied.

"Well, I realised he'd gone on the run," she explained, "so I took his papers and put them in the bin. As far as the Wehrbezirkskommando was concerned, he'd ceased to exist."

She had not only worked for the Nazis, she had also worked for the underground resistance movement. The risk she ran was incalculable!

My parents were speechless. Her generous act had saved our family.
"Perhaps that could be our little secret, eh?" she said with a broad grin.
And they carried on with the wedding celebrations.

RUBEN'S STRANGE CHRISTMAS GIFT

After breakfast, everyone on the farm was allotted tasks in the normal manner. On that day, my task was to plant potatoes in a plot which we called "the Rock." It is a place with a wonderful view of the Beskids Mountains. Since I was a young boy, I had often sat on that sheltered hill and enjoyed the majesty of the mountains and valleys. It was a place to listen to the "swoosh" the two rivers: the Black Wiselka and the White Wiselka and the other tributaries that flowed down the spruce-covered hills. It was a sight of great delight and wonder.

The morning calm was broken by the sound of a siren. Another siren joined in ... and another, then another. It seemed there was a siren or some other loud noise coming from every valley as far as ears could hear.

It was May 8, 1945.

Adolf Hitler was dead—and his war was over.

People in the fields stopped working and gathered in small groups. You could feel the relief bubbling up the valley. It was really all over! Down in town, some people paraded around in the madness of another celebration. Some people danced for joy. Others chatted excitedly with neighbours. There was the feeling that something new and wonderful was about to begin. There would be a fresh beginning! The days of horror, depression and melancholy had passed—or that is what we hoped.

The early morning sky was grey and the first blaze of a strong morning sun illuminated the sky above the spruce trees. Like we did on the first morning of the war, our family held the customary family worship.

As we sang, my mother burst into tears.

"What's wrong, Mum?" I asked her.

She spoke with great emotion, fighting back the tears as strongly as she could, striving for self-possession but not really getting there. Our hearts went out to her. We knew why she was crying.

Through the sobs that racked her body, she explained. "It's Ruben," she said. "My heart is breaking because he's been exposed to bullets probably every single day since he left. We've heard nothing about him for months. We don't know if he's alive or dead. If he is dead, we have no idea where he is buried."

I knew it was in vain but I would have given anything to console my mother. I tried to cheer her up by talking about how he had looked after his kit like a real soldier, how he had pressed his uniform to look smart and how he had polished his boots until they shone like glass. I looked into my mother's eyes to see if there was any glimmer of hope. There was none.

Trying another tack, I told her how I had prayed for Ruben when he left, especially that he would never have to use his bayonet on a human being. I looked at her deeply in the eyes. I spoke to her with as much love in my voice as I could muster.

"Mum, when Ruben left, you remember that day?" I tried to assure her. "Well, I prayed and prayed for him. When I had prayed, my heart was filled with a comforting peace and a total conviction that my prayers will be answered. He will be safe."

My mother wanted so much to believe that all would be well that she brightened up. I believe that I really raised her spirits, although there was no rational reason why I should have been able to do so. Wherever he was, human life was cheap and lives were being snuffed out by the hundreds of thousands. However, I did believe that Ruben would come through all right but I certainly wondered what his story might be.

* * *

"Mum! There's a letter in a Red Cross envelope. It might be about R . . ."

She had it out of my hands and had opened the envelope before I could say "Ruben."

I waited as she tore the letter open and began to read.

221

"He is alive," she said, finally allow herself to breathe again. "Ruben is alive." Then she was silent, overcome by emotion and unable to say another word.

I looked at the letter. He was indeed alive and had been taken prisoner in Italy by the British.

"The British?" we chorused. This news was almost too good to be true. The British were civilised in the way they dealt with prisoners. But the last we had heard he was on a train bound for the wilds of Russia.

Ruben had been in his uniform, with his kit and with his unit on a train at the Berlin main line terminus. The station was full of German soldiers, all of them in full kits and taking train after train to the east. By a strange irony, this station was called the Silesia Station. The station was filled with wives and girlfriends, brothers and mothers, all bidding tearful farewells.

"Don't forget to write."

"Don't forget to wear your woolly socks, it's cold over there."

"Bring us back one of those Russian hats."

"Do your utmost for the Fatherland, son!"

Ruben had been settling into his compartment with his friends from the battalion. Perhaps he was trying to find a little peace from the maelstrom outside. But any calm was broken by a shout: "Cieslar! Wo ist Cieslar? Where is Cieslar? Important orders! Important orders!"

"Cieslar! There's an officer looking for you," one of his fellow soliders said, relaying the message into the crowded carriage.

To his surprise, an officer came running down the platform.

"Did he say Cieslar?"

"Yes, that's you he's calling for."

"I'm here, sir, over here!"

"You are Ruben Cieslar?"

"Yes, sir."

"Well, get off the train quick, you've been posted."

Ruben looked around at his comrades.

"Some people have all the luck," someone must have said. His comrades would not have expected to return from Russia.

My brother, Ruben.

222

"Cieslar!" the officer shouted with impatience. "That is an order, young man! Get your bags and get off that train before it departs."

"Yes, sir!" he replied and swung his rifle off the rack, grabbing his kitbag and greatcoat.

"Come on," said one of his comrades said, "we'll give you a hand."

Ruben shuffled down the train corridor and jumped onto the platform just as the locomotive was letting off steam prior to departing.

"Goodbye, boys. We'll meet again."

"I wish I had your luck, Ruben, but orders are orders and you have to obey them!"

The station staff slammed the doors and the train headed eastward. Ruben was left standing on the platform watching the train disappear from sight. He never heard from any of his comrades again. It is unlikely that any survived.

The officer hurried him toward the administration offices on the station. "Come on, lad, come with me," he urged.

"Where am I posted, sir?" Ruben asked as they walked along.

The officer looked at the warrant in his hand. "It looks like you're going to Italy to see the signorinas," he said with a wink.

"Do you have any idea why, sir?"

The officer fixed him with a significant look in the eye.

"You've been to Russia before, is that right?"

"Yes, sir, I was there for six months last year."

"Come on, hurry up, they want you to go to Italy on the double. The policy is that if you have been to Russia you cannot return."

Ruben must have looked at him quizzically.

"I don't make the orders," he shrugged. "I just pass them on."

"Yes, sir."

This was a stroke of great fortune. He would still be in harm's way but meant that if he did become a prisoner of war, it would be with the British or Americans, away from the barbarism of Stalin's Red Army.

* * *

When I spent time with Ruben after the war, I discovered that he had sustained a head wound in Italy. On occasions, he had taken fearful personal risks. When the German army were planning to hang or shoot villagers to punish partisan activity, Ruben had tipped off the villagers on more than one occasion and saved their lives. However, one incident stood out above all others.

One day, while manning a high-powered machine gun, the officer-in-charge ordered him to shoot a peasant who was going to a well. "Go on, Cieslar, finish him off, he's the enemy," he goaded him.

But Ruben refused. "They're not doing anything, sir," he objected. "I didn't come here to fight civvies. I can't do it."

"Cieslar, that is an order! I order you to shoot them!"

"He's just a farmer, sir; he just wants water for his children. I'm not shooting him."

The officer was furious. He fumbled with his field pistol and was taking out of the holster.

Ruben was quicker. He picked up the machine gun and pointed it at the officer. "You try it and I'll try it!"

Having threatened the life of an officer and thereby committing a capital offence, Ruben was arrested, disarmed and put into a cell for safekeeping. He would most likely be court-martialled and shot the next morning.

He contemplated his end. He smiled to himself as he realised it was Christmas Eve. On the front line, there was no time or inclination to think of such things. He could not sleep. The night was noisy and he would face a firing squad in the morning.

Suddenly, there were shouts and screams. He heard the sound of running boots. He heard the sharp reports from small arms fire. Bullets zipped around the building, ricocheting with a whine and a final "splat." He heard the screams of men who had been shot, a sound he was too familiar with.

He heard orders in German and orders in a different language. He knew German, Polish, Russian and Italian but this was another language again. Ruben had no idea what was going on.

Suddenly, the cell-door was kicked open. A soldier stood in the doorway. He wore the round helmet of an American soldier and stood there pointing a gun at him. He saw that Ruben was not armed.

Ruben put up his arms and shouted, "Nicht schiessen! Don't shoot!"

"Keep your hands in the air or you are one dead Kraut!" ordered the soldier.

"No!" said Ruben. "Nicht Deutsch! Polsky! Polak."

"You Polish?"

"Polak! Polak!"

The American softened a little and pointed with his rifle. Ruben complied, glad to still be alive. He was herded out of the room, taken as a prisoner of war. He thought of it as his Christmas present. As he was taken away, he realised he was the only survivor. The Americans had killed all the others.

Some time later, Ruben was passed over to the British army. He was transferred from Italy to England shortly afterward and was set free. This was presumably because the British authorities classed him as a Pole rather than as a "sort-of" German.

Like thousands of Poles, he did not wish to return to a Communist country and found a haven in England. He was taken to a holding camp in Yorkshire and set free there. He was fortunate to find employment in Barnsley almost immediately, and he met a lovely girl, Grace, whom he married. Ruben and Grace continued to live in England and helped our family materially during the terrible post-war years when life in Communist Poland was so poverty-stricken.

I was not to see him until 1958 when my parents and I were allowed by the Communist authorities to visit him for a month. He told me when I saw him again that life on the front line was actually much easier than it had been at our farm with the ever-present danger of the SS picking up Józef and killing us all in some gruesome manner.

When he died, it was discovered that he had helped many old and needy people, as well as helping children from Chernobyl.

A VISIT TO AUSCHWITZ

Ｆifteen return tickets to Auschwitz, please."

We were fortunate to be asking for return tickets. Only months earlier, no-one was coming back from Auschwitz. Not so long ago, tens of thousands of terrified people travelled, crammed into cattle cars, to their death over these very train lines.

The young people of our church felt they had to see the truth of this camp at Auschwitz. One of our older members made the arrangements and led the trip. My sisters, Marta and Maria, and my brother Józef went with us.

Later, I was sorry I went. We did not realise the extent of brutality, suffering and death we would learn about on this tour. We had met people who had been imprisoned there and some who had escaped. Desperate people who were on the run had come to our farm, asking for food. They had told us Auschwitz was a place of unimaginable punishment, a slave-labour camp and a "death factory." People were being killed just for being Polish, Jewish, Gypsy or homosexual.

The camp in Auschwitz was established in 1940 for Polish political prisoners, mainly resistance movement members, representatives of intelligence and national leaders. Beginning in 1941, Nazis sent prisoners there from all countries conquered by the Third Reich. The camp was expanded to accommodate the increasing number of prisoners and soon became a huge death factory composed of three parts.

Auschwitz I was a mother camp, established on the grounds and in the original buildings of pre-war cavalry barracks in Oświęcim (Auschwitz). Auschwitz II–Birkenau was built by the SS in 1941 on the side of the Brzezinka, about 1 mile (1.5 kilometres) from Oświęcim. Auschwitz III–Monowitz was established in 1942 in the neighbourhood of the German IG Farbenindustrie factory in Dwory near Oświęcim. More than 40 sub-camps, exploiting the prisoners as slave labourers, were founded between 1942 and 1944 at various German industrial plants and farms.

As such, Auschwitz had two functions. It was the largest Nazi camp where prisoners died as a result of exhaustive work, hunger, inhumane punishment and torture, sustained beatings, murderous experiments, and single and collective executions.

In addition, from early 1942, Auschwitz became the largest centre of mass execution of European Jews, the majority of whom died in gas chambers immediately on arrival at the camp. The first transports of Jews condemned to death arrived in Auschwitz from Upper Silesia. In the spring, mass transports from Slovakia and France, then Belgium and Holland poured into the camp. In the autumn, still more came from Germany, Norway, Lithuania and other countries of occupied Europe.

The distance between the place of arrest and Auschwitz could be as far as 1500 miles (2400 kilometres). The journey was usually made in sealed and barbed-wired freight wagons. No food or drink was provided. People were crowded together like cattle, deportees travelling for as many as 10 days before reaching their final destination. Not surprisingly, when the bolts were drawn on arrival at the camp, frequently some of the victims, particularly elderly people and children, were already dead, while the rest were in a state of extreme exhaustion.

Auschwitz was also the place of the Gypsies' extermination. One proof of this crime is the Gypsy camp registration books, which were stolen and hidden by prisoners. They include approximately 21,000 surnames of the Gypsies registered in the camp. Our youth group studied copies of the pages, displayed on the tour.

Almost immediately after the Nazi's invasion of the Soviet Union, prisoners of war were sent to Auschwitz, which broke international legal regulations and laws. On the basis of issued prisoner numbers, it was found that some 12,000 prisoners of war were registered at the camp. In the period of five months, 8320 were killed—some by gas, some by firing squad, while others died of emaciation and exhaustion.

The newly arrived prisoners walked calmly into the gas chambers because the SS guards promised them a bath. Approximately 2000 victims at a time were led into the room. The people were ordered to undress, then sent to the second underground room that imitated a bathhouse. Showerheads dotted the walls but the expected cleansing water never came. After locking the gas-chamber doors, SS men discharged Zyklon B through vents in the ceilings of the gas chambers, down a shaft that led to the floor. People died in great pain within 20 minutes. The murdered had their teeth extracted, hair cut, rings and earrings removed, and their bodies were transported to crematory furnaces at the ground floor or to burning stacks.

We learned that when the Russians arrived at the camp they found many bodies lying in the snow. These had to be buried as quickly as possible because of the danger of disease breaking out.

The guide also showed us small coffin-like rooms, about 5 feet (1.5 metres) cubes, which the SS guards had bricked people into. They could not stand up, they could not lie down, and were left to die of starvation and asphyxiation.

The extent of the main camp at Auschwitz was huge. We saw endless rows of barracks in precise rows. We saw the original gas chambers, which had been used to test the concept of mass murder. We saw facilities for torturing people and hanging people in large numbers, designed in such a way that the remaining prisoners were able to view it all.

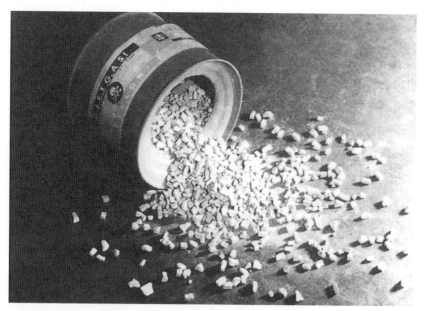

The granular form of the deadly Zyklon B gas used in Auschwitz.

We saw specially designed concrete operating tables. The "operator" would open up the victim's stomach to find if they had swallowed valuables. Some people were gutted alive. The tables were designed on a slope with channels so blood and bodily fluids would run away and be collected in a bucket beneath. The crematorium was next door so the body could be disposed of quickly and effectively.

Perhaps the most poignant story was that of a Czechoslovakian 12-year-old girl. She had committed the crime of sharing her bread with another inmate who was starving. The punishment was to stand barefoot on frozen ground in the middle of winter. The temperature was well below freezing. She was not allowed to move. Eventually she collapsed and died of exposure.

* * *

As we entered through the main gate into the camp, we were stopped by the guide to focus our attention on the infamous words displayed, in big letters on the gate: "Arbeit macht frei"—"The work makes you free."

From the guide's explanation, it was clear that these words set the alarm bells ringing for every prisoner who entered through the gate into the camp. It presented a challenge in the life of the prisoners. First, these words were

The infamous gates of the Auschwitz concentration camp.

deceptive. Its simple message—if you work enough, you can cherish the hope of being liberated from the prison camp—was a lie for almost all the prisoners.

The words also represented a warning for some prisoners at the camp. Many rich German farmers and businessmen depended on the workforce conscripted from the occupied countries by the Third Reich. If these "servants" seemed lazy, they would be taken to the Auschwitz camp for "re-education." As they watched the terrible suffering, brutality and death, they were challenged to make a wise choice: work hard enough and faithfully for the German masters or else finish life at the camp. After a few weeks, they were sent back to their original masters to continue their hard work.

As we continued our walk through the streets and narrow footpaths in the camp, we faced the horrifying evidence of human crime and inhumane suffering imposed on both adults and children. For example, the SS guards would bind people's hands behind them, then hang them by their wrists on the public gallows. It was a terribly painful and slow way to die! The shoulders of the victim would be dislocated from the body and the victim would find it very difficult to breath. Another punishment was flogging. Penalties between five and 25 lashes were administered liberally. The punished ones had painful wounds and bleeding from their backs and could not sit down.

Members of our group shed tears of sorrow and sympathy for those suffering

Flogging was also one of the common methods of punishment in Auwchwitz. Image used with permission of Anna Komorowska

victims. Our group felt the pain and the suffering of the countless innocent people who had died in such horrible circumstances. We experienced shock, fear, grief and, above all, anger toward the evildoers.

As our group took the train back to Wisła, no-one spoke a word. Some cried quietly. I was frozen with fear. Sobering questions plagued my mind: How can men be so brutal? How could they tell such lies? How could one of the most intelligent nations in central Europe perpetrate such atrocious crimes?

I came to a sobering realisation. The Auschwitz death camp is shocking proof of the magnitude of horror inflicted by modern men upon innocent men, women and children. Speaking of the unbelievable savagery at that time, one American observer stated to us: "If someone still dares do deny the devil exists, meet me at the death factory in Auschwitz."

Had I known all I would see that day, I would not have had the bravery to make the journey. Although my first visit to the death factory in Auschwitz took place only a short time after the liberation in 1945, the impact it made on me will stay with me for the rest of my days.

My grandchildren walking the railway lines leading to the Auschwitz II–Birkenau camp.

A COMPLEX
OF FEAR

As the post-war Polish government was set up in Warsaw, the people of Poland were forced to adapt to the brutal influence of Josef Stalin, whose inhumane nature was of a similar nature to the regime of Adolf Hitler.

The Gestapo and its loathsome sister organisations had gone but now we had the Ministry of Public Security—the Ministerstwo Bezpieczeństwa Publicznego or MBP. Its main goal was the disruption of any "anti-communist" structures in the new Polish state. The Nazi concentration camps had been abolished but the new state operated "labour camps" and "re-education camps," such as those at Swietochlowice and Potulice, in which thousands of people died.

Everyone in the world was glad that the war was over but, in Poland, life would not be particularly easier for some time. The younger people in the family had to rise at 2 am to walk the 4 miles (about 7 kilometres) to join the queue at the bread shop. It was mainly my younger brother, Jerzy, who got this job.

Our Adventist church in Silesia opened again soon after the Germans had gone. It had never really closed down but had lapsed into an underground existence in private homes and occasional in forest locations. However, we knew the Communist regime would readily classify us as "reactionary and unprofitable elements."

I was a trainee minister in the Adventist church in the early months of Polish

Communism. I soon discovered that if I used any words with possible political connotations, it would come to the attention of the secret police and I would be interrogated. We soon came to the harsh realisation that, in our congregation, there was someone who was informing on their own people.

The Communist secret police rejoiced in the name of Służba Bezpieczeństwa, Ministerstwa Spraw Wewnętrznych—or Security Service of the People's Republic of Poland. Their task was to identify, intimidate and, if necessary, punish people who were inconvenient to the state. While I was never actually arrested, I was interrogated on a number of occasions. They even knew details of what I had said in my sermons.

They took me to an interrogation room way below street level, where there was no natural light. The secret policeman pushed me into a small room and a large metal door slammed behind me. It was locked behind me. There would be no-one to hear my screams.

Nevertheless, in the first instant, they were terrifyingly polite. "Tell us about your parishioners," they prompted. "What do they say about the government?"

They encouraged me with access to a better life. They would ensure that, if I co-operated, I would receive an attractive apartment in the centre of Warsaw, access to better food and special shops for Communist party officials.

My reply did not please them. "I am satisfied with my life," I assured them. "I don't especially need any better quality of life."

At the second meeting, the stakes became higher.

"You are meeting people in your church and their private homes," the observed. "Do you have people who are against the government? You must have. Come on, tell us who does not like the government."

I replied that everyone I knew was content with the Communist government.

Eventually, at a later meeting, the gloves came off.

"Now young man, we know you do not like the rightful Communist government and we know that the influence of your church is negative to the people's government," they accused me. "Who are the ringleaders? If you don't give us any names, life will be very . . . shall we say 'unpleasant'? . . . for your family."

At no stage did they threaten any violence toward me. Their torture was of the psychological type. They would make me responsible for awful things that might befall my family.

* * *

By the time I was in my late teens, I had seen so much brutality. There seemed only two possibilities: either the world had gone mad or I had.

It was my absolute conviction that human beings have an innate appreciation of such things as justice, decency and honesty. But the everyday realities of the Third Reich and the Communist regime proclaimed that all of the values that my parents had carefully instilled in me were now invalid, past and forgotten. This was a terrible crime.

The values of both of those vile regimes had been obedience to authority, personal loyalty to the leader, survival by betraying others, and death and persecution to the disloyal or racially inconvenient. In either case, the individual's humanity, dignity and freedom of thought and freedom of choice were trampled into dust.

At 18 years of age, if I saw someone walking toward me, I immediately thought they were going to hurt me. I saw every human being as a potential killer. I developed stomach ulcers. I was depressed.

I was going downhill and knew it. I desperately needed an angel.

And an angel was at hand!

ANGEL OF A RUINED PARADISE

The inaugural church event in this new era was to be a get-together for Adventists from the local Cieszyn and Bielsko district. There were all the people we had expected to see—but also many more that we had not. There were people we had heard were dead. Some had disappeared but had now "miraculously" reappeared. One wondered where they had been for the past six years but they probably wondered where the rest of us had been for that time, too. It was a significant, joyous and historic occasion.

The Adventists all wanted to take stock. They tallied up who had survived, who had died and who was still missing. The older people were finding long-lost friends. People embraced, they kissed, they shook hands, they embraced again, they wept.

And they exchanged their stories. Some had been taken away in the army and never heard from again. In our neighbourhood alone, there were some dozen young men who did not come back. Others were taken to Auschwitz, had been shot or had simply disappeared.

The entire Adventist community had been under the most terrible threats. We had been told not to practice but we had kept on doing so out of sight of the Nazi invaders. Among all of the Adventists I knew, only two young men had thrown in their lot with the Germans—and both of these had been killed in the fighting. Otherwise, those of us who gathered had stayed strong, stayed steadfast and stayed alive.

Older members of the community rushed to embrace me. "Paweł, you are still alive, still alive!" they rejoiced. What a celebration it was!

The younger people were making new friends. Church gatherings and activities had been banned for almost as long as some of us could remember and we did not know many of the young people from adjoining churches.

So many people gave testimony of their survival experiences. Story after story challenged credibility. There were escapes from concentration camps. There were people jumping out of trains, dodging bullets, and escaping from the Gestapo and Sicherheitsdienst. There were stories of terrible betrayal but also stories of courage and bravery.

The euphoria was not destined to last but we did not think about that in those early days.

* * *

A second meeting took place sometime afterward. This second reunion was a much more high-profile event, which drew church members from all of southern Poland and was held in Bielsko. Chairs had to be found for 1400 people! It was our biggest church event for years and all the more exciting for coming after years of repression.

Pastor Babienko from the United States had come to address the meeting. He was a high-profile Adventist identity. Our new Communist masters had let him come because he was actually Russian born. Had he been American born, he would not have been admitted to the country.

As part of the seven-piece orchestra, my role was to play music during the two-hour lunch break. We played on a concrete stage in front of the main conference hall. The participants from the conference walked around and chatted, stopping from time to time to listen to us play.

Then it happened!

Two young girls worked their way through the crowd. I was playing my trumpet and noticed them as they came from the left-hand corner of the building. They were so pretty and had such disarming smiles. They stopped and listened for a while. One said something to her friend and then they disappeared. They reappeared a few minutes later from the other side of the building.

I surreptitiously kept my eye on them. At one point, I had to take the mouthpiece out of my mouth to take a short rest—and my eyes met the eyes of one of the girls.

I felt as if something life-changing had happened.

I can remember distinctly looking at the sky and saying, "God, how wonderful You are. You have created us to be so marvellous." I felt as if heaven had come down and touched me.

At the end of our performance, I decided I was not hungry in the slightest. I had to find that girl. I did not understand these feelings or where they came from. I only knew that there was something new in my life: something as beautiful as the scent of a May morning or the aroma of freshly-cut grass warmed by a benign sun.

I walked impatiently through the crowd, trying to look casual but walking faster and faster as I could not see her. Then, there she was.

I cast a few brief and demure glances toward her. She smiled in return.

I plucked up my courage and approached her with a few casual questions. Of course, what I most wanted was her name.

She was called Irena and was from Wapienica, with her mother Mrs Englert. Then her mother came over and talked to us. She must have seen the interest I was showing in her daughter and also—though I would not have dared hope for it—the interest Irena might have been showing in me.

I exchanged polite small talk with Irena and Mrs Englert for a few minutes. Then Mrs Englert took me by surprise. "You must come and visit us," she said.

I did not know how to respond.

The orchestra at the Bidlsko gathering.

She kindly said that, if I came over to Wapienica to visit, someone would collect me from the railway station, meaning they would meet me at the railway station and walk me back to their house so I would not get lost.

I started to count down the days until I could visit Irena.

I travelled back to Wisła with a strange collection of emotions. First, there was the happiness: I had met a beautiful girl *and* received an invitation from her mother. Second, there was the disturbing issue of how I would get permission from my parents to visit her. I knew exactly what they would say: "You are a child, only 17, what do you want with girls at your age?" This was not going to be easy. Diplomacy what was I needed—and lots of it. I was going to have to do something to secure that permission.

I found out from my parents that Irena's family were Reichsdeutsch. Under the new Communist regime, they had been dispossessed of their farm and Mr Englert had been arrested. Irena and her mother were now living in poor conditions in the garret of a house in Wapienica.

I talked to a few other boys of our church community. There was no doubt about it. She was possessed of a becoming shyness but clearly everyone liked her. I certainly liked her. From the first moment, I thought about little but her. I had just met her but already had a certainty that we had been destined to be together.

In the course of the next few days, my diplomatic strategy took shape. I was helpful to my parents. I was polite and charming to my siblings. No job around the house was too much. Within 48 hours, I had converted to the perfect son and brother. I was a new man. I had met Irena and the world had changed.

The change in me did not go unnoticed in the Cieslar household.

"What has happened to Paul?" asked my sister Marta.

"He is very helpful all of a sudden," said my mother.

I was dimly aware of suppressed smiles and exchanged glances around the household.

"He's in love," said someone.

I expect I blushed.

My mother soon realised what was going on. She saw that what was happening in me was genuine.

I told her about Irena. She thought for a moment and said, with great tenderness, "I do understand you, Paul"—so far, so good—"but you are too young for that kind of relationship."

My spirits sank like a brick in a deep river.

Yet, despite my mother's misgivings, she could see the enthusiasm I had for this girl. She was naturally feeling protective of me and did not want me to be exposed unnecessarily as I was still so young.

"I really like her, Mum," I said. "I really want to see her again."

My mother relented. "I will have a word with your father about it."

She put it to my father, mentioning how I had showed a lot more maturity of late, that I was being very helpful in the family and that now it might be appropriate that I should be allowed to visit a girl with the view to starting a romantic relationship.

My father's nod left me feeling as if I had achieved one of the great diplomatic coups of the 20th century.

SUDDENLY, THE WORLD IS DIFFERENT

I will remember the railway station at Wisła-Głębce as long as I live. I spent at least a thousand years there that Sunday morning. In reality, it must have been about three minutes between finding a seat and the train moving off. I remember the sulphurous, choking, black smoke from the ancient coffee-pot of a locomotive, which tugged snail-like and jolted my train through nine stations and 20 miles (about 30 kilometres) to Wapienica.

My heightened state of excitement was all because of that lovely girl, Irena!

In some strange, unknowable way, she seemed to transmit something profound and beautiful to me and something deep within my innermost being received it.

The carriage was one of the old-fashioned ones with compartments. It was always nice when you had a compartment to yourself. I stood by the open window. Outside, the steam engine clattered and banged and a white shroud of steam settled on the passing countryside. At the same time, a fine dust settled on my best suit. The "clackety-clack" of the wheels had a strange intoxicating quality.

I wanted to impress Irena in the most beautiful ways possible. As I climbed down the steps to the platform I knew deep inside me that I wanted to be loved by her. It also came to me in a flash that the complex of fear, which had dogged my existence over the years of war was now evaporating. That was due to Irena and the beauty she had brought into my life. After the privations of the war, she was the first person who ignited a spark of humanity and opened the wonderful vista of human relationships.

Now the train was in Jaworze—the last station before Wapienica. Was there ever a train that travelled so slowly? And I wondered who would meet me at the station. I reasoned that if Mrs Englert was there, it meant that she liked me but maybe not Irena. If Irena was there, it would mean they both liked me—which would be wonderful!

I took a small mirror out of my jacket pocket. A hair was out of place. I straightened it at once and combed my hair to a choirboy perfection.

Finally, we arrived in Wapienica and I jumped down from the carriage down to the ground. There were people milling about, but she would be there somewhere. There were people getting off the train and people getting on the train and people saying, "Goodbye—and look after yourselves."

After a few moments, the train jolted to a start and slowly clattered out of the station. Then the people had all gone. Irena had not come. I was alone and the disappointment chilled me to the marrow of my existence. Appropriately enough, the skies were grey and it drizzled miserably.

It was amazing how quickly my mood changed. Within minutes, the bitterness of this apparent betrayal brought back the old demons, filling me again with the bleakness of the war years. There was nothing for it but to pull myself together and return home. My desolation was so deep that I was not even bothered about the humiliation that such an event might bring in front of my family. I was confused, frustrated and disappointed. I went to the ticket office to buy a return ticket to Wisła.

In the waiting room with an hour before the return train home, my spirits sank. The other travellers in the waiting room were smoking cheap cigarettes, producing a fug that was little better than what came out of a steam engine's funnel.

I had to get outside but the dark clouds and rain outside echoed the misery I felt inside. As I walked desolately back down the empty platform, for some reason I looked to my left. There was a small person hiding from the rain under an umbrella. Every nerve inside my body screamed at me not to let my hopes get too high.

It was Irena! Again emotion surged inside me. I walked toward her, no longer noticing the falling rain. I did not notice all the railway paraphernalia or the self-important officials or the Ruritanian uniforms. I had eyes only for her smiling face.

My depression disappeared immediately. My heart jumped with delight. My spirits soared.

"How nice of you to come," she said with a smile.

No exquisite phrase penned by Shakespeare himself or Mozart ever sounded like that. I was enchanted, enthralled, transported.

* * *

We started out on the 20-minute walk along Międzyrzecka Street to Mrs Englert's house. My emotions were so heightened that I could hardly say a single word. Then we had to cross a road. Traffic was rare in Communist Poland, especially on a Sunday morning, but there was always the chance that Irena could be knocked down by a runaway horse. It seemed only reasonable to resuscitate my disinterested teenage benevolence. Inevitably, this meant that I should take her hand—very gently, of course—to help her cross this dangerous thoroughfare.

She let me take her hand. She did not pull away in the slightest. Again, I was speechless. Then our eyes met—and she smiled sweetly. She spoke so gently and in such a shy manner. I praised God in my heart and my soul and with everything in my being.

As we walked to Mrs Englert's house, Irena did not speak and nor did I. I do not think that Irena and I were worried about this, we were just happy to be together.

But the word "house" exaggerated the dwelling conditions of the Englerts. The place where they lived was an attic with only one small window in the roof. They slept on the floor.

"Come in, my dear," Mrs Englert greeted me warmly. She was a kindly woman with dark-brown hair and a friendly, welcoming disposition.

"I'm very pleased to meet you again, Mrs Englert," I replied. "My mother has sent you some butter." I gave her the package I had carried with me. "She hopes that you will all like it. It's her absolute best butter."

She thanked me profusely, then offered what I thought was a wonderful suggestion.

"Sweetheart, I'm making lunch, why don't you take Paul up to the interesting places in the forest?" Mrs Englert said. "You know where to go, up by the sluice. The rain seems to be easing off a bit."

"Come on, Paul, I'll show you our wood," Irena offered.

She could have showed me the coal cellar and I would have been enchanted, charmed and enraptured. The open road on which the Englerts lived gave way to a forest of fir and beech trees. We came across a small babbling stream, like one of those in a fairy tale but with some muddy patches left by the recent rain. We squelched across it, leaving muddy footprints and trying to keep our feet dry. Of course, it was only natural that I would help Irena across and took her hand in mine again. I even looked in a kindly way at the footprint her small foot left in the mud.

Sometimes we stopped to listen to the birds and commented on how sweetly they sang. Again, the lovely smile. I hoped it would go on forever.

I do not recall exactly what we talked about but there was one really important thing that happened that afternoon. It felt "right" being with Irena. I also felt comfortable with Mrs Englert and she was obviously pleased with me as a "special friend" of her Irena. The whole day was like a banquet that is stopped half-way through the first course.

"It's getting a bit dark, Paul," Mrs Englert said much too soon. "Will your mother be expecting you?"

"Probably, Mrs Englert, but thank you very much for a wonderful meal and for all of your hospitality this afternoon. I'll pass on your thanks for the butter."

"You'd better see Paul off, sweetheart, or he might take a wrong turning and miss the station. But do come again," she said to me.

Later I learned that the way from their home to the station has no side-turnings. I could not possibly have gotten lost and Mrs Englert knew that. This meant Mrs Englert was encouraging her daughter in this new-found relationship.

We walked the 1.5 miles (2.5 kilometres) back to the station at Wapienica as the evening settled into a grey murk. I need hardly add that we were hand in hand and smiling at each other at every possible opportunity. By the time we arrived at the station, it was becoming even more gloomy.

"I'd better see you home," I said, "it is really getting quite dark."

"Thank you," she said, "that's very kind of you."

I walked her back the 1.5 miles home, hand in hand through the evening turning into night.

When we got back to her house she said, "I had better see you off and make sure that you get the train home."

"That is very thoughtful of you, Irena, thank you very much"—and off we went, hand in hand again, walking the 1.5 miles back to the station.

Of course, I could not leave her to walk home from the station alone, so I also missed that train. And we continued walking together.

The moon came up, the stars shone brilliantly and we walked until 5 am. In the grey morning, I squeezed her hand gently and kissed her on the cheek. It took battlefield bravery to summon the courage to do it. And then our eyes met and the world changed for me.

This "love" thing, which I had heard about in a thousand corny songs, was now reality. But I had not a single thought in my head of any erotic nature. I simply wanted to talk with her and be with her. I pondered the utter beauty and kindness and Irena herself—and what she had done in one short day to my life. Beauty, kindness and an innocent love completely dominated my mind.

In the German language, there is a wonderful word "Weltanschauung." It does not matter how it is pronounced but what it means is important to this story. It means your own personal, subjective way of looking at the world. As I travelled back to Wisła amid the early morning workers, yawning and sighing, I became aware that my Weltanschauung had changed radically and, perhaps, forever. The demons of the complex of fear were vanquished, obliterated. I was starting to see wonderful things in people. I praised God in that moment of utter beauty.

* * *

But my parents were not amused.

"This is not good Paul, it is not moral." My mother was not angry as such, but for me to cause any disappointment was painful to me. "Why did you do it?" she scolded. "Your father will talk to you."

My heart sank. If my father forbade me to see Irena again, my Paradise had once again turned to an Inferno. What was worse, the depression would be back.

"Your father is not happy!" She did not need to add that, the picture was depressingly clear.

Irena, me and my sister Anna.

In my 17-year-old way, it had not gone through my mind that my parents would be worried at my non-appearance. But this was not a time to stay in childhood. This was a time to vault quickly, decisively and irrevocably into manhood.

There was no time to formulate strategies, all I could do was to open my heart and throw myself on my mother's mercy. She was a kind person and I could understand her concerns. I hoped she would understand.

"Mother, something has happened in my life, something really important," I ventured. "Will you listen while I tell you?"

She looked unconvinced. Her raised eyebrows suggested that she was prepared to be convinced if the argument was good enough but she had her doubts.

"Alright, darling, tell me what is going through your mind."

I told her the story, without embellishment. I expressed to my mother that I had met Irena, loved her and that, because of that love, my life was radically different from yesterday. My mother listened in silence but I could tell that her woman's instinct was in sympathy with what I was saying.

After listening, she responded with one of the most memorable sentences I have heard in my whole life. "Paul, I understand you. I will speak again to your father."

My father appeared some time later.

"What's all this about, son?" It was not the angry tirade I had been dreading.

I told the story again and could see that he related to what I was saying.

"Father, I love her. That is all I can tell you."

When I spoke of my love for Irena, I think they saw themselves in me. If so, they would have been delighted that I was now experiencing what they had experienced themselves.

For the first time, I realised I had gone a night without sleep and was dog tired. I fell into a deep sleep and slept for many dreamy hours.

* * *

I had mentioned to my parents that Mrs Englert was in a poor financial state and asked if our family could spare some food for Irena's family. My mother made up a parcel of homemade butter and cream. This meant that my mother was really trying to help me impress Irena and her mother! At any rate, she sent me on my second trip to Irena's mother with it.

I duly took the train again. I knew the way because I must have walked it 20 times on that wonderful, epic, operatic night with Irena. I knocked on the door with my heart thumping. Mrs Englert opened the door.

"She isn't here, Paul," Mrs Englert greeted me.

My heart sank and she must have noticed the profound disappointment that registered on my face. She invited me into the house. She must have known that I had intentions—of the most honourable kind—in relation to her daughter. Her kindness was her way of showing approval. But, of course, 17-year-olds never understand that their elders see through their every move. She thanked me and asked me to send her sincere thanks to my parents. I promised to pass on the message and returned home.

By now, however, my feelings were on the march. My feelings for Irena reached a point where nothing would stop me seeing her and squeezing her hand while she smiled at me.

I kept telling my parents of my feelings and received the immediate and not unexpected riposte that I was too young. My parents' coolness did, however, pose a problem. Their approval was crucial. I needed a strategy and I needed it quickly.

"These people are very poor," I nagged them. "We need to help them." This was not merely an artful strategy of getting to see Irena, I had been to their house and they were truly living in poverty. My father had nodded. The relief throughout my conscious mind, my spirit and my body was enormous.

After further negotiation, Irena came to our house, stayed with my family, and met my parents and brothers. She was accepted immediately with the status of "friend-of-my-sisters-and-prospective-girlfriend-to-me" but I had clear designs that the status might be upgraded in the near future.

Irena was changing my life in so many ways. If someone was short with me or rude to me, I would once have been angry. Now I thought, *Perhaps she had a bad day.*

My mother commented that I was suddenly volunteering to do jobs around the house. "You never did that before," she said. "What is happening to you, you never asked that before?"

My siblings most certainly knew and the words "Paweł's in love, you know" were heard around the house often. I was truly seeing—and enjoying—the nicer side of life.

"It was such a good idea to send Paweł over to Mrs Englert!" said my sister Marta with a knowing look.

LOVED
—AND LOST

Every so often, someone from the older generation proves to understand something that a teenager thought was their own discovery. My love for Irena was a case in point. Of course, I believed I had discovered love for the first time in human history. One day I blurted out my feelings for Irena once again to my mother.

To my surprise, my mother seemed not only to know all about it but to have a well-rounded philosophy on the subject. She knew exactly what question to ask. "Do you really know what love is?" she prompted.

This was a searching question. I had "discovered" this thing called love but my mother knew exactly how to put me on the spot. I had no answer. This was frustrating in one sense but I was also quite impressed.

"OK," I grinned, "I can't express it."

"The Bible tells us that God is the source of true and lasting love," my mother said.

I had to agree with her but wondered where was she going with this.

"As a teenage boy, you need to stabilise your feelings of love."

She was right and I knew it immediately. I knew my feelings for Irena were delicious and wonderful but inherently unstable.

My mother continued, "So stabilise your feelings of love within the love of God. If you can do that, your love will be in harmony with God and with all creation."

My mother was prompting me to think in a much bigger way.

I had known that my mind would be battered by waves of longing and blissful thoughts of Irena that would spark off sighs and even tears. My mother was showing me that all of this energy could be harnessed within the love of God. It would take me to a new level of humanity. Her words would have a deep and wonderful impact on my life, my whole view of the world and most of all on my future family.

Thanks to Irena and to the promptings of my mother, I could look into people's eyes again. Thanks to these women, I could believe in people again. Thanks to them, everything that was decent and beautiful would triumph in my life over the murder, the vileness and the inhumanity I had seen and experienced.

* * *

One day, my father and I were visiting a friend near Bielsko. Suddenly our quiet morning was shattered by an urgent banging on the front door, every bit as insistent as the SS or the Gestapo.

It was a good friend of mine.

"Paul," he said, panting after running, "they're deporting Irena. Get down to the station in Bielsko."

My spirits dropped like a lift in freefall down an elevator shaft. This news was a complete surprise. Many Germans had been deported from Silesia to Germany but we thought the deportations had finished.

"What do you mean?"

"There's another deportation of Germans," he explained urgently. "They rounded up Irena and her mother and they're sending them off somewhere. Get down to the station in Bielsko quickly."

I have never moved so quickly in my life. I a caught a bus to travel the 6 miles (10 kilometres) to Bielsko as

Portait of me at 17.

quickly as I could. As I rushed to the railway station, the harsh realities went through my mind.

The Polish Communist government were deporting ethnic Germans and sending them westward into the former Reich. The Germans had done this on a large scale to the Poles and now, in a hideous tit-for-tat, the Poles were doing it back to the Germans. If this happened to Irena, she would be sent to a displaced persons' camp. We could not even guess where she would end up, what dangers she would face or whether I would ever see her again.

I arrived at the station breathless and distressed. The sight that greeted me was one of the saddest I have ever seen. Under the watchful eye of the police, a line of some 20 miserable people sat on the platform benches, waiting for the train to oblivion. They had been allowed to take with them only one small suitcase. These people had been dispossessed of their farms, their property, their tables and chairs, their family photographs, their cats and dogs, their livelihoods and especially dispossessed of all human dignity. At their homes, their neighbours would be rifling through their house to loot their tools of trade, their property, their clothes, their underwear, their china jugs and anything that could be moved. Their homes and land would soon be reallocated.

Everything was under control. The people were quiet. The police were in plain clothes. There was no outward drama beyond the fact that I would never again see the girl I loved.

As I searched urgently through the deportation queue, I had to be careful that one of the vicious policemen did not think that I was being scheduled for deportation, in which case I would have been summarily thrown onto a train and my parents would never have seen me again.

In the middle of the throng on the station platform, I came across Mrs Englert in a state of total emotional breakdown. "They have taken Irena but I don't know where," she told me quietly. She was numb, broken.

My heart ached for her. My heart ached for myself. I kept on running up and down the station, looking for her, trying to see her for the last time. But I did not dare call her name aloud.

No-one paid the slightest attention to me. Their situation was so much worse than mine. The train chugged into the station. It was already full of displaced people from further up the line, who were also being deported. The queue of desperately sad, vanquished humanity shuffled forward and onto the train, made up of noticeably ancient carriages.

The station emptied rapidly as the train carriages filled. A whistle blew. The engine lurched forward with a slipping of massive driving wheels, a hiss of steam and a plume of evil black smoke. I looked into every window as they slid by. It was heart-rending to witness. They were on a one-way trip to an uncertain and unpredictable future.

There was no further sign of Mrs Englert. I did not see Irena at all.

The tail lights of the train disappeared around the bend, the signal dropped and the plume of black smoke from the locomotive disappeared toward the horizon.

I stood on the platform. It was as if an earthquake were shaking my body from the inside. I left the station and began trudging toward home.

When I was out of sight of the station and no-one could see me, I cried like a child. I cried because I loved her. I cried because her presence in my life had been critical at a very bad time. I cried at the sheer injustice, stupidity and inhumanity of losing her.

AT THE SEMINARY

I was always going to be a pastor. Earlier in life, I thought I would have liked to become a forest ranger, close to nature and with a magnificent uniform. But, as time went on, my mother's greatest ambition was for me to become a pastor and it worked. I really did want to become a pastor.

Fortunately, I met the entry requirements and was accepted to study at the theological seminary at Bielsko-Kamienica. Fortunately, again, this was not too far from home. I accepted the need to study hard and the seminary did not disappoint me. I sincerely prayed that I could meet any challenge that came my way.

Sometimes, something of the old "complex of fear" returned to trouble me and I would fret about whether my ministry would be successful or a failure. But, more importantly, I was inflamed with the love of God and love for other people. I was quite simply God's servant. My great strength was that I had seen the worst of humanity and the best of humanity, and knew with total certainty that the best was always better than the worst.

Two fires were burning inside me. One was the love of God; the other was the longing for Irena. Nothing could put them out. I had to find the inner strength to live with both, to cope with them and to put my life to practical use for my future congregations.

While all of this was going on inside me, the exterior world had changed dramatically. We did not have to say "Heil Hitler" anymore but we had to say

251

wonderful things about communism. To criticise Marxism was to fall foul of the secret police who sought to root out any dissent. To keep quiet was to invite suspicion. What was required was to tell lies and to be heard telling them.

* * *

One quiet Saturday, I asked the principal for permission to go for a walk for two hours through the woods. He was a kind man and knew of my love of nature. He gave his consent gladly. It was a wonderful experience and that beautiful, bitter-sweet afternoon came to have such significance in my life. I walked through the beautiful meadows and enjoyed the sights so much, enjoying being on my own.

I listened to the shrill piping of the birds as they darted among the trees. The air was full of bees as they went about their tasks.

Without realising my direction, I recognised that I was heading for Międzyrzecka Street, where Irena had lived. My heart missed a beat. It was as if I was ambushed again. Suddenly, my heart was heavy. I experienced again that sharp feeling I knew so well. I missed her so much.

It was as if my feet were taking me where they wanted. The sights of nature were still beautiful but now the beauty of the afternoon was shot through with that agony of separation. I repeated exactly that first walk we had taken together. I walked slowly with calm, precise steps.

I walked past the house where she and her mother had lived in the attic. I walked up to the wood. My face was fanned by a warm breeze, which was so fragrant as it wafted its way through the forest. As the breeze died down, I could hear the woodpeckers drumming their rhythm and I could even hear a gentle "cuckoo" somewhere in the depths of the forest.

The breeze should have made me happy in its simple beauty but with the memory of that separation, it filled my heart with sadness. I found the stream where we had negotiated the muddy bank after the rain. I saw the spot where she had left her footprint in the mud and searched to see if it might still be there.

For a moment, I felt that if I could find her footprint I would build a stone altar there and worship God for the happiness of that short but doomed love. The wood was as beautiful as ever. The fragrance of the forest was as wonderful as ever. The bird song was bright as ever. But there was no footprint.

I recalled the words we had spoken there. It was just a clearing in the forest and not special to anyone but me. To me, the clearing was the most emotionally charged place on this planet. The words Irena had spoken were not special words to anyone but me. They were her words and I remembered every one of them like jewels on a necklace.

I walked on to the dam and sat down slowly on a large log. My eyes drifted longingly over the rippling water. "My God, I am so sad," I said aloud to the trees, the cuckoos and the woodpeckers.

It was such a sensitive moment. I could not get over the loss of her and the questions it created. Why did she have to be deported? What did it achieve for anyone? Why did I have to be left so miserable?

I did not try to fight back the tears. I had not cried when the SS men threatened to shoot us. I had not cried when the policeman had taken me off to an unknown fate. I had not cried when Oberfeldwebel Weiss had injured my spine. But I cried for Irena.

Eventually, I walked back to the seminary, where I had promised to be back after two hours.

* * *

Worse was to come. A friend gave me an address for Irena in Germany. Whether this address was correct or whether she had moved on, I did not know. In a spirit of hope, I wrote to ask if she was all right. As a student for church ministry, I was of course a "person of interest" to the new secret police in Poland. The letter triggered the suspicions of the MBP. They commanded me to come so they could ask questions about it.

This did not come as a total surprise. The seminary principal had warned us that if we wrote letters to the West, they would be intercepted and read before being passed on. Files would be opened and information on us would be generated, graded and catalogued. "If you choose the wrong word, they will hound you as an enemy of the state," he warned us. "You will be in deep trouble."

The secret policemen were suspicious that my letter was an activity to cover independent acts hostile to their workers' paradise.

"Why are you in contact with the West?"

"You are a spy."

"Are you plotting against the state?"

"We know all about your friends."

"You had better tell us or it will be the worse for you."

It was an unpleasant interview and I knew a wrong word would lead to pain. But there was nothing they could catch me on. I explained that I was a student and Irena had been the girl I loved. I only wanted to know if she was all right. There was nothing else. I just loved her.

After the best part of an hour, they gave up with the air of hunters cheated by their quarry this time around—but they would get him next time.

Noticing the different approaches of the Nazis and the Communists, I was becoming a connoisseur of totalitarian regimes. It was with a great sigh of relief that I again breathed the cold air on the street outside.

* * *

But the period after World War II was not one for introspection. Amid the ongoing work of survival, there was not much time to reflect on what we had lost, what injustices had been done or even what was fair or not. But my new-found understanding of and faith in the love of God gave me a foundation and purpose.

I felt a drive within me to tell people about the caring love of God. It was not an easy or comfortable course of action. But when I looked inside myself, it was the best and most appropriate professional choice for me.

At our graduation ceremony, the keynote speaker was Pastor Frank Stekla, president of the Adventist Church in Poland. His message to the graduands was that we were not taking up an ordinary occupation. We were in God's work and our direct role model was that of Jesus, the Apostles and Saint Paul in "bringing souls into the kingdom of God."

We believed that this was what we had signed up for. But he continued in a more sombre mood. "If, after 12 months, your ministry has produced no fruit for God, some members of the church will tell you that God did not really call you into His ministry."

As he paused for effect, we realised the challenge he was laying before us to work with God to grow the church even amid the difficult times in which we were living.

"If your ministry is still fruitless after two years, then we at head office will tell you that you are not truly called by God and you will need to find other employment."

The audience was shocked.

"Another job!" he added by way of emphasis.

His words sounded harsh but this was a reflection of the situation in which the church found itself at that time. For the second time in my short lifetime, the church's survival was under threat.

MY EARLY MINISTRY

The situation was even worse than it appeared at face value. Poland had recently been taken over by a Stalinist government whose own "head office"—the Kremlin—had forbidden any form of public evangelism. We were not allowed to distribute tracts or papers. Possession of such matter was illegal and transgressions were severely punished. We could not speak in public.

But there were two publications that we were permitted. One was the Bible and the other was a book called *Steps to Christ*, which was attractively produced. In those poverty-stricken times, something that was nice-looking tended to attract attention. And, holding this little book in my hands, I had an idea of how I might be able to do evangelism.

I went to Bielsko railway station about 6 miles (10 kilometres) down the line from Kamienica. There were three working shifts in Communist Poland and most workers travelled by train. The first time I tried my idea was in the afternoon, just as the sirens sounded and the local plants were knocking off. There was the predictable rush to the trains.

But I was there first and was able to have a seat. Of course, the latecomers would have to stand all the way home. As the train jolted into movement, I would look around the workers and try to read their faces. I would find a kindly-looking lady or gentleman, speak in a friendly manner and offer my seat. Naturally, they would be grateful. I might ask, "How was work today?"—but would not push the conversation further.

At this point, I would open my briefcase and take out my copy of *Steps to Christ*. Then I would read it, holding it so the person could see the nice illustrations. "What is that you're reading?" the person would ask.

"This book makes me the happiest person in the world," I would reply.

This was no small claim. Poland had lost a third of its population. Auschwitz was just a few miles down the line. Happiness seemed a rare commodity.

"Really?" they would say. "How do I get a copy?"

"Well, I could lend it to you," I would offer.

The person would give me their address and I would then call on them a couple of weeks later. After travelling on a number of such trains in different carriages, I soon had many people reading the book, plus an invitation to their homes to collect the book.

When I went to their home, I would ask if they were interested in Bible study. Many of them were, so I had an invitation back to begin a Bible class. As often or not the person would have invited some friends and neighbours. The Bible classes went well and soon I was running a number of them and the groups were growing through word of mouth.

But various priests and ministers of other churches were not taking kindly to the competition of my Bible classes. I was starting to threaten their membership and they were not going to take it lying down.

One Wednesday evening, I was about to begin a cottage meeting and lead a study on the Ten Commandments. I noticed a hatchet-faced individual among the group. I sensed a threat and began to feel concerned about who or what he might be.

As soon as I started to teach, the man interrupted by shouting loudly. "This man is a deceiver," he boomed like an Old Testament prophet. "He is one of the deceiving Adventists who will tell you that you shouldn't eat pork, drink alcohol, go dancing or to the theatre, or have any pleasure in life!"

Myself at 30.

"Wait," I said, interrupting him back. "I ask everyone here, have I ever told you about anything other than the Bible and that alone?"

"No, you haven't," replied another member of the group.

The lady of the house also spoke up for me, addressing our interrupter, "Look, no-one invited you here and you come and insult our young speaker. That is not right!"

Then I realised this man was a former Adventist himself who had left for some reason and started his own congregation, some of whom were in the group to support him.

The meeting broke up with many of the group feeling disturbed. Some were saying that they would return to their original churches. Not to hoist the white flag, I said that whatever happened I would be there next week, same time, same place. Anyone who wanted to come would be welcome.

* * *

I reported back to my district supervisor, Pastor Siemienowicz. The situation seemed ominous. I didn't know if there would be anyone there the next week—or maybe only a couple. The awful thing with bad news is that all you can do is to get it off your chest and tell it like you believe it to be.

I wondered if this was God telling me not to be so pleased with myself. Perhaps I had been a little too proud. My supervisor did not really have an answer but suggested that we pray together.

"And keep on praying every day!" he added as I left.

A week later found me with a heavy heart as I walked to the Bible class. I didn't expect they would but I had to take responsibility and turn up, even if no-one else did. Then came the shock. I knocked on the door and, on entering, found the place packed.

"What happened?" I asked the lady of the house.

"Well, it's rather interesting," she explained excitedly. "Just after the last meeting, I had a dream."

"Really?" I asked.

"Yes," she continued. "There was a man—I don't know who he was but he was attending to a beautiful flower garden. The colours were wonderful and the fragrance was breathtaking."

I could not help but wonder where this story was going.

"Suddenly, a large and mentally disturbed pig jumped the fence," she reported.

I laughed at the absurdity of it, as she continued.

"It rolled in the flowers and wrecked the flower beds. It dug all over the place with its trotters and destroyed many of the beautiful plants."

"What an amazing dream," I agreed.

"Well," she said, "I knew it was a dream from the Lord and recognised our young Paweł as the gardener."

I smiled and felt flattered that she would think of me in this way.

"The pig," she continued, "was that horrible man who came last week and tried to destroy our meeting.

"Anyway, the dream was so vivid that I rounded up everyone I possible could and invited many new people as well."

She had invited so many people that it seemed impossible that she could have fitted even one more.

God certainly moves in mysterious ways, I thought.

With renewed enthusiasm, I carried on the Bible studies on a regular basis. Eventually, we had 51 people ready for baptism. The ceremony was conducted by Pastor Siemienowicz. Afterward, I shook his hand and thanked him warmly for the encouragement he had given to me when I really needed it. It had been a privilege for me to act in this small way in the service of God.

* * *

At that time, it seemed that the challenges came from all directions—and usually without warning. I was still only recently qualified when, in July, 1953, I was travelling on a crowded train. It was a normal Monday afternoon and the train clattered along from Bielsko to Jaworze. It was overcrowded to the point of being standing-room only.

One woman caught my eye. She was clearly tired after a long eight-hour shift. Her need was greater than mine so I offered her my seat. I soon pulled a copy of *Steps to Christ* out of my brief case and began to read it.

"What's that book that you are reading so attentively?" the woman asked.

I followed my script. "This book has changed my life and has given me so much comfort and peace that I like to read it again and again," I explained.

"Where could I get this book?" she asked. "I would like to read it myself."

"Tell you what," I said to her, "if you give me your address, I would either send it to you or deliver it to your home myself."

This was a normal interaction. She gladly gave me her address. I discovered her name was Mrs Stakla. I visited her home the next week and gave her a copy of the book. We easily began an extensive discussion on the subject of salvation.

Mrs Stakla was so excited that she invited me to her home the following week for another discussion on biblical subjects. It progressed into a weekly Bible study.

Four weeks later, she began attending the Adventist church. But my developing relationship with Mrs Stakla had happened so quickly that it seemed there had to be a catch. It was something I would never have foreseen.

When Mr Stakla realised that his wife was regularly attending the Adventist church, he was chilled to his boots. He was a member of the Nominal church and was close to the clergy. The situation quickly reached crisis-point.

"I command you to relinquish any further contact with the Adventist church," Mr Stakla ordered his wife. "I categorically forbid you to attend any of their meetings. Instead, every Sunday you will accompany me to our church. You will respect the words of our priest! Is there any of this which is unclear?' "

Mrs Stakla said she agreed with him and that she was happy to go with her husband to the church on Sunday. However, she insisted that she wished to go to the Adventist Church on Saturday. Her attempt at diplomacy was in vain.

Mr Stakla looked at her like the big silly bully he was and raised his voice: "You will do as you are told. That means that you will not go any more to that gang of heretics. Our church is the only true church. It is the only one that offers everlasting salvation. That is good enough for me and it is good enough for you!"

He then said something that shocked Mrs Stakla to the depth of her being, swearing violently as he made his threat.

"If this young what's-his-name turns up on my doorstep one more time, I will cut his head off with my axe," he said, brandishing his woodcutting axe in front of her. "This is how it is going to be. I am keeping my axe just inside the front door here—do you see? If Paweł Cieslar darkens my doorstep, I will cut his head off. Don't tell me about consequences because I do not care. I do not care how long I spend in jail. Tell him not to come back or he knows what he'll get."

Hearing the violence in his voice, Mrs Stakla believed he meant what he said. She was not only upset at her husband's barbarity but also worried for my safety. She knew her husband had a record of violence and was capable of doing what he threatened.

I was due at their house two days later for the next Bible study. Not having telephones, Mrs Stakla had to move quickly. That evening she went to the house of one of our church elders, Mr Tyrna.

"Please get in touch with Paweł and tell him not to come," she pleaded with him. "I am really scared as to what will happen."

"OK, Mrs Stakla," said Mr Tyrna. "Leave it with me and we'll sort it out, one way or another."

Later that evening, I opened the door to find Mr Tyrna standing there in a state of distress. "We seem to have a problem, Paweł," he greeted me.

"Really? Oh, do come in Mr Tyrna. What's the problem?"

He explained his understanding of the situation. It seemed grim, threatening and dangerous. I had to think fast.

"Thanks for coming around, Mr Tyrna," I replied. "I'll sleep on this and tomorrow, I'll run this past my supervisor, Pastor Siemienowicz. He's a good man to have on your side in a crisis."

* * *

"Come in, Paweł," said Pastor Siemienowicz, when I knocked on his door the next morning.

I related the whole crisis. He took it in his stride as I knew he would.

"Paweł, first of all, we shall pray to God for courage and wisdom to be able to deal with this man in the right way."

So we prayed together.

Then Pastor Siemienowicz said—with strong determination— "Paweł, on Thursday evening, at the appointed time for your Bible study with Mrs Stakla, we will go and face this man, in his home—with Christian courage!"

If he had proposed any less of a solution, I would have been disappointed. What he had proposed was the only correct solution and we

Pastor Siemienowicz

both knew it. But we would have to face this violent man and the axe behind his front door. And I was terrified—with a strange mix of faith and sheer human fear.

At the appointed time on Thursday afternoon, we took the local bus to Jaworze. From the terminal, we walked about 20 minutes to the Stakla home.

I remember the walk with such clarity. My heart was beating as if it would burst out of my rib cage. I imagine that Pastor Siemienowicz felt the same but he was a picture of calm and serenity outwardly.

As we walked into the small orchard in front of the house, he stopped.

"Paweł, this situation is very dangerous for both of us," he said. "We have to speak to God in prayer."

We stood under the spreading canopy of an apple tree and prayed intensely to God for the courage, wisdom and patience to deal with this angry and terrifying man.

"Ready?"

I nodded.

We walked down a slight dip to the small neat house. Pastor Siemienowicz knocked twice on the door. It opened rapidly and Mr Stakla, complete with his axe, looked at us coldly.

To our relief, he then dropped the axe on the floor. This was done with some violence but at least his offensive weapon was out of his hands.

"What are you doing here?" he asked with incredulity.

To our astonishment, he backed away and vanished into a side room.

At this point, hearing her husband's raised voice, Mrs Stakla emerged from the family room. She faced us with a mixture of fear and bewilderment.

"Gentlemen, for heaven's sake, why did you come here?" she asked with fear in her voice. "My husband will hurt you. I know him. He is perfectly capable of it."

"Can we just spend a few minutes with you in the family room?" asked Pastor Siemienowicz calmly.

Mrs Stakla was a kind person and asked us in, although with much misgiving as to what would happen next. Pastor Siemienowicz offered a short prayer.

"Now we are just going into the other room to see your husband," said Pastor Siemienowicz.

Mrs Stakla was very frightened. "He will kill you both in there," she said, extremely agitated.

Pastor Siemienowicz reminded Mrs Stakla that her husband did not have his axe with him. He encouraged her not to fear because everything was going to work out.

As we both entered the bedroom, Mr Stakla was lying on his bed. To our great relief, he seemed calm and controlled. The question was whether he would also be rational.

Pastor Siemienowicz slowly approached the edge of his bed, while I held my breath.

"Mr Stakla, we just come to ask you to grant us forgiveness for causing this unpleasantness in your family," he began.

Mr Stakla replied but we could not understand what he was saying.

"Mr Stakla," I offered, "we would really appreciate it if you could tell us how to remedy the situation in your family, so that you all could once again be happy." Pastor Siemienowicz slowly sat on the edge of the bed and continued talking to him in a kindly manner, again asking him to forgive us for causing this problem in his family.

After few tense minutes, the situation changed dramatically. We were suddenly in a friendly atmosphere. Mr Stakla sat up on his bed and began to talk with us in a relaxed and amicable manner. He invited us into the living room, where we sat and talked for some time.

Finally, he said to his wife, "Maria, you can go to the Adventist church!"

He turned to me and added, "And you are welcome to come for another Bible study next Thursday evening."

His wife was so happy and excited that she hugged him and kissed his cheek. We all felt that heaven had come down with such an amazing blessing!

The next Sabbath we were amazed and delighted to find the whole Stakla family—Mr Stakla, Mrs Stakla and all their children—worshipping with us in our church. When the congregation saw this family, many were moved to tears of joy.

"Knowing my husband, I can only say, this is a miracle of the grace of God!" Mrs Stakla told her new congregation.

That Sabbath morning in 1953 became a thanksgiving program of glory to God. Again, I had the privilege to learn what a wonderful thing it is to trust God in every situation of our lives.

* * *

We found out later that the crucial breakthrough had come about through our kindness. Pastor Siemienowicz had employed just the right approach: working with the power of God, we had melted him.

Little did I realise that this was the experience I still needed in my own life—even years later.

I LEARNED TO
FORGIVE

S ome three decades after the war, I was still cherishing my unhappy memories. I had seen so many terrible things during Hitler's war and. I had seen inside Auschwitz. I had had SS men pointing their machine guns at our family. And I could still feel the horror at seeing the SS man kick my mother with such brutality. That was the episode that most haunted me 30 years after it happened.

By that time—in 1971—I was living in England with my own wife and family. A man of 42, I had reached a point in life where I knew hatred is self-defeating. It is cancerous to the person who holds it; it is psychologically unhealthy. In my mind, I was clear I had to stop hating. But I could never fully achieve it.

My third bravura performance was looming. It would be harder than bamboozling the Gestapo man or Oberfeldwebel Weiss.

It began innocently. My boss—the president of the church in the Northern European and West African region, Pastor D Eva—received a phone call from The British and Foreign Bible Society in London. The caller introduced himself as Mr Gardner and asked, "Is it true that you have in your office a man who originally came from Eastern Europe, from beyond the Iron Curtain?"

Pastor Eva confirmed this and Mr Gardener made an appointment to visit our office.

Mr Gardner came into my office in St Albans the next day.

"Good morning, Mr Cieslar! I have a favour to ask of you."

"If I can help, I will do so in any way possible," I replied.

"We are running special interdenominational conferences in a couple of months' time and we would love it if you would be one of our keynote speakers," he explained. "We would all be very interested to hear about conditions in Eastern Europe and about your past experiences."

I was happy to accept the invitation and we talked further about these events. It was to take place in Lowestoft in Suffolk. Mr Gardner asked if I would outline some of the things I had seen in my life. He wanted me to talk about the destruction of Poland when Hitler invaded in 1939. Then he wanted me to describe the problems faced by Christians under the Nazis during the war. Before my address, he would show a documentary film about the destruction of Warsaw by German bombardment.

My halting English was getting better. I did not quite achieve a Londoner's nasal twang but I was achieving some fluency. It was pleasing that I now had enough command of the language to address such a formal gathering.

I felt I had a worthwhile story to share and I prepared my talk in my usual way. But I was not prepared for what would happen on the day.

Family portait taken while living in England.

I was introduced to the audience and invited to deliver my address. I mentioned some of the dramatic events in Poland. In particular, I told them about the SS man who took my sister and me away from our parents' home. I shared the painful experience in detail and finished my presentation with a testimony to the grace of God by which we survived those difficult years. And I also mentioned the millions who did not survive the war.

At the end, when I asked for questions, a middle-aged woman raised her hand.

"I am a German lady ..." she began.

Oh no! I thought. *I have probably offended her.*

"When the Nazis committed their crimes, I was 22," she continued. "As a German, I feel that I am guilty by association of these crimes. I am ashamed of what happened. It is burning me up. I feel such terrible guilt all the time."

From her manner, it was clear that my words had hit a nerve. Oberfeldwebel Weiss would have called it a Volltreffer—a bull's eye.

"My urgent question to you is: 'Can you forgive that SS man and can you forgive us Germans?'"

The sincerity in her eyes bored into me. I was in front of several hundred people and every eye was on me. I was in the spotlight as much as I was when that Gestapo man had asked, "Who said 'No Heil Hitler'?"

She repeated her question, stressing her point strongly. "Please, don't pretend! Give me an honest answer."

I realised that she had pushed me into a very narrow corner. I knew immediately that I would have to search deep within myself and find a level of honesty as I never done in my life before!

"Can you as a Christian forgive? Don't pretend," she asked again.

Her words chilled me somewhere deep inside, in some well-hidden psychological hiding place, which I did not know I possessed. I had to give a satisfactory answer in front of this crowd. I had no time to formulate a polite answer.

Looking for inspiration, I breathed a word of prayer. All I could do was to speak from the heart. But, as I stood at the lectern, I had no idea what I was going to say.

* * *

"Dear lady, my answer will be honest and truthful because I know that is what you need."

I spoke slowly and emphatically to ensure there could be no misunderstanding of my purpose. It also bought me three extra seconds in which to frame an answer. I wished the room was not so quiet. I felt as if I were under a microscope.

"It is a most difficult question and one that I have not faced in this way before."

I paused again to collect my thoughts further. The sight of the SS man's boot crashing into my mother's body flashed through my mind.

"From a human perspective, it is not possible to forgive these terrible things."

I paused.

"It is just not possible. It is not in human nature. To forgive is divine."

I had to pause again to compose my thoughts in the most honest and accurate manner possible.

Then in an equally emphatic way I said, "But when I come to the foot of the cross of Calvary and realise how my beloved Redeemer washed away my sins, it is a different picture. Then forgiveness is possible!"

It was a tense stand off and I could see a number of risks in speaking from the heart. At least I had been honest. My emotional and intellectual tanks were empty. I had nothing more to give to her. I looked at her to gauge her response.

"Thank you very much," the woman responded. "I am satisfied with your answer. God bless you!"

But I knew in the next instant that my somewhat rushed answer did not go far enough. She should not have been satisfied with my answer.

After the meeting concluded, we met at the front of the room and talked further on this issue. I told her that her question had made me see these matters with clarity for the first time.

"If this SS man ever had a moment of truth and asked God for forgiveness and if he is in heaven, then I would like him to be my neighbour," I finally was able to say to her. "Having said that, he would have had to first find a God other than Adolf Hitler."

It was a moment that would illuminate the rest of my life. Her question had brought me to a moment of truth. We both felt the emotional intensity of the moment.

As I came to empathise further with the feelings of this German woman, I came to yet another level of understanding. Forgiveness is not simply forgetfulness. To pretend that something painful did not happen is usually dishonest and nearly always dangerous.

Forgiveness does not hide the reality but it is a kind of letting go. But there is no forgiveness without pain. If someone has shot you with an arrow, you can expect the extraction to be excruciating. The pain is normal and healthy. Allow yourself to feel the pain and then turn it over to God. This is the example of the cross of Calvary.

As I spoke to that German woman, I gave the feeling of "unforgiveness" to Jesus and it worked. It had taken 30 years—but I got there!

Our wedding day, the happiest day of my life!

EPILOGUE

The final defence of Berlin between April 25 and May 2, 1945, expended some 55,000 Hitler Youth boys and Bund Deutscher Mädel girls. The oldest were 16, the youngest 13. About half of them are buried at Waldfriedhof Cemetry, the others simply ceased to exist without their parents—or indeed anyone—ever knowing what happened. I have lived my life knowing that, but for the grace of God, I would have been among them.

Through both success and trials, I served as a pastor in Poland until 1970. In 1963, I met the true and lasting love of my life, Halina. She was singing in a choir at a church event and immediately caught my attention. We were married eight months later and we still are, more than 50 years later.

Then on that golden day in 1970 the request by the General Conference of the Seventh-day Adventist Church, the worldwide body, gave me the call to work in the Northern European–West African regional headquarters, based in England.

The communists would approve my departure to get rid of me. Like most people, I would grab the opportunity to be away from Communism. Most importantly, Halina and our two children, Peter and Margaret, had a much greater chance of receiving a higher quality of life if we lived in England rather than Communist Poland.

Later, when my father and mother both died, I applied for a visa on my British travel document to attend their funerals. The Polish Communist government refused entry. This was extremely painful for me. To prevent me attending their funeral was yet another act of the cruel vindictiveness, which passed for normality under the Communist regimes.

With Halina and our children, we lived and worked in England for 14 years, until I was invited to pastor in Australia in 1984. We continued in pastoral work in Polish-speaking and English-speaking Adventist churches in Melbourne, Victoria, until we finally retired in 2002. In retirement, we live just to the east of Melbourne and continue to be active in ministry.

* * *

In June, 2008, I had the privilege of visiting my Wisła again. On one wonderful, sunny Friday afternoon, I strolled down the hill on my parents' farm. I loved anew the quiet picturesque green of the meadows, the dappled shady paths beneath the trees and the magical quality of the bird song. The feeling was one of tranquillity and peace.

The day was again a golden Polish autumn day, much like that on which this story began.

On this day, I had to visit the graves of my parents. As I saw my parents' names on the gravestones, I had to close my eyes. Seeing those names on the solid grey stones emphasised that they had passed away. Of course, I had known this for many years but now it was as if it hit me for the first time.

In my mind's eye, I enjoyed again the happiness of our Christian home, the great gift our parents had bestowed on us. Despite the dreadful memories of

My parents on their 60th wedding anniversary. Sadly, the communist Polish government did not allow me to attend my parents' funerals.

wartime, it was a journey to a delightful era. Memories flooded back of brothers and sisters, some still with us but some not.

I reflected how much I would have liked to have spent just a few minutes with them before they died, to tell them of the pain of missing them and how much I still love them. I wanted so much to tell them of the anguish that I had been unable to keep my promise to be at their memorial service.

As I came back from the cemetery to my parents' farm and strolled along on my own, I came to the significant spot where we used to meet as a family for worship on so many Sabbath afternoons. In my imagination, I could see Jan, Jerzy, Ann, Ruben, Józef, Maria, Ruth and Marta—all of them.

Then there was that dark and secret place where my parents hid their devotional books from the prying eyes of the Nazis' evil agents. There were the buildings of the farm: the buildings I had known as a child and which had withstood the change from Poland to Germany and back to Poland again.

As I reacquainted myself with the places of my childhood and youth, I could only give thanks again to God for what we had and how He brought our family through. These memories are precious—and the faith and hope that are so much a part of them are more precious still.

The farmhouse in which I grew up, looking from the east.

A photo of our farm taken on a recent visit to Poland.

Halina and me, now retired and living in Australia.

SOME IMPORTANT PEOPLE

I have observed that people often do not realise the influence they exercise over others. They do it by what they do, what they say and how they say it. Their energy radiates enthusiasm and holds the attention of the people who listen to them. Their bright conversation attracts people wherever they go.

Apart from my parents, I want to mention four significant people in my life who exerted a positive influence on me. In most cases this was during some of the most confronting periods of my life.

I suspect that none of them had any inkling as to the positive effect they had on me. Nevertheless, there were times, especially when I was a young man, when my life circumstances were very tough but their benign influence helped pull me through.

Pastor Andrzej Maszczak: As director of the Seventh-day Adventist seminary in Poland, Pastor Maszczak would often talk to me privately. He would raise important issues of the day concerning the work of the minister in a local church. I recollect one day, especially, when he gave me a significant caution. He told me to watch out for the poisoned chalices of self-satisfaction and self-congratulation in a minister's life. He warned me against the uncritical readiness to settle for peaceful coexistence. His words have had a life-long influence on my ministry.

Pastor Włodzimierz Siememowicz: It was my privilege to work for my first two years as an intern pastor under his dedicated leadership. He was a powerful, persuasive and influential speaker. He was also skilful in handling difficult people. His talents made a huge impression on me. He often reminded me that "he who has no concern for others will sooner or later discover that others, including his erstwhile friends, have no concern for him." These words encouraged me to develop the right attitude toward others but above all to my beloved wife, children and grandchildren.

Pastor Marian Kot: He was the leader of the church in the region of eastern Poland, where I worked under his leadership. I was impressed by his friendliness and kindness as a person. Often he and Mrs Kot would invite me to their home for a meal. They became, in a sense, my spiritual parents and I appreciate their influence on me to this day. One of his most endearing traits was that when he realised he had made a mistake he would always say, "How silly I am for jumping to such a conclusion." This sort of acknowledgment showed that he possessed a natural modesty, which is a sign of a noble character.

Pastor Alf Jorgenson: He was a quiet man with a clear vision of what God promises us. After his wife died, Halina and I had a close and ongoing relationship with him. We visited him often in his home and, later, in hospital. Often we would drive him to his preaching engagements. My wife invited him to our home for lunch many times. As we listened to his conversation, we found that we could always learn valuable things from his many years of experience and wisdom.

ACKNOWLEDGMENTS

I am indebted also to the following people for their contributions to this book:

First and foremost, I want to thank one of the most courteous gentlemen I have been privileged to know: Jeff Steel. He believed in the project of this book from the start. He was unstinting in giving his time. His valuable help is much appreciated in accomplishing this task. He was not only my co-writer but also helped me with the use of English language, translated various texts from German and added a substantial body of material into the book from his own research.

Special thanks go to my good friend, Jan Kropp, a school principal in Wisła. I am indebted to him for helping me find some of the medieval historical material of the Counter-Reformation in Cieszyn and Bielsko.

I thank also Michael Pilch who lives in Ustron, Poland, for being so kind as to provide me with some of the photographs of the forest churches in the Beskiden Mountains.

I thank also Kazimierz Smoleń, the former director of the Museum of the Concentration Camp in Auschwitz for his valuable information I needed for this book.

I must thank Jan Wójcicki from Cieszyn for his kind cooperation in obtaining much useful information for this book.

It is also fitting that I give thanks to my good friend, Romney King, for his help and inspiration.

Thanks also to Pastor Jeff Youlden for special encouragement in writing this book. I had already written seven chapters in Polish but Pastor Youlden encouraged me to tell my story in English to make it more widely available.

And I thank my beloved wife, Halina, for providing a supportive environment in our home for the three years it took us to write this book and the further time it took until publication.

WHEN GOD CALLS, EXPECT ADVENTURE

LESTER HAWKES *with BRAD WATSON*

From coral-fringed Papua to the incredible Highlands
of New Guinea and remote Pitcairn Island . . .

Lester and Freda Hawkes worked tirelessly to share
the love of God as medical missionaries.

**Answering God's call really does lead to
incredible adventure.**

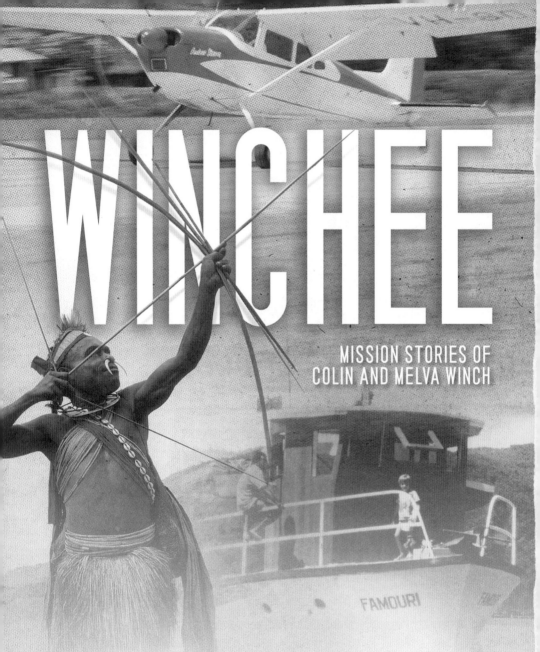

WINCHEE

MISSION STORIES OF
COLIN AND MELVA WINCH

FAMOURI

*"Close landings, lives being changed, hope being shared, the gospel
going to the Pacific islands. These stories are worth treasuring.
An inspiring record of pioneer aviation and mission, and what God
can do when we go on an adventure with Him."*
—Gary Krause, Director, Office of Adventist Mission,
General Conference of Seventh-day Adventists